Planning an Appropriate Curriculum in the Early Years

A guide for early years practitioners and leaders, students and parents

Fourth edition

Rosemary Rodger

 Routledge
Taylor & Francis Group

LONDON AND NEW YORK

Fourth edition published 2016
by Routledge
2 Park Square, Milton Park, Abingdon, Oxon OX14 4RN

and by Routledge
711 Third Avenue, New York, NY 10017

Routledge is an imprint of the Taylor & Francis Group, an informa business

First edition published by David Fulton Publishers Ltd 1999
Third edition published by Routledge 2012

British Library Cataloguing in Publication Data
A catalogue record for this book is available from the British Library

Library of Congress Cataloging in Publication Data
Names: Rodger, Rosemary, 1946-
Title: Planning an appropriate curriculum in the early years : a guide for early years practitioners and leaders, students and parents / Rosemary Rodger.
Description: Fourth edition. | New York, NY : Routledge, 2016.
Identifiers: LCCN 2015040845| ISBN 9781138905740 (hardback) | ISBN 9781138905757 (pbk.) | ISBN 9781315695754 (e-book)
Subjects: LCSH: Education, Preschool--Curricula--Great Britain. | Curriculum planning--Great Britain.
Classification: LCC LB1140.4 .R63 2016 | DDC 372.21--dc23LC record available at http://lccn.loc.gov/2015040845

ISBN: 978-1-138-90574-0 (hbk)
ISBN: 978-1-138-90575-7 (pbk)
ISBN: 978-1-315-69575-4 (ebk)

Typeset in Bembo
by Saxon Graphics Ltd, Derby

Planning an Appropriate Curriculum in the Early Years

Now its fourth edition, *Planning an Appropriate Curriculum in the Early Years* offers a comprehensive guide for early years practitioners and students on how to plan and implement a suitable curriculum for the children in an early years setting. It examines the key roles and responsibilities of practitioners working in early years settings and those with responsibility for leading and managing provision for EYFS in primary schools.

Completely revised and updated in line with the Statutory Framework for the Early Years Foundation Stage, latest research evidence and OFSTED requirements, this book covers the following aspects of the early years including:

- what we mean by planning an appropriate curriculum in the early years;
- transition from nursery to school and into Year 1;
- defining quality learning and play in the early years;
- assessment procedures and examples;
- integration of 2-year-olds into school;
- the role played by parents and carers in children's learning and development;
- the ways in which vulnerable children are provided for;
- examples of planning material developed by practitioners.

With case studies of good practice and questions for reflective practice and group work, this timely fourth edition will be welcomed by students and practitioners looking to provide high-quality and effective learning experiences for the under-5s.

Rosemary Rodger is an early years consultant and trainer. She works with schools, nurseries and children's centres in the UK. She was previously Senior Lecturer in Early Years Education at Edge Hill University and Manchester Metropolitan University before becoming a Registered Inspector of primary and nursery schools and an Additional Inspector working with schools causing concern.

Dedication

This book is dedicated to the children in my family, Adam, Alexander and Kirsten, and my grandchildren Jake, Ethan and Estelle, as well as to my husband Iain for his patience and support. I also wish to extend my thanks for the contributions by the headteachers and staff at Trimdon Grange Nursery and Infant School, Durham, Kidmore End Primary School and Kidmore End Pre-school, Oxfordshire. I appreciate the encouragement by Annamarie Kino and her colleagues at Taylor and Francis. A special thank you to Janice Baiton for her patience and guidance throughout the editing process.

Contents

Illustrations

Preface

The first edition of this book was published in 1999, with editions two and three following in 2003 and 2012. This edition includes details of the statutory framework for the Early Years Foundation Stage (EYFS) (DfE, 2014a), what constitutes a curriculum for the early years and how practitioners work with pre-school children, in particular 2-year-olds. There is reference to outstanding provision as appropriate. The new chapter on vulnerable children is included to reflect and support the need for high-quality early years provision for those children the most at risk in our society. The pattern of priority given to early years provision in this period is very varied, from the widespread closure of Sure Start/Children's Centres, to 2-year-olds in school and increases in pre-school nursery provision for the children of working parents. The priority to early years is marked, particularly by Ofsted in their dedicated early years reports (Ofsted, 2015a).

I first started working as a teacher of children under 5, opening a new nursery unit attached to a primary school in the early 1980s in northeast England. Then worked with children under 3 in their homes in Knowsley as part of a government-funded home pre-school link project for disadvantaged children, followed by heading up the infant department in a very large Lancashire primary school. A secondment to Edge Hill University to prepare reception class teachers to teach 4-year-olds across schools in the northwest followed. A permanent post as senior lecturer in Primary Education gave me the opportunity to work with early years teachers wishing to study for Early Years Master's degree and diplomas. My work took me to Manchester Metropolitan University, where as a senior lecturer in Early Years Education I edited *Quality Education in the Early Years* (1994) with Professor Lesley Abbot, was involved in several research projects – *An Identification of Factors Contributing to Quality Educare for Children under Five* – with the early years team, researched into promoting language development through structured play in Manchester schools as well as supervising serving teachers studying for higher degrees and preparing postgraduate students to teach in the early years, which has been invaluable in understanding the dilemmas many students face, particularly at the end of the first term of the PGCE course. The writing of a Sure Start bid for a local authority in the Northeast was a gratifying experience, being able to plan for early years provision across a wide range of areas and meet the needs of many disadvantaged families via a play bus and drop-in centres across the authority. The final years of my career were spent leading inspections of primary and nursery schools as well as training inspectors for early years inspections. My role as an assessor of advanced skills teachers has undoubtedly provided me with many superb examples of excellence in the early years. However, time to observe the development of my own three children as they moved to adulthood and parenthood of their children has perhaps provided me with the greatest impetus to revise this publication.

Introduction

I am prompted to introduce this edition with a quotation and comments from Margaret Donaldson: 'People turn to wondering whether schooling really does begin as well as it seems to do or whether the brightness of the early years carries within itself the shadow of the darkness that is to come' (1978: 14). Her views led me into a career working with trainee early years teachers and those wishing to increase their knowledge and understanding of young children through further professional development. As far as what is appropriate for young children, Margaret Donaldson spoke from considerable experience and understanding of child development at a time when it was felt imperative to get it right in the very early years. The 'darkness that is to come' refers to the ways in which children are unprepared by pre-school and subsequently make less progress as they go through primary school. The key role played by adults in working with the very youngest children to ensure that all children are prepared for statutory school at 5 years of age has subsequently been found to be crucial in laying the foundations for early learning, particularly with regard to language development and early literacy. It has taken many years for a priority to be given to what happens with the under-3s in the early years. It now has an increasingly high profile. At this point in time there is certainly much consternation in early years settings as to how to accommodate 2-year-olds and the 30 hours a week provision for the pre-school children of working parents in the near future. The National Association of Head Teachers (NAHT) recently stated that the plans to extend the free childcare could backfire and leave fewer children attending nurseries. This is due primarily to the lack of funding provided to cover the cost of nursery provision. Another continuing concern relates to the plans to improve the level of staff qualifications in the early years sector. Cathy Nutbrown's review (DfE, 2012c) highlighted the lack of qualifications in several early years sectors but many of her recommendations were rejected. There are plans to introduce non-qualified teacher status (QTS) early years teachers to relax ratios, and not require childminders to hold formal qualifications. The strength of early years in England has been in the quality of our staffing compared with other countries. The government now claims that the reforms to staffing will bring us into line with countries such as France and Denmark.

The *Early Years Foundation Stage* (EYFS) (DfE, 2014a) sets the standard that all early years providers must meet to ensure that children learn and develop well and are kept healthy and safe. It aims to promote teaching and learning to ensure children's 'school readiness', so states the statutory framework. The EYFS seeks to provide:

- *Quality and consistency* in all early years settings, so that every child makes good progress and no child is left behind;
- *A secure foundation* through learning and development opportunities which are planned around the needs and interests of each individual child and are assessed and reviewed regularly;
- *Partnership working* between practitioners and with parents and/or carers;
- *Equality of opportunity* and anti-discriminatory practice, ensuring that every child is included and supported.

(DfE, 2014a: 5)

This edition includes details of the statutory EYFS framework (DfE, 2014a), what a curriculum for the early years must include and how adults aim to teach, plan and play with children up to the age of 5 before the children transfer to Year 1 to follow the National Curriculum. A chapter on meeting the needs of 2-year-olds covers how outstanding practitioners are able to effectively integrate the youngest children in pre-schools and schools. The statutory requirements for the prime and specific areas of learning and the safeguarding and welfare requirements are also are included. The assessment chapter outlines the recently introduced *baseline assessment* for children starting reception class in 2016. There are chapters too on defining quality in the early years with a particular focus on the features of strong leadership, planning and assessing learning, and involving parents and carers. The addition of a new chapter, 'Vulnerable children', is included to throw light on how various organisations are helping families tackle living in poverty and the ways in which many of these initiatives are contributing to making a marked impact on disadvantaged children's well-being and education. Children from poorer families achieve less well than their peers. In 2012, just over a third of children were not working securely in communication, language and literacy and in deprived areas this rose to more than four in ten children. Links to specific websites for planning examples are provided as well as the inclusion of some examples in this edition. There is a vast amount of guidance from the Department of Education and Science (DfES, 2012) and local authorities available on various websites as well as the most recent statutory guidance from the Department for Education (DfE, 2014a). This new edition includes greater emphasis on how children learn in the early years and highlights the opportunities provided for children to play and how practitioners engage with children as they play. The curriculum chapters describe research, teaching and good practice in communication, language development and literacy and the increased use and contribution of technology in the early years. There is some debate in the early years sector as to the use of, and meaning of, the word 'curriculum' and what is meant by this in the early years. This is discussed further in Chapter 3, which tackles this sometimes contentious but recognised and well-used word worldwide in relation to early years. Those working in the early years are referred to as practitioners. All adults working in the early years also teach. Use of the word 'teach' does not only refer to qualified teachers.

Indications that civil servants are beginning to take greater interest in the early years is evident in a series of Ofsted reports that evaluate how settings achieve and maintain high-quality early years provision (Ofsted, 2013a, 2015b, 2015c) and a second yearly report from HMCI with an exclusive focus on early years (Ofsted, 2015a). Hopefully, this may help to highlight the imperative need to have appropriately qualified practitioners working in all early years sectors. The pattern of priority given to the early years in recent years varies from the ambitious launch of the Sure Start project across the country, to changes in government and reduction in the numbers of Sure Start centres and Children's Centres. The reasons for the reduction are outlined in the recent cross-party government report *Foundation Years: Sure Start Children's Centres* (House of Commons Education Committee, 2013) and from my own delving into of the minutes, which state very clearly that there is a lack of clarity about their purpose and what centres should offer. It is further claimed that accountability is needed both at centre level and at local authority level. The findings of this report are outlined in more detail in Chapter 2.

The priority of this publication is to provide trainee early years practitioners with current developments in the early years and the implications of this for their practice in whatever route they take to work with children under 5. Recent research and government reports stating the statutory guidelines for early years are included. The key role of the practitioner as a teacher is given a high priority, with the aim of equipping readers with a framework to guide their own practice and a theoretical underpinning as to effective teaching and learning in the early years and how this takes place in settings now required to implement the statutory early years curriculum from birth to 5 years old. Teaching and play along with the links between the two is given a high priority. Being mindful of the guidance from Ofsted (2014a) that there is no requirement to see planning when inspected, there is less priority given to planning examples than in previous editions. The pressures put on practitioners previously to plan in detail is a view supported too by the critical views of practitioners in a DfE evaluation in 2011, citing the demands of increased paperwork. My more recent experience of what happens in early years settings regarding planning identifies child-friendly topics that require resourcing by the pre-school and reception class. Assessment becomes the means by which next steps for learning are identified. Discussions with the children to establish a starting point as to their understanding of a suggested topic and some leading exploration of first steps and prepared activities are commonplace. This may be less common in a pre-school where assessment of a child's learning journey may form the starting point and content of their learning and development. A higher priority to the impact of learning in the outdoors is a major feature in many settings.

The early years sector is, without doubt, a political football wavering as it does between priorities of opposing political parties. However, it is reassuring to note that since the introduction of *the Early Years Foundation Stage* the proportion of good or better providers has risen from 64 per cent in 2008 to 74 per cent in 2012 with a year-on-year improvement in children's attainment as evidenced by the *Early Years Foundation Stage Profile* scores: a rise from 49 per cent reaching a good level of development in 2008 to 64 per cent in 2012 across all types of early years settings. The allocation of funding for childcare for 2-year-olds from less advantaged backgrounds as a result of the findings from Sure Start evaluations (DfE, 2008, 2010) over several years is a positive development, but nevertheless poses additional challenges for practitioners. Partly, this is because of a lack of funding, but also because of the implications for accommodating the particular needs of 2-year-olds, as recommended by Ofsted. Examples of exemplary practice along with findings of good practice publications by Ofsted are included. More recently, the allocation of 30 hours of free childcare for the children of working parents announced in the 2015 budget from 2016 will add to the demands placed on existing early years provision. Research by the charity 4Children identified an 11 per cent increase in families using centres in 2012. Nevertheless, it is likely that around sixty Children's Centres could close over the next twelve months due to acute financial pressure. My own authority reflects this well having started with forty-three Sure Start Centres and recently reduced that number to fifteen with the twenty-eight closures of buildings for Sure Start being transferred to other community groups. The rationale for this being the failure to reach disadvantaged parents with children who were not accessing the provision provided by the Sure Start Centres, along with the mixed evaluations of the impact of Sure Start on supporting children from disadvantaged families. One of the reasons given for the closure of so many Sure Start Centres was because, by the end of the Foundation Stage, children in this authority were achieving in the bottom 10 per cent based on the EYFS profile results. However, as in all local authorities, the reduction in their budgets is likely to be the main reason for so many closures. There is a difference between the charity findings and statements from DfE spokespersons who claimed that funding for Sure Start centres increased from £2.2 billion to £2.5 billion in 2014/15. This edition provides information about the many schemes evolving to compensate for cuts to funding leading to the closure of Children's Centres. The key role played by parents and how practitioners can work to support parenting is vital, particularly for those with children up to 24 months old. The responsibility for this is increasingly via the charitable sector and Lottery-funded projects across the most deprived areas of the country. The extent to which schools will provide for 2-year-olds remains to be seen, but is certainly becoming more of a feature across the country due, in part to its promotion by Ofsted (2015b).

As a very practical academic driven by a professional life spent observing children and practitioners together in many different settings, the key to successful provision is the ability to achieve a balance between meeting children's social, emotional, physical and intellectual needs, liaising and working together with parents and providing a happy and productive environment for young children. This book aims to identify high-quality provision and to provide support to practitioners and students planning a career in the early years. Priority is given to the contexts in which newly qualified practitioners find themselves and the aims to keep you up to date with government changes. The key to becoming a successful early years practitioner has many strands. I hope this publication will help to contribute towards your journey.

Quality in the early years

Introduction

Defining quality in the early years is an elusive concept that early years educators have wrestled with for many years (Abbott and Rodger, 1994). Cathy Nutbrown defines very firmly the importance of excellent pedagogical leadership, which is vital in improving the quality of provision, and suggests that all early years practitioners can aspire to be pedagogical leaders (DfE, 2012c). Different government policies have sought to define what counts for quality in the early years over the past fifteen years. This chapter aims to examine more recent definitions of quality with a particular emphasis on the crucial role played by those who work directly with young children as the leaders of a team. Primarily, this is because effective leaders make the greatest contribution to quality learning for children. Successful provision and outcomes for children is a very mixed and diverse picture, mainly because the range of provision is so vast and the needs of children from 2 years old to starting school in the year in which they are 5 years old covers a wide range of settings. While not always possible, I will be making a distinction between early years practice for children attending pre-school and those in reception classes. Also, where appropriate, the distinction between education and childcare is more variable: the former settings are staffed by qualified teachers or early years professionals (EYP) in maintained nurseries and reception classes and the latter in the private, voluntary and independent (PVI) settings where staffing qualifications may be unqualified. Learning is most successful when there is a combination of qualified practitioners and children working together to ensure that planned and spontaneous activities reflect the needs and interests of the children as well as providing the enriching experiences that allow children to grow and develop. All these practitioners also 'teach'. Recent research builds on previous findings as to what constitutes quality provision, such as the positive impact of qualified teachers or EYPs. The free entitlement to childcare was raised from 37 per cent in 1999 to 88 per cent in 2007, with the majority of growth in the private, voluntary and independent settings. A large proportion of 3-year-olds (44 per cent) were paying to access early education in a PVI setting. Cathy Nutbrown's review for the DfE (2012c), *Supporting Families in the Foundation Years* (DfE, 2012a) and Mathers et al. (2014) spell out very clearly what needs to become standard practice when working with very young children. The distinction between childcare and education continues. Generally, childcare takes place in the PVI sector and education in maintained nursery schools, classes and reception classes. According to the statistics in Her Majesty's Chief Inspectors (HMCI) annual early years report (Ofsted, 2015a), a third of Children's Centres were judged to require improvement according to the outcomes of their inspections. This was a slight improvement on previous years, but compared to maintained nursery schools having only 3 per cent requiring improvement, the difference is worrying. Children's Centres are often in areas of disadvantage where their impact needs to be considerable on the development of their children. Could this be part of the reason for encouraging access to school for 2-year-olds? The findings of the Marmot Review (2010) found that nearly half of all children in England are not ready for school when they finish reception at the age of 5. Recent Ofsted reports and comments by HMCI suggest that the quality of provision in the early years sector is better than it was (Ofsted, 2015a). However, the reality is that too many of our youngest children's lives are linked to poverty. Children from more deprived areas are more likely to than those from affluent families to fall short of the developmental and educational milestones set down by the Department of Education. These include being able to listen to stories, pay attention, use the toilet and dress themselves, and having started to read and write and do simple sums. As all the evidence shows, children who struggle in primary school are less likely to do well later on. Marmot cites the closing of Sure Start Children's Centres, which were set up for families in deprived areas, as 'not a good way to improve early childhood development'. Reading this I am conscious of some emerging concerns as I sign yet another petition against the closure of a Children's Centre, this time in Barnsley. Internationally, there are very positive views of early years in England, particularly early years pedagogy. The strengths mentioned include the approach outlined in the curriculum, the emphasis on age-appropriateness and play in pedagogy, the encouragement to staff to employ different approaches flexibly and the continuous child development for the whole of the early years education and childcare age range, due to the overarching curriculum framework and the favourable staff ratios.

Barriers to quality provision

So what are the barriers to ensuring there is high-quality early years provision across the country? It is difficult not to become political at this point, but the reality is that local authorities struggle to deal with budget cuts, and Children's Centres across the country are closing at an alarming rate. Reading the valedictory report from the outgoing president of Early Education, Helen Moylett, reminds one that, 'children and families all over the UK are suffering, and poverty and inequality are getting worse'. A disturbing further claim she makes is that she meets too many practitioners who do not understand the core processes of child development sufficiently well to support and extend learning for all children. There is a difference between the findings of various charities: 4Children, for example, compared with statements from a DfE spokesperson's claims that funding for Sure Start centres increased from £2.2 billion to £2.5 billion in 2014/15. Much can be made of conflicting figures. However, there are data showing that the UK scores badly on children's development compared with other wealthy countries. In 2007, Unicef put the UK at the bottom of twenty-one developed countries for child well-being, judged on measures throughout childhood and adolescence, including infant deaths, teenage pregnancy and young people out of education, employment and training. Although Marmot (2010) does not directly criticise specific governments, he does quote the French economist Thomas Piketty, author of *Capital in the 21st Century*. The message here can be applied to current government priorities, whilst agreeing to increase free education and childcare for the children of working parents by 2020, there are no plans to improve the quality of provision or level of training for staff:

> It seems to me wherever you are on the political spectrum; we should be looking at this huge concentration of capital and income and thinking that this is not good for our society ... If we want a healthy economy, a healthy population, a fair society, a population with lower crime, we ought to be very concerned.
>
> (Piketty, 2014)

A survey of practitioners' experiences of *The Early Years Foundation Stage* (DfE, 2011b) hinted very clearly at some of the drawbacks to their work in the EYFS. It posed challenges to staff in a range of early years settings in relation to the demands for increased paperwork when practitioners already have to observe, assess, record keep and carry out risk assessments. A typical grumble, too, by headteachers was the need to free up staff to have time to do planning to fit into EYFS and the work it entailed. Comments such as:

> Then along with all the monitoring and all the paperwork, and the observations, and everything that goes with it, it's a lot of work for staff ... It takes them away from the children.

The demands of the paperwork was seen very much as an obstacle for play workers attached to Children's Centres. The difference in staffing ratios between pre-school and reception classes was also perceived to be a barrier. Comments such as:

> Obviously in reception you have only yourself and the teaching assistant; and you've got inside and outside and ongoing planning for individual learning. Differentiation thirty ways is almost impossible.
>
> (Reception class teacher: DfE, 2011b)

The range of concerns regarding end of year assessment in the reception class was a major time-consuming activity too (DfE, 2011b). Fortunately this requirement may have been lifted with the introduction of observational baseline assessment as the children come into the reception class. However, I am aware of some schools that are still planning to carry out assessment using the *Early Years Foundation Stage Profile* to provide information for Year 1 teachers. The EYFS is now much more manageable with the reduced need to have detailed planning information and the ease of access to readymade planning via the internet. It is too easy to say that there are no barriers to ensuring quality following the revisions of the EYFS and the reduction in paperwork required.

A major barrier remains and is linked to the quality of staffing in PVI settings according to research. This situation is well documented in Cathy Nutbrown's report to the DfE (2012c) in which she states as a basic principle that all children deserve the very best early education and care. Currently, the level of qualifications in some early years settings are not of a high enough standard or quality of content. She suggests that more is needed on child development and play, children with special educational needs, inclusivity and diversity and the age range from birth to age 7. It is reassuring that there are developing settings that take account of all these factors, but the issue is that there are not enough of them. The major barrier currently lies in the lack of qualifications held by some staff in settings and by those who train aspiring early years staff. It is advised that all new members of staff are given time to be inducted into a setting and their role, and have good support and mentoring for at least their first six months.

Defining quality leadership

The crux to having more quality lies with the qualifications of those leading and working in early years settings. Nutbrown sets out her vision for early education and care as one where:

- every child is able to experience high quality care and education whatever type of home or group setting they attend;
- early years staff have a strong professional identity, take pride in their work, and are recognised and valued by parents, other professionals and society as a whole;
- high quality early education and care is led by well qualified early years practitioners and
- the importance of childhood is understood, respected and valued.

(Nutbrown, 2012c: 10)

The quality of early years leadership and the effectiveness of the relationship between child and adult in settings need to be of prime importance if we are to equip our youngest children for the twenty-first century. All practitioners working in the early years as a head of a Children's Centre, nursery, pre-school setting, reception class, or childminder have leadership responsibilities. In a primary school, the reception class or classes should be distinctive from Years 1 and 2. In some situations the reception class teacher could be part of the early years team or even leader of that team in a small school. Consequently, leadership is not a remote activity from staff in the classroom. Aspiring early years teachers should be familiar with the key features of leadership too:

Excellent pedagogical leadership is vital in improving the quality of provision, and all early years practitioners can aspire to be pedagogical leaders.

(Nutbrown, 2012c)

The observations by Ofsted (2013a) of leadership in action highlights very clearly where children's experiences are falling short of where they need to be to give children a secure start. Table 2.1 is an example of an issue identified by the head of an Early Excellence Centre and added to the list of priorities in the centre development plan. A key requirement identified by the leaders themselves is that they are only as good as the quality of the interactions between adults and children. This means that they must:

- set high expectations
- put in place structures that help children's learning
- set out clear routines and procedures
- help to build self-assurances as well as awareness of others' needs
- teach – ensure children improve vocabulary, social and cognitive skills.

(Sir Michael Wilshaw, HMCI, in Ofsted, 2013a)

TABLE 2.1 An exemplary section from a Children's Centre development plan and evaluation

Centre Improvement Plan – a 3-Year Forecast
Priority 2 – Leading Learning and Development
To provide improvement in outcomes for child and family through Learning, Teaching and Care Practices

ACTION TO BE TAKEN	PERSONNEL	PLANNED PROGRAMME AND OUTCOME	SUCCESS CRITERIA	MONITORING (CHECKING THAT IT IS HAPPENING)	EVALUATION (HOW EFFECTIVE WERE ACTIONS)	COST/FINANCE
To improve boys' thinking and learning. Ask question: Does this early years setting meet the needs and interests of boys?	■ Lead – head and all key workers – x and y	Observe, track and monitor current activity by boys to gain a clearer picture of take up and use of provision. Complete an in-depth study of learning stories and ask question: Do we meet the needs/interests of boys under the remit of the Unique Child? Attend training to support boys' achievements. Share with staff. Develop expertise amongst staff to identify dispositions and how to promote/extend boys PSED.	■ Staff are aware of the needs/ interests of boys and reflect this in the learning environment ■ Tracking and monitoring ■ Identified boys AEN/SEN registration and intervention ■ Raise staff awareness through in-house training and impact on practice ■ Unique Child needs are met	■ Planning ■ Learning stories ■ Reflections ■ Through increased identification of need and response ■ Practice records ■ Baseline strands ■ SIO reports	■ Whole staff review ■ Gender equality scheme action plan review ■ Staff competent and confident in supporting the 'Unique Child' ■ Effective movement through Code of Practice.	None

What is emerging with regard to early years leadership is the tendency for definitions to focus on the collaborative nature of leadership with leadership capacities more widely distributed to the team (Dunlop, 2008). As she says, 'the relationship between effective leadership and children's achievement is strongly evidenced'. She would also claim that leadership is most effective when it is shared and developed widely with a team. This is not universal, as claimed by Pen Green, 'if we are to transform children's life chances, this can only be done through visionary leadership'. The Effective Provision of Pre-school Education Project (EPPE; Sylva et al., 2004) found a strong relationship between the qualifications of the centre manager and the quality of service provision in early childhood settings. In the recent past, DCSF produced many examples of ways in which leaders needed to, for example, carry out observations of learning and playing (see Table 2.2 as an example of the prompts provided by the DCSF (2010)). Traditionally, kindness and warmth are valued by parents and in past years less emphasis was placed on academic rigour with almost exclusively females as leaders (Dunlop, 2008). The early years leader plays a vital role in ensuring quality provision in Swedish settings. The key to effective leadership can be seen where the leader is working directly with children in the setting: leading by example and supporting other staff with their practice, encouraging reflection and refinement. Pedagogical leaders are those practitioners who have extensive knowledge and understanding of child development, of play and of the individual needs of children and their families and how to support them all. Evangelou and Soukakou (2012) discuss the quality of both the home learning environment (HLE) and the setting as having measurable and independent effects on children's development. Quality indicators included relationships and interactions, but also pedagogical routines and structures for learning. A recent Ofsted survey (2015b), *Teaching and Play in the Early Years: A Balancing Act?*, explores the perceptions of play and teaching in the early years. This survey was based on a sample of the most successful early years providers. The criteria for their selection were that the children were achieving good or better outcomes for children in some of the most deprived areas of the country. Notable in this survey was that leaders:

- recognised accurate assessment of what a child could do being at the heart of any decision regarding their learning;
- formed powerful, professional networks to collaborate with a wide range of colleagues, and these networks were seen as the 'hub' within the community;
- did not think of teaching and play as separate endeavors. In every playful encounter observed, adults, consciously or otherwise, were teaching;
- had prioritized mathematics for improvement to ensure that learning experiences were challenging children to reach their full potential.

(Ofsted, 2015b: 7)

Some universities are developing specific part-time degrees in early years leadership (Edge Hill University) following on from a foundation degree. This particular early years leadership degree may give the student the opportunity to acquire QTS. Its particular focus is the study of the context of leadership and management in different settings both in the UK and further afield. There were a raft of publications and courses linked to Sure Start centre leadership in 2007 with specific publications on leadership (DFES, 2007) that continue to be useful. The list below is taken from this publication. Leaders are expected to make a difference by:

TABLE 2.2 Observation of learning, playing and interacting

Practitioner observed..................... Observer		
Date......................... Context......................... Purpose.....................		
POSSIBLE PROMPTS	OBSERVATIONS	REFLECTION: IMPACT ON LEARNING
Close, caring and respectful relationships.		
Encourage and support children to relate to others.		
Support children to resolve conflicts through problem-solving.		
Observe children as a natural part of all normal activity.		
Interpret children's actions and words to try to understand the child's thinking and learning.		
Scaffold children's learning through, talk, discuss strategies and ideas, suggest possibilities and model approaches.		
Provide brief, well-planned focused learning opportunities in response to observed interests, learning and development.		
Use daily events within the routine to provide to provide worthwhile real-life experiences.		
Vary experiences, using fresh, creative and playful approaches.		
Provide first-hand experiences to explore and discover.		
Directly teach through demonstrating or explaining.		
Support children to persevere through difficulties to take risks, to ask questions and problem-solve.		
Use the language of learning to focus children on themselves as learners.		
Identify and support the next steps in learning.		

Source: DCSF, 2010

Observation evaluation/discussion notes	
Strengths:	
Areas for development:	
Agreed actions by:	**Timescales:**
Leader/Manager:	
Practitioner:	

Source: DCSF, 2010

- Establishing and sustaining an environment of challenge and support where children are safe, can flourish and learn.
- Providing the vision, direction and leadership vital to the creation of integrated and comprehensive services for children, mothers, fathers and families.
- Leading the work of the centre to secure its success, its accountability and its continuous improvement. Central to such success is the quality and level of collaboration with other services and the whole of the community.
- Working with and through others to design and shape flexible, responsive services to meet the changing needs of children and families.
- Ensuring that all staff understands children's developing needs within the context of the family and provides appropriate services that respond to those needs.
- Ensuring that the centre collects and uses all available data to gain a better understanding of the nature and complexity of the local community served by the Children's Centre.

- Using such knowledge and understanding to inform how services are organised and how to offer differentiated services that are responsive to all groups including fathers, children or parents with disabilities or additional needs, and black and minority ethnic communities.

(DfES, 2007: 5)

In order to be confident and knowledgeable about the above, leaders need to have the following systems in place to be most effective and be able to justify their position within the local authority and aim to squash the threat of changes to their status. I am only too aware of the reality at this time given the reduction in Sure Start centres in the past few years. Nevertheless, times may change. Below is a checklist of the roles and responsibilities of leaders in the early years based on Ofsted criteria and a list of the evidence that leaders may be asked to supply or given the shortage of notice given for inspections. Table 2.3 lists the DfES (2010) standards that heads of Children's Centres are expected to meet. When evaluating the quality of leadership and management, inspectors must consider the extent to which providers:

- fulfil their responsibilities in meeting the learning and development requirements of the Early Years Foundation Stage, including overseeing the educational programmes;
- have rigorous and effective systems for self-evaluation that inform the settings priorities and are used to set challenging targets for improvement;
- have effective systems for supervision, performance management and the continuous professional development of staff which have a positive impact on teaching and children's learning and development;
- have effective partnership with parents and external agencies that help to secure appropriate interventions for children to receive the support they need.

(Ofsted, 2013: 14)

The evidence that leaders are required to provide to an inspector will mostly come from interviews with a manager or member and/or registered provider. They are likely to be asked about how well practitioners and any trainees are monitored, coached, mentored and supported, and how under performance is tackled. Qualification levels and the effectiveness of any programme of professional development arising from identified staff needs and improving relevant qualifications are checked. The deployment of staff taking account of qualifications, skills and experience is also checked. Expect to be asked about:

- the extent and range of completed training, including child protection and safeguarding training which fully meets statutory requirements, and the impact of training in improving children's well-being;
- the effectiveness of the monitoring of children's progress and interventions where needed to ensure that gaps are narrowing for groups of children or individual children indentified as being in need of support;
- the effectiveness of arrangements for safeguarding, including recruitment practices and how safe practices and a culture of safety are promoted and understood are checked;
- how effective self-evaluation includes parents' contributions, carers and other stakeholders
- how improvement plans are checked for engagement with staff, children, parents and carers;

■ how effective the arrangements are for sharing information and working in partnership with other providers, schools and professionals in order to identify children's needs and to help them make good progress.

The closure of many Sure Start and Children's Centres is of great concern. The reasons for this are evident in the most recent government report *Foundation Years: Sure Start Children's Centres* (House of Commons Education Committee, 2013), which found a lack of clarity about their purpose and what centres could offer. The opening statement in the report's summary was based on the identification of three types of centre offering different levels of service: full centres based around nursery schools, centres as parts of schools and centres that operate as family centres. The report stated categorically that accountability was needed at both the centre level and the local authority. The local authority must provide stronger accountability for how well they perform through their Children's Centres in improving outcomes for children. The findings of Ofsted also stated that Children's Centres needed to be treated with the same seriousness by authorities as are those for schools or other services for children. This report suggested that Children's Centres need to identify the kinds of parental engagement in the home environment which makes most difference in narrowing the gap. A further more recent finding by Ofsted was that they found a third of centres required improvement (Ofsted, 2015a: 34).

TABLE 2.3 Standards for leading Sure Start Centres (DfES 2010)

Standards **The head of the Children's Centre must be able to show they can:**
■ Review and evaluate learning, teaching and care practices to promote improvement in outcomes for children and families with a particular focus on the most disadvantaged.
■ Identify, promote and encourage effective practice.
■ Establish a safe environment in which children can develop and learn.
■ Develop and foster a learning culture that enables children, families and staff to become, successful, enthusiastic and independent learners.
■ Ensure that staff acknowledge the expertise of parents and find ways to share this knowledge and understanding of individual children's learning at home, in order to work together and improve learning opportunities in the Centre.
■ Help parents to overcome barriers such as lack of confidence or poor basic skills and support them to take decisive action to return to study, graining and employment.
■ Respect diversity and respond with sensitivity to different cultures and beliefs and ensure equality of access to learning opportunities.
■ Regularly review their own practice and take responsibility for their own personal and professional development, seeking support where appropriate.
■ Create experiences that will inspire children, their families and staff to raise expectations for their own achievement, enjoyment and economic success and make a positive contribution to the community.

Source: DfES, 2010

Defining quality: pedagogy and reflective practitioners

> The key variable in improving quality and raising outcomes for children is the competent, reflective, well-qualified practitioner.
>
> (Bertram and Owen, 2014)

A key area that early years leaders have found less easy to evaluate is the day-to-day quality of teaching and learning in their settings. A typical comment is that because headteachers or managers are working alongside their colleagues on a daily basis there is less need to carry out a formal evaluation of teaching. There is a statutory requirement linked to performance management that monitoring should be carried out. A review of this has taken place recently to remove the limit to the number of times that a practitioner may be observed. However, that is the least of the reasons why there needs to be a professional dialogue between colleagues about the way they interact and extend children's learning. I have worked with settings that have videoed aspects of teaching and learning in their own setting and used it as a basis for staff development. Informal discussions of the key learning taking place leads naturally into evaluative comments about teaching. This paves the way to creating a trusting atmosphere between colleagues as they work together to provide the best for the children in their care. The standards for the early years professional status award also provide useful guidance on evaluating teaching and learning. The following list combines some of the professional standards for all qualified teachers and the standard for Early Years Professional Status (EYPS):

- Demonstrate professional knowledge and understanding. As already mentioned this relates to the practitioners familiarity with the principles and content of EYFS. This is manifest in practice through reference to development matters statements in planning, an understanding of observational assessment techniques.
- Provide safe and imaginative use of new technology that supports learning.
- Understanding how to monitor progress and share this information with parents.
- Create an environment of challenge and support where children can flourish and learn.
- Apply professional qualities and skills.
- Radiate personal enthusiasm for and commitment to learning by, for example, participating in research, analysis and debate about effective learning and how to improve achievement.
- Engage parents and help them to adopt practices that will promote their children's health and development.
- Identify and challenge discrimination that obstructs access to and engagement with learning.

The guidance to inspectors in the revised document *Conducting Early Years Inspections* (Ofsted, 2014) provides a less direct approach relating to the evaluation of teaching. Judgements relating to the quality of teaching in EYFS are less concerned about the quality of teaching and more about the impact of teaching on the progress that children are making in their setting. Practitioners are expected to understand and know the EYFS learning and development requirements and will observe to check that children are performing at typical levels of development and whether children who are disadvantaged or underperforming are catching up quickly. The publication of *Sound Foundations* (Mather et al., 2014) identified the four key dimensions of good-quality pedagogy for all children under three:

- Stable relationships and interactions with sensitive and responsive adults.
- A focus on play-based activities and routines which allow children to take the lead in their own learning.
- Support for communication and language.
- Opportunities to move and be physically active.

The key conditions for quality to take place include:

- knowledgeable and capable practitioners, supported by strong leaders;
- a stable staff team with low turnover;
- effective staff deployment (e.g. favourable ratios and staff continuity);
- secure yet stimulating physical environments;
- engaged and involved families.

Characteristics of effective teachers of language and literacy

The Ofsted survey *From Training to Teaching Early Language and Literacy* (2012) aimed to identify the characteristics of the best newly qualified teachers of language and literacy. As a result of their effective support, teachers were judged to have:

- a deep understanding of children's language development and understanding of the links between language skills and literacy skills;
- sufficient knowledge of language and literacy skills across the age groups, so that they were able to adapt their teaching for different age groups as well as pupils with a range of abilities and attainment;
- good questioning skills which helped pupils to develop their thinking skills through talking and listening;
- a good knowledge of phonics and how this supports reading and spelling – they understood how to help pupils use the skills they have learnt throughout the curriculum.

Along with all the above qualities the teachers also had the ability to:

- create interesting experiences and activities that promote the use of language and children's listening skills;
- assess learning in language and literacy accurately and understand what to teach next to enable pupils to progress quickly;
- provide good models of spoken as well as written language;
- use accurate and precise pronunciation;
- blend and segment words when teaching phonics;
- use a wide range of well considered resources to help to extend vocabulary and create enthusiasm for writing;
- assess pupils throughout lessons and target their questioning, providing sufficient challenge and support for different pupils;

- understand how to support pupils with special educational needs and those who are at an early stage of acquiring English;
- be proficient in teaching language and literacy skills across the curriculum;
- be highly reflective practitioners.

(Ofsted, 2012)

The findings from a later Ofsted survey provide further examples of the characteristics of effective pedagogy in the early years. The quality of early years teaching is defined by Ofsted as:

- communicating and modelling language
- showing, explaining, demonstrating
- exploring ideas, encouraging, questioning, recalling
- providing a narrative for what they are doing
- facilitating and setting challenges.

(Ofsted, 2015a: 10)

Quality pedagogy in Sweden

What can be learned from other countries? A relatively recent review of provision for young children in Sweden (Taguma et al., 2013) channels its main priorities to identifying the level of quality that children experience. The *Quality Toolbox for Early Childhood Education and Care* identified five policy levers that can encourage quality in Early Childhood Education Centres (ECEC), which is Sweden's early childhood curriculum. The five levers that ensure quality provision are:

- setting out quality goals and regulations;
- designing and implementing curriculum and standards;
- improving qualifications, training and working conditions;
- engaging families and communities;
- advancing data collection, research and monitor.

The art of effective early years practice is getting the balance right between guided and self-initiated learning either in homes or settings. Excellent settings according to Evangelou and Soukakou (2012) encouraged more 'sustained shared thinking'. Two or more individuals work together to solve a problem, clarify a concept, evaluate activities or extend a narrative. The review found that this does not happen very frequently, although in some adult modelling there is limited use of open-ended questioning. Freely chosen play activities often provided the best opportunities for adults to extend children's thinking. It is important that adults extend child-initiated play as well as teacher-initiated group work, as both are important for promoting effective learning. Chapter 5 provides examples of exemplary approaches to teaching and learning for 2-year-olds in school settings.

But is it as straightforward as this? What are the key dimensions and barriers to overcome in your settings? The knowledge and understanding of the adults working in the setting, the resources available, relationships with all the stakeholders, parents, fellow professionals, the children, the accommodation and what the children have available for their learning. All have an impact on helping to define quality. To tease out the vital elements of quality in relation not only to how children learn but also what is provided for them, we can turn to recent and longer enduring research that helps define quality and also provides a theoretical base for giving aspiring practitioners confidence and security in how they relate to young children, engage with them to encourage participation and explain and discuss with parents how their child is settling in and beginning to learn.

Ofsted may provide a framework, but does not instill beliefs into early years practitioners, hence the use of showing effective practices on YouTube. An understanding of the underlying knowledge about the nature of children's learning becomes integral to understanding how children learn. The early years experts relating to early childhood development and learning provide a solid theoretical base substantiated by extensive, recent research. One of the main dilemmas that early years practitioners may have is the conflicting opinions of early years researchers and the strength that each may effectively demonstrate in their research outcomes into what is best for young children's development. There are differences, too, in the ways in which teaching and learning are approached depending on whether the children are in a preschool or school/reception class environment. From a personal viewpoint I have been swayed by very recent Ofsted surveys (2015a, 2015b) in which there is to some extent an extension to Evangelou's finding quoted earlier stating that 'freely chosen play is the best way for adults to extend children's thinking'. To quote, 'play provides the natural, imaginative and motivating contexts for children to learn about themselves, one another and the world around them' (Ofsted, 2015b: 8). Play and the need to teach were equally important. While this may be a straightforward finding, the leaders of the exemplary settings held conflicting views about this based on their personal beliefs and philosophies. This is to be expected as over the years this has always been the case.

The reflective practitioner

> An individual does not stop learning and developing once they have completed their initial training and become qualified…They need further training to enhance and develop that knowledge, skills and to keep pace with new research and developments. This is well recognised by professions such as teaching and nursing, and it must be equally true in the early years.
>
> (DfE 2012c: 4.23)

In order to build on the emphasis made by Ofsted of the importance of being a 'reflective practitioner', the following actions are considered. Reflective practice is the process of thinking about and analysing your practice, leading to a continuous cycle of reflection and improvement. PACEY (Professional association for childcare and early years) suggest asking yourself the following questions.

- Do you take a balanced view of your practice?
- Do you recognise and celebrate your strengths?
- Do you acknowledge what could be improved?
- Eventually your practice will help to develop your professional development needs.

(PACEY, 2013)

How then do you embark on evaluating and reflecting on your practice? Is it something to be done on your own or reflecting with colleagues? There are statutory requirements linked to self-evaluation from Ofsted in the form of the early years evaluation form and an evaluation schedule for inspecting registered early years provision. There are also various early years rating scales that can act as a starting point and are worthy of examination of the national data gathered by researchers over the years. However, as recently qualified practitioners, this is unlikely to be your responsibility. For newly qualified staff the first six months are a time when much new knowledge and experience is acquired and assimilated, and confidence around child and family is being developed. During this time, leaders and other experienced staff in a setting have a crucial role to play in creating an environment that is welcoming and supportive to new colleagues, and ensure all staff are able to learn, reflect on and improve their practice. New staff need time to reflect on their practice, to link it to their understanding of theory and the time to be able to discuss this with more experienced practitioners. The single reception class teacher in a primary school may have difficulties with this, so it is important that you are able to contact other practitioners in the same position or get together with heads and/or staff of feeder nursery schools. Do this after checking the quality of their most recent Ofsted report as, according to Nutbrown (DfE, 2012c: 4.28), a member of staff will not benefit from being mentored by a practitioner whose own practice is not good enough. That, according to Nutbrown (2012c), would be someone working in a setting with an Ofsted rating below 'Good'.

Measuring quality

There are some very recent research projects that have addressed the issue of 'quality in the early years'. Mathers, Roberts and Silva (Pugh and Duffy, 2014) discuss conceptualising quality. They distinguish between process, structure and outcome. Measuring quality in this way is difficult and time consuming. Ofsted, for example, tended in the past to focus very much on structure and outcome to measure quality in this way. It is still a widely regarded benchmark on which to gauge quality. There are other well-known early years tools such as the Environment Rating Scale, which have been in use for many years as a measure of quality. The Effective Pre-School, Primary and Secondary Education study (EPPE: Sylva et al., 2004) also assessed the effects of early education and care on children's development. The quality of the pre-school setting attended by these children was a major factor in the outcomes for the children. A further indicator of quality is the level of qualifications of the staff and the level of staff to child ratios. The Nutbrown Review (DfE, 2012c) focused on childcare qualifications as well as early education to corroborate other reviews regarding the importance of staffing expectations and the minimum standard expected of those working in the early years sector. In all she made nineteen recommendations to the government related to staffing, the routes into the profession and the status of various qualifications. Academics and others are critical of the Ofsted model used to measure the performance of pre-school settings. However, this is the model that all early years practitioners are likely to come up against and therefore it is relevant that would-be practitioners have a grasp of the main strands of this. The research by Mathers et al. (2014) compares the usefulness of Ofsted reports and makes recommendations as to how useful reports need to be for parents. The Environment Rating Scales are also evaluated along with Quality Assurance (QA) schemes run by local authorities.

A question they asked in the Nuffield research was 'Who helps to improve quality?' Their findings go beyond the 'process, structure and outcome' statements to some extent. They found that parents help to determine quality by their choices based on information available on websites and how much information they can access. Local authorities (LAs) also help to improve quality in how funding is granted for free places. Indeed, this research identified many dimensions of quality such as:

- quality of interactions between staff and children;
- the ratio of staff to children and their qualifications;
- leadership and management;
- the setting's own improvement agenda;
- children attending settings that scored higher in ECEKS and ITERS do better than children in lower-quality settings.

There are several challenges to Ofsted scores for early years settings which do not predict children's later outcomes, based on research by Hopkins et al. (2010). A high Ofsted grade, he suggests, does not guarantee that children are experiencing high-quality provision, particularly for the children under 30 months. This is a finding discussed further in Chapter 6. A major criticism by Hopkins relates to how parents perceive the information they receive. For example, it is suggested that Ofsted and LAs should share more information with parents and make more use of the knowledge of the early years professionals. Parents should be provided with guidance on what to look for when visiting settings. The most recent guidance for Ofsted inspectors is a useful tool to modify for parents. What does high-quality childcare look like? Do parents understand the new EYFS? Research suggests that Ofsted reports need to be clearer in the language they use and a distinction needs to be made for 2-year-olds in reports. This criticism is excellently refuted in two very recent publications: *Parents as Partners in Teaching* (Ofsted, 2015c), a good practice example of a small, rural infant school, and *Teaching and Play in the Early Years: A Balancing Act* (Ofsted, 2015b). There are excellent examples to be found of how LAs achieved quality within an authority (DCSF, 2008a) The example in Figure 2.1 comes from Bolton LA and was given as an example in a National Strategy publication (DFES, 2008a) to show how quality can be organised around three key factors: workforce, practice and environment. With children at the centre, these factors interact and enable the children's enjoyment, well-being, learning, development and better long-term outcomes.

Sustained shared thinking

The Effective Provision for Preschool Education (Siraj-Blatchford et al., 2007) project has provided an effective baseline on which to judge quality based on the hypothesis that children whose thinking skills have been nurtured in the company of supportive adults will do better than children whose thinking has been developed alone or in the company of their peers. This finding is very much corroborated in recent examples of outstanding practice (Ofsted, 2015b, 2015c). The project was instrumental in identifying the effects on children of different types of pre-school provision and the characteristics of more effective pre-school settings, such as interaction styles, pedagogy and staff training. The crucial factor in excellent settings is the encouragement of more 'sustained shared thinking' (Syraj-Blatchford et al., 2007). This is defined as 'an episode in which two or more individuals "work together" in an intellectual way to solve a problem, clarify a concept, evaluate activities, extend narrative etc'. A child and an adult are expected to contribute to the thinking and it must develop and extend *that* thinking. The EPPE research project found that generally this did not happen very frequently. In excellent settings there were more than in good settings. This led the research team to conclude that periods of 'sustained shared thinking' are a necessary prerequisite for excellent early years practice, especially where this is encouraged in the home through parent support. The evidence suggests that 'adult modelling' is often combined with periods of 'sustained shared thinking', and that open-ended questioning is also associated with better cognitive development. The research found that open-ended questions made up only 5.1 per cent of the questioning used in even the excellent settings. Another crucial finding is that there is an equal balance between who initiates activities, staff or a child, in the excellent settings. Staff in excellent settings regularly extend child-initiated activities but do not dominate them. The balance in reception classes changes with much greater emphasis on adult-initiated episodes. Children spend much of their time in small groups. However, episodes of sustained shared thinking were most likely to occur when children were interacting one-to-one with an adult or a single peer partner. Freely chosen play activities provide the best opportunities for adults to extend children's thinking. Adults have to create opportunities to extend child-initiated play as well as teacher-initiated group work as both have been found to be important for promoting learning.

Learning from research

The research by Mathers et al. (2012, 2014) and Evangelou et al. (2012), along with the theories of Bruner (1983), Vygotsky (1978) and Sarah Meadows (1993) are included to provide a theoretical and practical basis to underpin and develop the intuitive beliefs and understandings of aspiring and qualified early years practitioners to inform their day-to-day work with young children. The expectations of Ofsted surveys and reports are referred to as a steer to early years providers in whatever setting they work, whether registered early years providers or not. These are the guidance documents on the evaluation schedule (Ofsted, 2014) and guidance for inspecting early years provision required to deliver the Early Years Foundation Stage. Despite shortcomings, according to research (Mathers et al., 2012), that Ofsted inspections do not provide an accurate account of settings in their reports, there is still a wealth of very helpful information to leaders and staff in settings in their guidance. It is not my intention to celebrate or even recommend guidance from Ofsted, but having spent many years observing and inspecting early years settings and providing training to serving and trainee teachers, I know that this is the kind of information they find helpful and, along with other sources of research into the early years, provide clear indicators of quality and pertinent signposts to help readers develop their professional system of beliefs.

The key to improving quality lies in improvements to staffing in every sector. Graduate leadership makes a marked impact on improvements to provision for the least and most advantaged 3- and 4-year-olds. Less than half of private and voluntary nurseries employ a graduate (Mathers and Smee, 2014).

The issues relating to quality childcare have become critical in the past ten years. Due to the increase in the PVI settings with 44 per cent of 3-year-olds paying to access early education in a PVI setting. The consequences of free provision of 30 hours a week for working parents of 3- and 4-year-olds could have devastating effects on access to provision for disadvantaged children as they are more likely to come from families where parents are lower wage earners, unemployed or do not work. Research found there was only a small impact on children at age 5 and age 7 who had attended childcare. However, the small positive impact came mostly from children who would not have attended early education without the free entitlement. The less advantaged children did almost 15 points better on the FSP (Foundation Stage Profile) than they would have done. Nevertheless, the overall findings of the EPPE project found that a sizeable proportion of 3-year-olds were already in early education due to mothers working, and therefore it might have been more cost effective to target the financial resources to high-quality intervention for the poorest children. This is questionable because what did happen was a greater mixing of children from different backgrounds in the same early education setting. EPPE formed the bedrock of the government's evidence base by concluding that children who received pre-school education in the later 1990s had better cognitive development. What will happen in the future is not clear. There is the commitment of a Conservative government increasing free childcare to 30 hours per week in the recent manifesto and due to commence in 2016, which is a year earlier than planned and for some families this will be earlier. This is reported to also increase the funding rate to providers, although this not yet finalised as headteachers in the maintained sector are expressing considerable concern that their budgets cannot pay for the additional children. The dilemma is that many providers will not have the capacity to take on children for a 30 hour week, especially in the smaller settings. The gainers in this are likely to be working mothers, who historically are those who have lamented the high costs of childcare in recent years. All other 3- and 4-year-olds can have 570 hours of free childcare, usually taken as 15 hours each week for 38 weeks of the year. How can early years settings be expected to pay for this without parents' contributions as in the past in the PVI sectors? A research topic by Mathers and Smee (2014) was to investigate the quality of early years provision for 3- and 4-year-olds in deprived areas. The 'quality gap' between nurseries catering for the least and most advantaged 3- and 4-year-olds is widest in relation to support for language skills. They stress that their findings were showing that disadvantaged children are already a year behind those from wealthier backgrounds in terms of their vocabulary by the time they are age 5, with the gap increasing as they move through school. Their conclusion is significant regarding language skills. Evidence from further afield by Gambaro et al. (2013) asked the question: Do children from disadvantaged backgrounds receive lower quality early years education and care in England? The findings of this research makes dismal reading when English provision is compared to that of several other countries: Australia, France, Germany, Netherlands, New Zealand, Norway and USA. However, I am less disheartened by this as I begin to recognise that, at last, someone is beginning to listen to the early years lobby and raise its profile in government and across the country as a whole, albeit at a time of financial restraint and welfare reductions. To return to the question, 'Generally how well are we doing using the 'Childcare triangle' of quality, cost and access?' England almost has universal enrolment for children aged 3+, with the US and Australia being exceptions. For under-3s, England is lower than Norway and Netherlands, similar to France and New Zealand and above Germany and the US. The quality indicators of qualifications show that English requirements are lower than Norway, France and New Zealand but higher than Germany, Netherlands, Australia and the US. England has the lowest staff ratio (fewest children to staff) and a curriculum as do Norway and

New Zealand. Currently provision in the UK is most expressive for the unders-3s. Many threads relating to quality mentioned in this chapter are dealt with in more detail in the relevant chapters; for example, 2-year-olds and the curriculum.

Topics for discussion

- What are the main barriers to achieving quality in your setting?
- If you have overcome barriers to quality provision or children's progress, what were the key features of your success?
- Discuss the most effective strategies for staff development.

Further reading

Abbott, L. and Rodger, R. (1994) *Quality Education in the Early Years*. Buckingham: Oxford University Press.

Vygotsky, L. (1978) Interaction between learning and development. *Mind in Society* (pp. 79–91) Cambridge, MA: Harvard University Press. Printed in Gauvain, G. and Cole, M. (2008) *Readings on the Development of Children*. New York: Worth Publishers.

What is an early years curriculum?

Introduction

Using the term 'curriculum' for this age is about giving the youngest children the same status as older children. It is showing that the learning and development of a 1-year-old is as important as that of a 15-year-old (Pugh and Duffy, 2014: 17). The use of words such as 'curriculum', 'areas of learning', 'prime' and 'specific' are educational jargon that do not always relate too well to what children under 5 are about as they learn, play and develop. However, those practitioners entering the profession will need to familiarise themselves with this jargon. It is important not to lose sight of the key principles of the early years. This chapter aims to provide an overview of the *Statutory Framework for the Early Years Foundation Stage* (EYFS) which became mandatory for all early years providers from 1 September 2014. It will also debate the use of the word 'curriculum' and attempt to define what it means in the early years and why it is a valid term to use. A curriculum is the framework from which learning experiences emerge planned and unplanned. Children are the prime agents of learning based on their interests and abilities, which vary depending on their age and stage of development. This is now encapsulated in the statutory framework for the early years. It is worthwhile exploring the focus on 'prime areas of learning' as examples of what children enjoy doing the most – talking and singing, being active and playing, both within a secure environment where they feel safe, confident and happy. Adult intervention adds the cognitive dimension in communication, language literacy, mathematics, knowledge of the world, and expressive arts and design of the specific areas of learning. It is reassuring to know that the evidence base for inspectors when inspecting early years settings is based on direct observation of the way in which children demonstrate the characteristics of effective learning:

- Playing and exploring
- Active learning
- Creative and critical thinking.

(Ofsted, 2014: 7)

The key role of play in the early years has an appropriate status in the dissemination of recent Ofsted surveys (2015a, 2015b). The ways in which other countries provide for their youngest children in an educational context is also described and the views of early years practitioners are shared. Over many years, early years practitioners have adapted early years practices from several countries, some of which remain embedded in current early years practice such as the Reggio Emilia and High/Scope curricula. Australia, New Zealand and Sweden may also have influenced our practice, which is why the principal philosophies of these well-known models are included in this chapter. Examples of ways to organise your space indoors and outdoors are suggested to assist practitioners about to start their careers in the early years.

An appropriate curriculum

The inclusion of this chapter is prompted because of a response by an early years academic who rejected the idea that there can be a 'curriculum' for the early years. There is plenty of justification for using the familiar word 'curriculum'. The quotation from *The Early Years Curriculum* (Pugh and Duffy, 2014: 117) suggests that the use of 'curriculum' accords early years practices the same status as all learning for children. The activities and resources provided for children will vary depending on the age of the children in a setting. The word 'curriculum' fits well too when making comparisons with other countries. It is an internationally used word in the early years field, widespread and familiar, for example, as in *Scottish Curriculum for Excellence, High/Scope Curriculum* in Sweden and New Zealand's *curriculum*. In Sweden, a high status is given to the 'curriculum' as the basis of a common framework as it helps staff to clarify their pedagogical aims, keep progression in mind and provide a structure for the child's day.

The use of the word 'curriculum' becomes more relevant also when used alongside the word 'appropriate'. This is particularly crucial now that there are likely to be a fair proportion of 2-year-olds in settings learning and playing alongside 3- and 4-year-olds. A definition of curriculum used in national publications over the years is 'the term used to describe everything that children do, see, hear or feel in their setting, both planned and unplanned' (DCFS, 2009). What is valued most highly? The appropriateness of the experiences provided to help children learn and develop in situations that are most suitable goes some way towards answering this question. Practitioners may shy away from the use of the word 'curriculum' because of the connotations it has with a formal approach to learning and is therefore an inappropriate term to use in the early years. In the past Sylva (1992) warned of the detrimental effect of the National Curriculum on children under 5, citing evidence which revealed that formal pre-school education impedes progress. Her concern rightly was that over emphasis on an academic orientation linked to the then 'desirable learning outcomes' was at the expense of children's social and collaborative skills. There are critics of the use of the word 'curriculum' in an early years context; for example, Abbot and Langston (2005) wrote of the formal learning that could be implied by using the word 'curriculum', which is, as they see it, very much a term for older children in school. The early years professionals have debated and reviewed what the priorities should be for learning and development in children under 5. This is now encapsulated in the *Statutory Framework for the Early Years* (DfE, 2014a) and provides a common structure for early learning.

The Statutory Framework for the Early Years Foundation Stage in England

The Early Years Foundation Stage (DfE 2014a) sets the standards that all early years providers must meet to ensure that children learn and develop well and are kept healthy and safe. It promotes teaching and learning to ensure 'school readiness' and gives children the broad range of knowledge and skills that provide the right foundation for good future progress throughout school and life. The EYFS seeks to provide:

- *quality and consistency* in all early years settings, so that every child makes good progress and no child gets left behind;
- *secure foundation* through learning and development opportunities;
- *partnership working* between practitioners and with parents and/or carers;
- *equality of opportunity* and anti-discriminatory practices ensuring that every child is included and supported.

There is research that praises those countries that have a clear policy vision and coordinating frameworks for children from birth to 8 and a lifelong learning approach from birth onwards, encouraging smooth transitions for children (Bennet, 2004). More recent views suggest that the EYFS curriculum is held in high regard by practitioners in other countries, precisely because there is a uniformity across settings that is valued by parents and practitioners alike (Oberhuemer, 2005). Other researchers have compared other well-known curricula: Reggio Emilia, Te Whariki (New Zealand), EE (Belgium), High/Scope and the Swedish National Curriculum for Pre-school. There are a number of similarities with the EYFS (DfE, 2014a). These are:

- A child is seen as an 'active child who initiates communication and who is interested in the surrounding world'.
- They visualise the child's rights, but children's needs form the basis of rights in EE and High/Scope and children's rights are stated in Reggio Emilia, Te Whariki and the Swedish National Curriculum (LPFO).
- Interaction and communication play a central role in learning and well-being, particularly in Te Whariki.
- They emphasise the importance of parental involvement, which was most evident in Te Whariki.
- Staff should be encouraged to develop their understanding of child development and of each child through reflective practice.

(Samuelsson et al., 2006)

The EYFS framework sets the standards for learning, development and care for children from birth to 5. The statutory guidance provides a section (DfE, 2014a: 7) defining what practitioners must do. There is the expectation of working in partnership with parents and carers (see Chapter 7). The learning and development requirements are informed by the best available evidence on how children learn. The areas of learning and development are: communication and language, physical development and personal, and social and emotional development as the prime areas. The prime areas are applied through the specific areas, literacy, mathematics, understanding the world, expressive arts and design. (Table 3.1). This publication focuses primarily on the first two sections of the framework, that is, the learning and development requirements and assessment in separate chapters.

The final section of the framework covers the safeguarding and welfare requirements, which includes child protection, suitable people, staff qualifications, training, support and skills, key person, staff–child ratios, health and managing behaviour. Aspects of each of the safeguarding and welfare requirements are included throughout other chapters. The critical section of the framework for practitioners is 1.8 of the EYFS, which states very explicitly how children under 5 learn and the ways in which practitioners are expected to relate to their children in all settings:

> Each area of learning and development must be implemented through planned, purposeful play and through a mix of adult-led and child-initiated activity. Play is essential for children's development, building their confidence as they learn to explore, to think about problems, and relate to others.

> (DfE, 2014a: 9)

The framework applies to all early years providers: maintained schools; non-maintained schools; independent schools; all providers on the early years register; and all providers registered with an early years childminder agency. The next section reviews some of the recent research that has informed the EYFS framework and the increased reference to the key role of play in developing children's learning. Case studies are included from pre-school and reception class settings to highlight outstanding practices. The impact of the Reggio Emilia

TABLE 3.1 The prime and specific areas of learning and development

AREAS OF LEARNING AND DEVELOPMENT	ASPECT
Prime areas	
Personal, social and emotional development	Making relationships Self-confidence and self-awareness Managing feelings and behaviour
Physical development	Moving and handling Health and self-care
Communication and language	Listening and attention Understanding Speaking
Specific areas	
Literacy	Reading Writing
Mathematics	Numbers Shape, space and measures
Understanding the world	People and communities The World Technology
Expressive arts and design	Exploring and using media and materials Being imaginative

approach, High/Scope and early years practices in other countries are cited. English early years practices have developed and improved considerably in the past few years and are held in high regard by early years providers in other countries. According to Ofsted, 80 per cent of early years settings are currently good or outstanding. Ofsted's priority to early years is evident in the publications over the past two years of a dedicated early years publication. *Early Years* (Ofsted, 2015a). The reality is that to ensure children make progress, 'teaching' needs to encompass adults providing worthwhile activities in a play-centred environment. My own experience suggests that there are many early years settings that have planned topics to enable children to enjoy where they play and learn, and also to provide a context in which to learn and apply basic skills, particularly communication, language and literacy skills, especially in reception classes. This is less likely in pre-schools but even there it is probably necessary to plan, at least in the mind of the adult, what is going to be provided for the children to enable resources to be gathered or visits organised. As a result, practitioners are able to build on children's experiences and to extend their learning through their explanations, observations, demonstrations and direct engagement with children to ask questions, model language and solve problems.

The learning and development requirements cover:

- the areas of learning and development which must shape activities and experiences (educational programmes) for children in all early years settings;
- the early learning goals that providers must help children work towards (the knowledge, skills and understanding children should have at the end of the academic year in which they turn five;
- assessment arrangements for measuring progress (a requirement for reporting to parents and/or carers).

(DfE, 2014a: 5)

There are seven areas of learning and development (Table 3.1) which capture the fundamental intellectual and social needs of children. The early learning goals set out the knowledge, skills and understanding children should have by the time they leave reception class. All areas of learning are important and inter-connected. Three areas of learning are particularly crucial for inspiring children's curiosity and enthusiasm for learning. These are the prime areas which are fundamental to children's successful learning in the specific areas. The specific areas cannot be encountered in isolation from communication and language or personal, social, emotional and physical development since children always experience the world through communication, physical and sensory involvement. The focus needs to be on the prime areas of learning for younger children.

This is a reassuring development and one which should help practitioners develop their practices with young children to fully reflect 'playing and exploring', 'active learning' and developing 'creative and critical thinking'. Hopefully, there will be less emphasis on unnecessary paperwork. The guidance for inspecting early years settings states very clearly that:

The inspector should not routinely expect to see detailed written plans for the activities they observe, although they must look at plans when they are offered by practitioners.

(Ofsted, 2014a: 11)

The next section reviews some of the recent research that has informed the EYFS framework and the increased reference to the status of play in the statutory guidance.

Learning through play

> We know that play is fundamental to children's wellbeing, learning and development, and it is essential that early years practitioners understand, value and support young children's play in its various forms.
>
> (DfE, 2012c)

Learning through play is given a high status in the EYFS framework (DfE, 2014a) and in recent Ofsted guidance documents (Ofsted, 2013a, 2015b) for inspectors and in very recent surveys of good practice in early years settings with 2-year-olds (Ofsted, 2015c). Research (Evangelou et al., 2009) supports the valuable contribution adults or more knowledgeable others can make to improving children's cognitive and language development as a result of their interaction with children as they play or as Ofsted describe it to 'Teach and Play'. One of the main objectives of Evangelou's research review was to identify the best supportive contexts for children's early learning and development. How does pre-school/nursery class provide that context? Has play always been given such a high status? Recent observations of practice, where 2-year-olds are attending early years units or nursery classes corroborate the key role played by adults and older children in inducting the youngest children:

> Play is a prime context for development.
>
> (Evangelou et al., 2009: 4)

Studies of the different kinds of play, especially the ways it can be enriched by guiding, planning and resourcing on the part of staffing settings, is fully reflected in Ofsted's guidance to inspectors:

> the main evidence comes from inspectors' direct observations of the ways in which children demonstrate the key characteristics of effective learning – playing and exploring, for example.
>
> (Ofsted, 2014: 7)

The Evangelou review acknowledges new developmental theories which assume that development proceeds in a web of multiple strands, with different children following different pathways:

> the art of early years practice is getting the balance right between guided and self-initiated learning.
>
> (Evangelou et al., 2009)

Here's the rub. At what point do practitioners intervene, in their minds, to extend learning or possibly, from a child's viewpoint, interrupt a sequence of play? One can read over and over again of how 'play can be used to enrich and enhance children's learning and development'. On whose terms should intervention take place – the child's or the adult's? It is vital to engage with children on their terms (Wood, 2014: 98). The EPPE research by Sylva et al (2004) over recent years provides some clues as to the strategies adults need to adopt to sustain children's play. The phrase 'sustained shared thinking' (SST) defined as instances where two or more children work together in an intellectual way to solve a problem, clarify a concept, evaluate activities or extend a narrative. SST can also occur between an adult and a child/children. The familiarity of a child with the source of the activity is critical. From experience, to be in a situation where a child is in a more knowledgeable position than the adult creates an appropriate environment for 'solving problems, evaluating an activity and extending a narrative'.

Kwom (2002) offered a word of caution about the value of free play as research shows that it does not maximise cognitive development because there may be a lack of challenge since children do not always persist at tasks and conversation between adult and child may be limited. This potential finding about free play is wisely addressed in Sweden, where the ECEC curriculum puts the child and play at the centre of the curriculum, balancing content by addressing academic and socio-economic development. The longitudinal study of a national sample of young children's development between the ages of 3 and 7 years (Siraj-Blatchford et al., 2004) has indentified a range of characteristics that make an impact on children's successful development. In the context of this publication and what practitioners found important was the definition of an effective pedagogy including interaction traditionally associated with the term 'teaching' and the provision of instructive learning environments and the 'sustained shared thinking' (SST) studies of the different kinds of play, especially the ways it can be enriched by guiding, planning and resourcing on the part of staffing. The philosophical views are captured well in the discussion below with a serving headteacher of an outstanding school and exemplary provider of integrated provision for 2-year-olds. Her aim is to develop a philosophy to meet the needs of the children in the community. This involves three strands:

- the adult leading the teaching of activities deemed to be worthwhile for the children;
- children exploring on their own with no adult direction as they explore having a go, retry and begin to understand;
- a meeting point between the two as children's interest is used to take an activity to the next level and draw the children into what happens next.

Model making, painting, exploring and features of the natural environment all contribute to the challenges children need to face. Adults need to make sensitive interactions with children. Play is something that needs to be taking place to enable the teaching of specific skills. Adult input into play praises children's efforts, provides key vocabulary and encouragement to develop new language. A key principle of the headteacher is that parents are the first teachers of children and all she achieves is in partnership with parents, helping their children and as a result her pupils attain exceptionally well. Supporting learning is teaching in the early years and everything adults are doing is promoting children's learning. They are doing things such as:

- communicating
- modelling language
- setting challenges
- explaining
- demonstrating
- solving problems

It is imperative that children are able to use the whole physical environment inside and outside. Teachers want children to learn at the highest level and are likely to succeed where there is direct questioning and some overt modelling. The case study below demonstrates how an English-speaking child is able to support a bilingual learner in a Manchester reception class.

CASE STUDY 3.1 Supporting bilingual learners

In the Foundation Stage classroom, the structured play area was developed to extend the topic 'Light and Dark' by setting up as a bear's cave. The space to do this in the classroom was very restricted, but as it turned out, this was a bonus because of the security and intimacy provided for the children in the cave. Ingeniously designed walls and flaps over the entrances ensured there was a high degree of privacy and authenticity for a small number of children to play together. The stimulus for the story was 'Do Little Bears Sleep?', copies of which were displayed inside the cave along with other stories familiar to the children. Creatures suspended from the ceiling and cushions on the floor provided a comfortable concealed environment away from the hustle and bustle of the classroom. Torches of various sizes and colours were available for the children to see the pictures in the book. Clipboards with outlines of Mr Blobby were available for children's use. The class teacher routinely targeted pairs of children with EAL to explore and work in the cave. Her intentions were to encourage the children to construct their own literacy and play experiences. Her curriculum plans identified the ways in which this environment was planned to support children's literacy learning. She encouraged the children to share a story, always pairing a linguistically capable child with a less confident one. Children who spoke the same home language were encouraged to work together, thus providing support and encouragement for the less fluent speaker of English and also enabling the children to share the story in their home language (Rodger, 1998: 158).

Learning from other countries

There are several areas across the world with innovative early years practices that have stood the test of time and are making an impact on the daily practices in many pre-schools across the UK. In particular I would want to share the strengths of the High/Scope curriculum from the USA, the Reggio Emilia Approach from Italy, and the Swedish early years curriculum. There also follows an account of the way in which Scotland approaches defining their early years provision.

The High/Scope curriculum

The cornerstone of the High/Scope approach to early childhood education is the belief that *active participatory learning through play* is fundamental to the full development of the human potential.

(www.highscope.org)

The High/Scope curriculum is defined as a cultural construct derived from what we as a nation value most highly for all our children. What is valued most highly? The appropriateness of the experiences provided to help children learn and develop in situations that are most suitable goes some way towards answering this question.

The High/Scope model of learning originated in the USA with the aim of improving life chances of children by promoting a high-quality educational programme. It was developed as a result of the concern about the failure of high school students from Ypsilanti's poorest neighbourhood in 1962. A key basis of the High/Scope curriculum is that the children are active learners. The approach requires practitioners to have a particular classroom arrangement, a daily schedule, an assessment and a curriculum (content). The philosophy behind High/Scope was originally based on Piaget's research on child development and John Dewey's philosophy of progressive education. Currently, High/Scope is underpinned by more recent research. Its teaching draws very much on the work of Lev Vygotsky (1978), especially the strategy of adult scaffolding – supporting children at their current developmental level and helping them build on it. Crucially, the adults working with the children see themselves more as facilitators or partners than as mangers or supervisors. The High/Scope curriculum provides a range of experiences appropriate to young children's stage of development. It is based on three principles:

- Active participation of children in choosing, organising and evaluating learning activities. Practitioners observe and guide children towards various classroom learning centres, based on the children's wishes.
- Regular daily planning by practitioners linked to a development-based curriculum model and child observations.
- Developmentally sequenced goals and materials for children based on the High/Scope key experiences.

The children have a daily programme of *plan-do-review* which is unique to High/Scope, and enables children to express their intentions, carry them out and reflect on what they have done. *Small group time* provides educator-initiated learning experiences based on their observations of children's interests, key developmental indicators and local events. In *large group time*, educators and children initiate music and movement activities, storytelling and so on. Alongside this, the key role played by parents is fostered, especially to encourage fathers, as well as mothers and other carers. Regular observations and assessment of children's learning as they take part in activities is essential to the approach. Staff teams share their observations and assessments to plan further learning experiences and interactions. High/Scope has had and continues to have a major impact on the ways in which settings are organised.

A US view of setting core standards for the early years (2015)

In January 2015, Defending the Early Years and the Alliance for Childhood released a report entitled Reading Instruction in Kindergarten: Little to Gain and Much to Lose (www.allianceforchildhood.org), outlining the potentially damaging effects of the Common Core standards for kindergarten students in the US. It cited several research studies published over the past several years. The report makes several key recommendations, most notably that the Common Core Standards are dropped immediately. There was a shift away from play-based learning in American kindergarten over the past few years to a more direct instruction. This emphasis on academic skills is seen to have ignored the research on how young children learn best. Studies show that students who attended play-based pre-schools and kindergartens perform better on cognitive and social-emotional development than their peers who attended more academic programmes. The High/Scope Preschool Curriculum Comparison Study (Schweinhart, 1997) found that, by age 15, students who attended direct instruction pre-schools were more than twice as likely to have exhibited delinquent behaviour. These findings give further weight to the validity of the revised EYFS (2014).

The Reggio Emilia Approach

This approach is reputed to be one of the best educational programmes in the world. Based in northern Italy, it is built around core beliefs about how children learn, introduced by the former founder, Loris Malaguzzi, directly after World War II. The more recent publication, *The Hundred Languages of Children* (Edwards et al., 1998) provides a set of essays on his unique approach to early childhood education. There are less academic accounts of the Reggio Emilia approach online, such as *An Every Day Story*. It is recommended to anyone who has an interest in the education of young children. The Reggio system has been described as follows:

> It is a collection of schools for young children in which each child's intellectual, emotional, social and moral potentials are carefully cultivated and guided. The principal educational vehicle involves youngsters in long term engrossing projects which are carried out in a beautiful, healthy, love-filled setting.

The approach is relevant in this publication because of the impact it has had and continues to have on successful early years provision across the world, particularly the key role played by access to the outdoor learning environment, including Forest School approaches to early learning. Table 3.2 outlines the Reggio Emilia principles which are central to learning for the young children in Reggio Emilia.

The Reggio Emilia Approach principles

There are several factors that are inherent in the Reggio Approach: the image of the child; the expressive arts in the pre-school establishment; *progettazione*; community and parent–school relationships; environment and teachers as learners. A difference perhaps from our own images of children as 'empty vessels' is that the Reggio Approach educators believe strongly in a child with unlimited potential who is eager to interact with and contribute to the world. The child is driven by curiosity and imagination, a capable child who delights in taking responsibility for his or her own learning, a child who listens to, and listens. Unlike other pedagogies that treat infancy as preparation for later childhood, the Reggio Approach considers early infancy to be a distinct developmental phase in which children develop and demonstrate a distinctive curiosity about the world. The well-known term 'The Hundred Languages' was encapsulated by Loris Malaguzzi:

> The child is made of one hundred. The child has a hundred languages, a hundred hands, a hundred thoughts, a hundred ways of thinking of playing of speaking.

Progettazione is often understood to mean emergent curriculum or child-centred curriculum. What children want to do is expected to come from the child and the adult observes, listens and values the ideas to assist in deciding how to support as they give value to the children's

TABLE 3.2 Fundamental principles of Reggio Emilia (1998)

Children are capable of constructing their own learning They are driven by their interests to understand and know more.
Children form an understanding of themselves and their place in the world through their actions with others There is a strong focus on social collaboration, working in groups, where each child is an equal participant, having their thoughts and questions valued. The adult is not the giver of knowledge. Children search out knowledge through their own investigations.
Children are communicators Communication is a process, a way of discovering things, asking questions, using language as play. Playing with sounds and rhythm and rhyme; delighting in the process of communicating.
The environment is the third teacher The environment is recognised for its potential to inspire children. An environment filled with natural light, order and beauty. Open spaces free from clutter, where every material is considered for its purpose, every corner is ever-evolving to encourage children to delve deeper and deeper into their interests.
The adult is a mentor and guide Our role as adults is to observe (our) children, listen to their questions and their stories, find what interests them and then provide them with opportunities to explore those interests further.
An emphasis on documenting children's thoughts You will notice in Reggio and Reggio-inspired settings that there is an emphasis on carefully displaying and documenting children's thoughts and progression of thinking; making their thoughts visible in many different ways to show their understanding and express their thoughts and creativity.
The Hundred Languages of Children Probably the most well-known aspect of the Reggio Approach. The belief that children use many different ways to show their understanding and express their thoughts and creativity. A hundred different ways of thinking, of discovering, of learning through drawing and sculpting. Through dance and movement, through painting and pretend play, through modelling and music, and that each one of these Hundred Languages must be valued and nurtured. These languages or ways of learning are all part of the child. Learning and play are not separated. The Reggio Emilia Approach emphasises hands on discovery learning that allows the child to use all their senses and all their languages to learn.

own ideas. The programme or curriculum gives a high priority to the cultivation and guidance of children's intellectual, emotional, social and moral development. The educational vehicles for this are the long-term projects in which practitioners work alongside children encouraging initiative, listening to children's views and guiding them appropriately. The curriculum has a strong child-directed leaning with teachers following children's interests and not providing focused instruction in reading and writing. The outdoor environment plays a key role.

The Swedish ECE curriculum

A common curriculum framework helps ensure an even level of quality across different forms of provision and for different groups of children.

(Taguma et al., 2013: 9)

Readers may be surprised to read this account of the Swedish Early Childhood Education and Care (ECEC) Curriculum curriculum, which is so at odds with their previous reputation of a family model of pre-school centres and an interest in the holistic development and well-being of children, vividly described in a previous edition of this book. Sweden's guide to improving quality in the early childhood education and care (ECEC) curriculum rests with giving the curriculum the highest priority. Their use of the word 'curriculum' is quite explicit and refers to the content and methods that substantiate children's learning and development. Not only is it an aid to practitioners but it also provides guidance for parents to help them to learn about child development and encourages them to ensure a good home learning environment. Furthermore, their understanding of research into brain development supports its sensitivity to language, numeracy, social skills and emotional control all peaking at the age of 4. The foundations of key skills and abilities are thus deemed to be of great importance at this stage. Sweden suggests that their high-quality curriculum frameworks are related to practice in which cognitive and social development are viewed as complementary and of equal importance. Sweden also considers more overt linking of the ECEC curriculum with that of the primary school, which is in line with the EYFS to some extent. Similar to the English system, there is a process of research reviews to inform their ECEC policy.

In Sweden, however, a strong argument for a common framework for the ECEC was put forward which applies equally appropriately to the EYFS in England. There is a consensus on the importance of an explicit curriculum with a clear purpose, goals and approaches for zero to school-age children. Some structuring and orientation of children's experience towards educational aims is generally expected. There is little pedagogical direction for younger children. The curriculum is influenced by many factors: societies' values, content standards, research findings, community expectations, culture and language. The ECEC curricula provide developmentally appropriate support and cognitive challenges that can lead to positive child outcomes. A common framework can help ensure an even level of quality across different forms of provision and for different groups of children. Guidelines for practice in the form of curricula framework help staff to clarify their pedagogical aims, keep progression in mind, provide a structure for the child's day and focus observation on the most important aspects of child development. This account could not differ more from the description of 'free' schools, which have largely been abandoned in Sweden. It is reassuring to be able to see similarities in early years practices in another country whose early years policies have generally been highly regarded in the UK.

The Scottish early years curriculum

The Scottish early years policy is also based on recent research that has pinpointed the importance of play, reflected in the publication *Play Strategy for Scotland: Our Vision* and *Play Strategy for Scotland: Our Action Plan* (Scottish Government, 2013). The opening quote in these documents is:

> We want Scotland to be the best place to grow up. A nation which values play as a life-enhancing daily experience for all our children and young people; in their homes, nurseries, schools and communities.

The rationale to improve play experiences for all children is based on children's right to play as set out in the United Nations Convention on the Rights of the Child. In some ways it is similar to the EYFS but with a much stronger emphasis on play. The Early Years Framework (EYF) has improving outcomes and children's quality of life through play, as one of the ten elements of transformation change set out in the EYF. Again there is reference to play in this document: 'Free play has the potential to contribute powerfully and positively to the most significant areas of life in schools, nurseries, early years and childcare.'

In Scotland, the use of the term *Curriculum for Excellence* is described as, 'flexible and meaningful, promotes real life learning and focuses on the needs of every child and young person'. It further includes play and active learning, transitions and playing and learning at home. Scotland does not have a centrally prescribed compulsory curriculum for the early years as in England. It has an *Early Years Framework* (2008). The early years phase is defined as pre-birth to 8 years old. This extension of the age span deliberately recognises the importance of pregnancy influencing outcomes and that the transition into primary school is a critical period in children's lives. The role of parents and the community are central with the development of nurseries, schools and childcare centres, giving this high priority and developing their role in family and community learning. There are strong elements of the Reggio Approach in Scottish pre-schools, evident in their publication *Early Education Support: The Reggio Emilia Approach to Early Education* (Learning and Teaching Scotland, 2006). Practitioners are guided to asking the question 'What can the Scottish early education system learn from the Reggio Approach?' There is strong encouragement to look at adapting pedagogical approaches and reflect on current practice.

This recent reappraisal of the goals for early learning may in part be a reflection of research data that show the home learning environment in the early years as the largest factor in attainment and achievement at age 10. In order to support the staff as they implement the key principles nine features of practice are suggested, all of which are deemed to be equally significant. They were not presented hierarchically.

- role of staff
- attachments
- transitions
- observation, assessment and planning
- partnership working
- health and well-being
- literacy and numeracy

- play
- environments.

It is very evident that there is no prescribed curriculum content as in England at this time. The development process has involved unparalleled engagement with teachers and practitioners. The professionalism of teachers and the importance of this in exercising the freedom and responsibility associated with broader guidance was a key position in 2008. However, more recently *The Early Years Strategy Progress Report* (Education Children and Families Committee, 2014) reported on the quality of services assessed by inspections of nursery classes, partner providers and Under Five Centres in Edinburgh. The most successful providers were praised for:

> The ethos based on trust and mutual respect which reflects the strong vision and shared values of the centres and the exceptional skills of staff in responding to individual children's needs and interests.

> High quality children's learning and achievement, and the commitment of staff to supporting children and families.

The two areas identified for development in most inspections were curriculum and self-evaluation. To develop the implementation of the curriculum, a range of resource materials has been produced and shared with early years centres; for example, literacy rich environment tool kits (indoors and outdoors) and a numeracy rich environment tool kit, as well as conferences on literacy and mathematics. Scotland's first national play strategy is supported by Aileen Campbell, the Minister for Children and Young People. She admirably supports the changing priorities in early years education.

> Play, as we know it, is an essential part of a healhy, happy childhood, taking place within the home from birth, through formal and informal learning and in community settings through the use of public spaces and services.

Organising your learning environment

A key decision needed when deciding how to organise an early years environment is what is the best for your children. There is no doubt that free choice activities need to dominate as that is the way to respond to where children want to play. This was backed up by American research covering ten countries (Montie et al., 2006) who found that when free choice activities had predominated in pre-school, children had significantly higher language development at age 7. They also found that less time spent in whole group pre-school activities was linked with higher cognitive development by age 7.

Practitioners will be constrained to some extent by the limitations of the classroom space available for the under-5s. However, there are very basic requirements for the youngest group of children in a primary school reception class. These are:

- free flow for children indoors and outdoors (to create equal status for learning);

- multi-purpose area for the whole class sessions but versatile for child-centred activities (not always needed in a nursery environment);
- reading area well supplied with easily accessible books and room for small group work;
- technology area (smart boards, computers);
- creative area – model-making, painting, clay, baking;
- exploratory area;
- children's area – lockers, coat pegs, space to put own things;
- snack area;
- some tables for table-top activities;
- role play/dressing up, maybe musical too;
- sand and water (inside and/or outside).

Mathematics is an area of learning that needs to permeate everywhere. There may be specific resources gathered in one place but children use their mathematical knowledge as they play games indoors and outdoors, so number lines, numbers on walls all need to be scattered indoors and outdoors. All areas need to be set up so staff can observe the children at a glance wherever they are playing. A large school may have a reception unit with as many as sixty to ninety children to enable sharing of resources. Ideally, the outdoor learning environment should mirror the indoor environment.

Discussion topics

- Discuss your definitions of curriculum and identify your priorities for learning.
- Share the differences between a pre-school and reception class with colleagues.
- What strategies are used to maintain visibility of the children in your setting?
- What are your key priorities in the early years?

Further reading

Nutbrown, C. (1999) *Threads of Thinking,* 2nd edition. London: Sage.
Pugh, G. and Duffy, B. (2014) *Contemporary Issues in the Early Years,* 6th edition. London: Sage.
Wood, E. (2013) *Play, Learning and the Early Childhood Curriculum,* 3rd edition. London: Sage.
Mirac Ozar (2012) Curriculum of Preschool Education: Swedish Approach, *International Journal of Business and Social Science* 3(22) (Special Issue).

Useful websites

Department of Education https://www.gov.uk
HighScope www.highscope.org
Ofsted www.ofsted.gov.uk
Play Strategy for Scotland: Our Action Plan, www.gov.scot

CHAPTER

4

Planning for children's learning

Introduction

This chapter aims to discuss planning methods and the ways in which nurseries and schools handle transition from one phase to another. It is important to recognise that the starting points for whatever children are learning are the children themselves, what they are interested in and how skilled practitioners build on those interests to extend learning. Careful planning and development of the child's experiences, with sensitive and appropriate intervention by the educator, will help nurture an eagerness to learn as well as enabling the child to learn effectively (Abbott and Rodger, 1994). This statement reflects the need to take account of what children are interested in doing and what practitioners know they need to learn. This may result in a framework to guide others and to assist assessment of learning, taking account of the prime and specific areas of learning as appropriate. Activities should be designed to build on regular, accurate assessments of children's learning, knowledge and skills, and adjusting activities to meet the needs of individual children and groups who are most at risk of falling behind. As stated in a recent Ofsted report:

> The most powerful learning occurs when more and less experienced learners work together to achieve a common goal.
>
> (Ofsted, 2015c: 1)

Each area of learning and development must be implemented through planned and purposeful play together with skilled teaching as this is the way children's language is developed, their communication skills are improved and a context is established to engage children in learning. Play is essential for children's development, building their confidence as they learn to explore, think about problems and relate to others. Practitioners vary in how they approach planning with a more formal approach to planning and teaching phonological awareness being more typical in reception classes where what children are expected to learn may be clearly planned out week-by-week, particularly the statutory requirement to teach children to read in a particular way. This is endorsed by Ofsted who found that approaches to early reading to be viewed as the most formal approach to learning. Schools generally had a dedicated time each day to teaching communication, language and literacy with short, sharp, focused teaching sessions. The opportunity for nursery- and reception-aged children to work together in an integrated early years unit is also a popular option, where children from the ages of 2 to 5 learn and play together. It is important to involve the children in planning. To quote the statutory guidance:

> Practitioners must respond to each child's emerging needs and interests, guiding their development through warm and positive interaction.
>
> (DfE, 2014a: 9)

Examples of starting points and the stimuli used by practitioners to introduce a topic are included in this chapter. Small group brainstorming with children to detect their interests and experiences, discussion with parents and events in the local community are all likely to provide potential starting points to enrich children's learning and interests. Practitioners need to consider the individual needs, interests and stage of development of each child in their care, and must use this information to plan a challenging and enjoyable experience in all areas of learning and development. Practitioners working with the youngest children are expected to focus strongly on the three prime areas which are the basis for the successful learning in the other four specific areas. The three prime areas reflect the key skills and capacities all children need to develop and learn effectively, and become ready for school. That is, a move to Year 1 (DFE, 2014a: 8).

The importance of the role play makes in developing children's early learning is fully endorsed in the revised Early Years Foundation Stage (EYFS) statutory guidance and is central to this chapter along with discussion of how a balance between play and teaching is achieved. Various strategies used by schools to ensure that transition from the early years to Year 1 is a smooth experience for children are suggested. There is little recent research evidence to confirm what works best, but certainly the views of practitioners are available. Links to appropriate websites and YouTube are provided to show outstanding provision and to provide planning examples.

Planning for Statutory Early Years Foundation Stage (DfE, 2014a)

- Planning should be based on observation of what has gone before and finds out how each child's learning development will or might progress.
- Planning should be sufficiently flexible to keep a focus on children's individual needs and interests – children learn in a range of ways, many not planned for at all.

In planning and guiding children's activities, practitioners must reflect on the different ways that children learn and reflect these in their practices. The three characteristics of effective teaching and learning are:

- *Playing and exploring* – children investigate and experience things, and 'have a go'.
- *Active learning* – children concentrate and keep on trying if they encounter difficulties, and enjoy achievements.
- *Creating and thinking critically* – children have and develop their own ideas, make links between ideas, and develop strategies for doing things.

(DfE, 2014a: 9)

The main changes in the EYFS have been in the way practitioners are planning. Before the statutory framework for EYFS, it was more or less staff-initiated planning, now it is more child-inspired: 'we observe the children then we plan and we take ideas from the children, parents and staff' (Brooker et al., 2010). This approach is very evident in childminder groups, who express views that generally intuitive methods of supporting development and learning were validated by the framework with practice being 'child led'. EYFS sets the standard that all early years providers must meet to ensure that children learn and develop well and are kept healthy and safe. It promotes teaching and learning to ensure children's 'school readiness' and gives children a broad range of knowledge and skills that provide the right foundation for good future progress through school life. The EYFS requirements for learning and development cover:

- the areas of learning and development which must shape activities and experiences (educational programmes) for children in all early years settings;
- the early learning goals that providers must help children to work towards (the knowledge, skills and understanding children should have at the end of the academic year in which they turn five);
- assessment arrangements for measuring progress (and requirements for reporting to parents and/or carers).

As children grow older, and as their development allows, it is expected they will gradually move towards more activities led and guided by adults, to ensure they are meeting all the requirements of the statutory EYFS curriculum. The planning and learning cycle is illustrated in Figure 4.1.

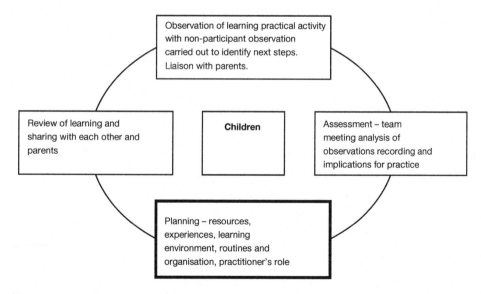

FIGURE 4.1 The planning and learning cycle

Planning principles

The statutory guidance identifies four guiding principles which should shape practice in early years settings. These are:

- Every child is a *unique child*, who is constantly learning and can be resilient, capable, confident and self-assured.
- Children learn to be strong and independent through *positive relationships*.
- Children learn and develop well in *enabling environments*, in which their experiences respond to their individual needs and there is a strong partnership between practitioners and parents and/or carers.
- *Children develop and learn in different ways and at different rates*. The framework covers the education and care of all children in early years provision, including children with special educational needs and disabilities.

The four principles are given a high status and can be used as a guarantee of high quality provision without the need for so much detailed or prescriptive guidance. Practitioners are now more likely to appreciate the focus on personal, social and emotional development (PSED) as a prime area of learning. This is a view well supported by parents. However, they are much less happy about the expectations of letters and sounds, which causes anxiety amongst parents as schools appear to spend too much time on this, which may be a misconception of parents. Although from my own experience this view is held because it is an area where parent support is important. Possibly too, the prospect of the phonic check in Year 1 puts reception class teachers under pressure. By comparing several planning formats, I have put together the following list of planning principles as being the most useful to aspiring early years practitioners:

- Brainstorm with children all they know about a suggested topic to find a starting point.
- Provide a stimulus to engage your children – a walk in the park, to the shops, a problem to solve, a mystery visitor, an unusual object discovered outside.
- Include what you want children to learn, particularly the links to communication, language and literacy.
- Be flexible in the use of ready prepared plans to ensure 'magic learning moments' are not missed.
- Identify the next steps based on prior learning.
- Include activities planned in response to children's interests.

The above are not in order of priority. In my experience there remains a difference in what is expected of an early years child in a reception class compared with a pre-school. Reception teachers are likely to be following different pedagogical practices to the rest of the school. This is as it should be, as the reception class is still part of the EYFS with their own clearly defined statutory curriculum that places play in a central role. A shift has taken place with the revised EYFS guidance. However, there is a clearly defined range of experiences for children from birth to 5. Children need to acquire a range of skills to meet the learning goals provided in the statutory EYFS guidance. Reception teachers have generally valued the principles and the flexible indoor and outdoor pedagogy, but found it difficult at times because sometimes Key Stage 1 colleagues lacked an understanding of the differences in EYFS compared to National Curriculum requirements (DfE, 2010). Ofsted too are picking up this dilemma for Year 1 teachers faced with a new group of pupils possibly unfamiliar with the classroom organisation and rituals in a Year 1 class. Not so many years ago before the EYFS, this situation was dealt with by carrying on some Foundation Stage activities into Years 1 and 2, such as the structured play area or home corner to help children make a gradual transition from reception to Year 1. Suggestions on how to facilitate transitions are outlined later in the chapter. Tables 4.1, 4.2 and 4.3 outline the requirements of the prime areas of learning.

TABLE 4.1 The prime areas of learning (communication and language)

PRIME AREAS: COMMUNICATION AND LANGUAGE
Listening and attention
■ Children listen attentively in a range of situations. ■ Children listen to stories, accurately anticipating key events. ■ Children respond to what they hear with relevant comments, questions or actions. ■ Children give their attention to what others say and respond appropriately, while engaged in another activity.
Understanding
■ Children follow instructions involving several ideas or actions. ■ Children answer 'how' and 'why' questions about their experiences in response to stories or events.
Speaking
■ Children express themselves effectively, showing awareness of listeners' needs. ■ Children use past, present and future forms accurately when talking about events that have happened or are about to happen in the future. ■ Children develop their own narratives and explanations by connecting ideas and events.

TABLE 4.2 Physical development early learning goals

PHYSICAL DEVELOPMENT
Moving and handling
■ Children show good control and coordination in large and small movements. ■ Children move confidently in a range of ways, safely negotiating space. ■ Children handle equipment and tools effectively, including pencils for writing.
Health and self-care
■ Children know the importance for good health of physical exercise, and a healthy diet. ■ Children talk about the ways to keep healthy and safe. ■ Children manage their own basic hygiene and personal needs successfully, including dressing and going to the toilet.

TABLE 4.3 Personal, social and emotional development

PERSONAL, SOCIAL AND EMOTIONAL DEVELOPMENT
Self-confidence and self-awareness ■ Children are confident to try new activities, and say why they like some activities more than others. ■ Children are confident to speak in a familiar group, will talk about their ideas and will select the resources they need for their chosen activities. ■ Children say when they do or don't need help.
Managing feelings and behaviour ■ Children talk about how they and others show feelings, talk about their own and others' behaviour, and its consequences, and know that some behaviour is unacceptable. ■ Children work as part of a group or class and understand and follow the rules. ■ Children adjust their behaviour to different situations, and take changes to their routine in their stride.
Making relationships ■ Children play cooperatively, taking turns with others. ■ Children take account of one another's ideas about how to organise their activity. ■ Children show sensitively to one another's needs and feelings. ■ Children form positive relationships with adults and other children.

Adult-led and child-initiated learning

The terms 'adult-led' and 'child-initiated' learning are familiar to early years practitioners. Despite encouragement to define what adults do when working with young children as 'teaching' and 'play', leaders maintained their preference for the terms 'adult-led' and 'child-initiated' in a third of settings involved in the survey *Teaching and Play in the Early Years: A Balancing Act?* (Ofsted 2015b). Their definitions are likely to be familiar to many readers. The following comments by leaders define teaching as being about adult-led activities, where the adult has a pre-defined purpose in mind, they know what they want children to learn and have usually selected the specific group or individual who will benefit the most. The adult in this scenario decides everything. In contrast, a child-initiated activity is firmly based on play. Children are the masters here. They choose when and where and what they want to do. The activity lasts as long as the activity interests and engages them. Children are free to select the resources and materials they want to use. The aim primarily is about the process not the end product.

An example of how an adult develops the learning of a single 2-year-old child is the way in which she responded to the child's interest in a sheep by verbally recalling what he was doing and saying, so providing a model for the child to copy verbally. The member of staff observing this activity had used it as an opportunity to assess his development against the early years outcome for communication and language – talking and using simple sentences to communicate. He was beginning to make believe by pretending (to be a sheep). This is a good example of the child's ability to be imaginative, one of the Expressive arts and design outcomes.

As a result of my own beliefs, corroborated to some extent by the findings of the EPPE Project (Sylva et al., 2004), 'effective pedagogy includes provision of instructive learning environments and "sustained shared thinking" to extend children's learning'. I cannot emphasise strongly enough the key role of the adult in promoting early learning, whatever the age of the child. A view developing from the work of Vygotsky (1978) that pays tribute to the prime role played by an adult in young children's development. Perhaps more significantly, dire consequences result when developing children do not have an adult to share experiences with, to help children make sense of the world and to aid the social and emotional development that is so pivotal to successful readiness for the challenges of life. The use of the word 'support' is evident in the statutory guidance, where previously practitioners were unsure of the extent to which they needed to be involved in children's learning. I can concur with this based on my own work supporting schools in difficulty. Clarification of what learning through play actually means, and what the implications of this are for the role of adults is much clearer. The answer lies in the use of play-based approaches combined with instructional yet playful teaching, as described in the example of the 'sheep' earlier. Practitioners need to have a flexible approach to teaching, based on the level of development of the individual child. Is it possible to separate out child-initiated from adult-guided or direct learning? When working with young children, the exchange between adults and children should be fluid, moving interchangeably between activities initiated by children and adult responses helping build the children's learning and understanding. I have intentionally still included the following comments from the Tickell review (Tickell, 2011) where she says that throughout the early years, adults should be modelling, demonstrating and questioning. To exclude elements of teaching from the early years would increase the risk of children not being ready to move to Key Stage 1. The research review supports this view wholeheartedly. The key for practitioners is the quality of their interaction with children to extend their learning. Adults are the ones that intervene and make a difference. In practice, adults and children may be part of a small group activity building on where children have chosen to play, possibly leading to enrichment of vocabulary and challenge by an adult. The views of practitioners were listened to, as can be seen from the statutory guidance. Previously, many practitioners provided evidence to the EYFS review that they wished to see the early learning goals – which define the level of development most children should have reached by the end of the year in which they are 5 – reduced and simplified; also, to be made more sensitive to the needs of summer-born children and to those who are fast developers. The planning example (Table 4.4) is an example of the preparation by an early years teacher. At the end of the chapter are further planning examples (Figures 4.3 and 4.4).

Currently there are seven areas of learning with a marked emphasis on the ways in which all the areas of learning are inter-connected. The degree of detail in the current statutory requirements is much reduced. Practitioners will see that the phrasing of the new learning goals are less specific and much more user-friendly, which should make planning and assessment less onerous and, importantly, be easily understood by parents. However, students and others entering into the early years profession may find it very useful to consult the breakdown of the expectations of children at different stages that were part of the previous EYFS but are less dominant in the current statutory framework (DfE, 2014a: 10–12). How do we talk to children? The list below gives an indication of all one expects of children as they develop cognition in discussion with a practitioner. The demands are in ascending order from simple to complex.

TABLE 4.4 Beech Hill Primary School Early Years Foundation Stage: outline of provision week beginning 16.5.11

CP = Continuous provision & child initiated (see potential learning plans in areas)   E = Enhancements linked to children's interests

	MONDAY	TUESDAY	WEDNESDAY	THURSDAY	FRIDAY
Tinkering table (problem solving)	Cauldron counting (adding 1 more to 5) E-interest in making spells	As Monday – continued interest/ planned observation opportunity	Sorting jewels/ buttons according to more than one criteria E-interest in Winnie's jewels	CP (consolidation time)	Cauldron counting (adding 1 more to 10) E-interest in making spells
Role play (Winnie's house)	Establish roles of characters from Winnie the Witch (focus text)	As Monday – adults to support play with S&L focus (turn taking/ using magic vocabulary)	As Monday – adults to support play with S&L focus (turn taking/ using magic vocabulary)	CP (consolidation time)	CP (consolidation time)
Cosy story area	Selection of books about magic E-interest in witches and magicians	Selection of books about magic E-interest in 'Room on the Broom'	Re telling 'Room on a Broom' using story sack and props (adult focus)	CP (consolidation time)	CP (consolidation time)
ICT/smart board	Cbeebies site E-interest in 'Grandpa in my pocket' so focus to be on this/ navigation skills	Cbeebies site E-interest in 'Grandpa in my pocket' so focus to be on this/ navigation skills	Magic paintings on smart notebook- selecting tools to use (stars, rainbows, etc) E-interest in 'magic finger'	Magic paintings on smart notebook- selecting tools to use (stars, rainbows, etc)	CP (consolidation time)
Construction/small world (carpet)	Black fabric, mini beasts, cauldron to make spells E-interest in spell making		CP (consolidation time)	CP (consolidation time)	CP (consolidation time)

	MONDAY	TUESDAY	WEDNESDAY	THURSDAY	FRIDAY
Creative area (messy table)	Glitter in the paint-thin brushes E-interest in sparkle	Glitter in the paint-thin brushes E-interest in sparkle	CP (consolidation time)	CP (consolidation time)	CP (consolidation time)
Workshop	CP (consolidation time)	CP (consolidation time)	Making witches hats E-Winnie the witch	CP (consolidation time)	CP (consolidation time)
Sand	CP (consolidation time)	Wet sand E-interest in shape moulds	Wet sand E-interest in shape moulds	Wet sand E-interest in shape moulds	CP (consolidation time)
Role play (magic carpet)	Adult focus – model going on a magic carpet ride	Adult focus – model going on a magic carpet ride	CP (consolidation time)	CP (consolidation time)	CP (consolidation time)
Mark making area	CP (consolidation time)	Writing spells (rhyming focus)	Writing spells (rhyming focus)	CP (consolidation time)	CP (consolidation time)
Investigation station	Torches, magic set (rings, pots and balls, cards) E-interest in magic shows	Torches, magic set (rings, pots and balls, cards) E-interest in magic shows	Torches, magic set (rings, pots and balls, cards) E-interest in magic shows	CP (consolidation time)	CP (consolidation time)
Busy fingers	Black sparkly play dough CP	CP (consolidation time)	CP (consolidation time)	CP (consolidation time)	CP (consolidation time)
Water	Spell making – glitter, jewels, green colouring	Spell making – glitter, jewels, green colouring	Spell making – glitter, jewels, green colouring	CP (consolidation time)	CP (consolidation time)
Outdoor area	Fairy ring, campfire, tyre play, witch den making, making potions CP	Fairy ring, campfire, tyre play, witch den making, making potions CP	Fairy ring, campfire, tyre play, witch den making, making potions CP	Fairy ring, campfire, tyre play, witch den making, making potions CP	Fairy ring, campfire, tyre play, witch den making, making potions CP

- What is it? What do we do with it? (labelling and simple function)
- What did you see? What was that over there? (memory)
- What is happening in the picture? (description)
- Feel that. What is it? (non-verbal demand)
- Demonstration. Now do what I did. (imitation)
- What else was there on the tray? (incidental memory)
- Before you build the tower show me the bricks. (delay)
- Look at this picture. Find me the rabbit. (visual search)

(Meadows and Cashdan, 1988: 69)

There are many ideas about how children learn that are relevant to early childhood education. A common strategy used by parents in the home may be a model of learning that emphasises passiveness. A small child is surrounded by happenings and has experiences. If two events are close together the child learns to associate them. For example, exploring and touching the television controls triggers an immediate 'No!' from a parent. Thus, the child may learn to associate touching the controls with parental disapproval and stop doing it. However, this does not help the child interpret or work out why. There are lots of examples of things that children learn passively that leads ultimately to knowledge, for example, the names of colours. But do children passively soak up information all the time? I think not! Piaget suggested some of the ways in which children handle information. Assimilation and accommodation are what children do, but what children assimilate is governed by what they already know, and as they become aware of additional information that may then accommodate the concept. However, the drawback of this theory of learning is that children will have limits to what they can assimilate and accommodate. Young children will find some information too strange or too distant from what they already know and will have great difficulty learning it. This is why current thinking about learning emphasises the activity of the learner. Hence we have 'hands on' experiences and the practical activities that abound in early years settings. Children learn too from observing others – adults and children alike. They imitate others. They learn that a radiator is hot by observing someone else getting burned by it. Children, as stated earlier, do learn when they are told something. I do not propose to go into the Piagetian theories that justify play, although the third concept of 'readiness' is worthy of further explanation. Piaget saw learning as controlled and limited by development: unless children had developed to a point where they were ready, they would not be able to do the thinking, assimilation and accommodation that are necessary for learning. To try to teach might harm the child's own development was the theory. Thus we have the reason for encouraging play as the medium for early childhood education. When one applies this approach to learning to read, it can be seen that 'readiness' is not the issue, but that the practitioner presents the opportunity to learn to read by helping the child to learn to recognise words – labels or the child's name for example.

Teaching and play

To quote the headteacher of a small infant school:

> Everyone is an educator. Children, parents, grandparents and other professionals all have something they can contribute (teach) in any scenario.
>
> (Headteacher, Trimdon Grange Infant and Nursery School)

Teaching is not separate from play, to define teaching to mean one fixed view of how things should be done. Play provides the context for teaching. Teaching is the many different ways in which adults consciously or otherwise help children to learn. There are many terms for how children learn. A curriculum with a high level of child-initiated activities can have long-term benefits, including increased levels of community service and motivation. Child-initiated and free-flow play are almost synonymous but will both include children choosing what to do and where they want to play in the setting not directed by an adult. The reality is that free-flow play or self-initiated learning often provides a crucial context for learning. The role of the adult is to extend learning, as the more knowledgeable other (Vygotsky, 1978). This scaffolding by an adult can build on what the children already know. Generally play and/or learning which is self-initiated and seen to be worthwhile from the child's point of view by providing a secure platform for the child to develop in many ways, benefitting by the adult's involvement. The key is to create a situation whereby the developing independence of the child is not compromised. According to the research (Garrick et al., 2011) that identified children's views, many children in the sample often saw themselves as capable of being involved in planning their own activities. There are suggestions that there is a reluctance to use the word 'teaching' among leaders and staff in pre-school settings, who often viewed teaching as a very formal approach to learning that involved adults passing down knowledge to children through their focused direction of activities. The word 'teaching' was seen to be synonymous with qualified teacher status and schools. To try to create an alternative to defining working with young children as one or another, a much more fluid view of teaching was held by leaders and the settings generally. To take the phrase 'Everyone is an educator' sums up the reality of the school because children, parents, grandparents and other professionals all have something to contribute. All the staff working in any setting with children 'teach'. Ofsted (2015b: 11) defines teaching in the early years sector as:

> Teaching should not be taken to imply a 'top down' or formal way of working. It is a broad term which covers the many different ways in which adults help children learn. It includes their interactions with children during planned and child-initiated play and activities: communication and modelling language, showing, explaining, demonstrating, exploring ideas, encouraging, questioning, recalling, providing a narrative for what they are doing, facilitating and setting challenges…Integral to teaching is how practitioners assess what children know, understand and can do well as take account of their interests and dispositions to learning, and use this information to plan the next steps in learning and monitor their progress.

This may seem very ambitious. It works in this particular setting because parents all receive a weekly learning letter informing them of the themes for the week and suggest what can be done at home to echo and complement the learning that is taking place in school. When necessary, these learning letters also include examples of particular strategies used by staff so that those at home can be sure they are working in complete tandem with school. For example, when children are learning about addition, staff send home detailed information about the stages of development children will go through so that parents can reinforce these ways of working at home. The staff can be seen therefore to be acting as facilitators to ensure children are confident enough to apply their basic skills to enhance and cement their learning of, for example, reading, writing, cooperating, sharing and concentrating on what interests them. The chosen topics may be adult selected based on what they know their children are interested in through discussions. Staff also engage with parents to gather the children's learning stories to help select topics. Typical ones might be:

- A light and dark party
- Minibeasts linked to familiar stories such as *Along Came a Spider*
- Building repairs
- Dragons
- Forest walks (Forest school with own forested area).

Research by Garrick et al. (2011) asked the question:

> To what extent do children's views inform planning and delivery of the Early Years Foundation Stage by practitioners?

In a sample of 146 children aged between 3 and 5, the children saw themselves as capable of being involved in their own activities. As indeed would be expected, as many children are given choices and/or options as to what they can do in their home environment. The research found that children seemed to find it easier to choose and lead their own activities when the space was less clearly organised into areas designated for specific play themes. Although children enjoyed planning their own activities, they were often not as involved as they would like to have been. Nor were many children happy not to know the setting and some were unhappy because they did not understand some of the written information (Roulstone et al., 2010).

Outdoor learning

In some early years settings, learning is equally provided for inside and outside. The outside space is planned for in as much detail as the inside area with the same opportunities for learning in the outdoor area. Provision for mark-making, for example, often includes large implements and surfaces on which to mark. Outdoor play is an excellent catalyst for child-initiated learning. Watching children outside investigating with their magnifying lens, a 4-year-old spotted a ladybird and immediately started to count its spots. Several hasty questions started to flow as the boy's curiosity was aroused and by this time two other children arrived on the scene and they verbally described what the ladybird was doing – crawling, then flying away. This proved to be a very effective starting point for a minibeast's topic and led to a hunt for all the ladybird stories indoors.

Outdoor learning aptly suits some children's learning styles, particularly boys. I can vouch for this from a comment by the reception class teacher of my 5-year-old grandson that, 'he is certainly an outdoor boy!' Reception classes are where the freedom for indoor/outdoor learning may not be so common. A few years ago practitioners in all groups believed that the high profile given to outdoor learning in the EYFS validated their principles for children's learning and development (Brooker et al., 2010).

The access to free-flow has vastly developed in schools with reception classes. Generally, the outdoor provision mirrored indoor activities. Provision for mark-making often includes large implements and surfaces to make marks and develop early writing skills.

Forest schools

There is a steadily growing forest school movement developing throughout the UK. Generally a forest school is part of the outdoor experience that children enjoy on a regular basis. Figure 4.2 is an example of the way in which a small infant school brought the outdoors inside. However, there is more to it than this. It is based on Scandinavian principles of open-air play-based education and earlier European pedagogical theories on the importance of outdoor learning. The chair of the Forest School Association offers some tips for schools wishing to develop the forest school ethos. In relation to early years there is already an organisation that suggests resources, namely, Learning Through Landscapes. It is advised that as a first step schools should just consider the importance of the outdoor environment as a learning resource and ensure children get outside. This is certainly happening in the early years. A basic requirement of a forest school is that there are a few trees. Hmm! Maybe this is not so easy to create in more urban areas. Ofsted have praised the high level of curiosity and imagination promoted in children. To quote a Danish teacher, 'Children start school so young in this country: they would get much more from being outside and socialising improving their language and physical development.' The National Trust have suggested there is a decline in

FIGURE 4.2 Indoor forest

outdoor play and see the forest school approach as a way of reconnecting children with the natural world. A forest school in a pre-school setting is likely to be an area of the outdoors that children access at any time and be likely to include a natural wildlife area, some willow tunnels or structures, poly tunnels, raised flower beds to grow flowers and vegetables. There may be a forest trail or footpath through a wild area with bird feeders, sensory areas. A very pertinent quote from Elizabeth Wood:

> Outdoor play is important in its own right, not as a safety valve for inappropriate pedagogies.
>
> (Wood, 2013: 124)

The forest school concept was brought to England by the staff of Bridgewater College, Somerset following an exchange visit to Denmark in 1993. The rationale for this approach to learning and development chimes well with traditional views of 'good' early childhood education (Maynard, 2007) and the EYFS curriculum framework. The importance of outdoor play cannot be underestimated given the decline in children's freedom to play outdoors safely. It has been given a tremendous boost with the EYFS framework's expectations that indoor and outdoor learning complement one another. Others have written widely of the benefits of outdoor learning (Bilton, 2010; Maynard, 2007). Children have more space to move around, greater opportunities for fantasy play, especially boys. A major finding from Maynard's research is the attention given to small achievable tasks in which children succeed, become more confident and have a greater level of self-esteem as a result. The forest school is an outdoor approach to education and play in which the outdoor environment becomes the classroom. This is reputed to increase children's self-confidence and self-esteem. This is particularly true for children who do not do well in a school classroom. The findings of research into changes in twenty-four children in three case study areas over eight months identified the following impact:

- Confidence – this was developed by the children having the freedom, time and space to learn and demonstrate independence.
- Social skills – children gained increased awareness of the consequences of their actions on peers through team activities, such as sharing tools and participating in play.
- Communication – language development was prompted by the children's sensory experiences.
- Motivation and concentration – the woodland tended to fascinate the children and they developed a keenness to participate and the ability to concentrate over longer periods of time.
- Physical skills – these improvements were characterised by the development of physical stamina and gross and fine motor skills.
- Knowledge and understanding – the children developed an interest in the natural surroundings and respect for the environment.

(O'Brian and Murray, 2007)

Many practitioners make use of published planning to guide children's learning. The examples in Figures 4.3 and 4.4 are suggested outlines.

| Year group: | Time Allocation: 1/2 Term | Date: SPRING TERM 2a Cycle 1 | Teachers: |

Communication and Language:
We will listen to and participate in a wide variety of fact and fiction books about snow and ice. Small groups of children will create their own 'Ice Emergency' stories using the Interactive white Board software or puppets and props. We will watch images from Frozen Planet and Google Earth, comparing the Artic, Antarctic with our weather at home using new words to describe weather conditions.

Mathematics:
The Children will be counting and recording how many animals attend the vets and carry cases to fit the pet. In our cold weather activities we will be sorting clothes for size and purpose as well as working with pairs of socks, boots and gloves. In the Freezer Shop and Vets Reception we will be using and beginning to recognise coins and notes and recording numbers. We will be using timers to see how long it takes for an ice cube to melt, play pass the ice cube and add together two sets of 'snowballs' to find a total.

Literacy:
The children will write and mark make to record pets arriving at our Vets as well as putting our names on 'registration forms'. In groups we will create snow and ice stories. We will listen to a wide variety of fact and fiction books about snow and ice. In the Freezer Shop we will identify well known brands and shop logos as well as write order forms and shopping lists.

Frosty Fun

WHY?
The children will discover what happens to water when the temperature is below freezing. They will also find out what happens to ice in warm temperatures. The children will learn about staying safe in snow and ice.

SMSC
The children will learn about 'New Beginnings' when looking at new growth in our garden and changes on the pond. Children will learn about different cultures through celebrating 'Chinese New Year', and the Jewish traditions of Sabbat.

Understanding of the World:
We will learn about x-rays and broken bones when role playing in The Vets. The children will begin to understand about caring for their pets. We will explore and discover water, ice and snow, looking at immediate and gradual change inside and outdoors. We will experience and have fun 'melting' chocolate when making crispy cakes and cheese pizza. We will be finding out about the traditions and customs of Chinese New Year, including tasting some Chinese food.

Expressive Art and Design:
The children will make ice sculptures using natural and man made materials, evergreen sticks and pebbles from outside or glitter, stars and shiny treasures from the making trolley. We will look at colours and patterns. We will make footprints in the 'snow' either the real experience or black paint on white paper. Once frozen we will be able to go outside to observe and photograph frosty images in the garden. We will make an interactive display of Chinese artefacts.

Personal, Social and Emotional Development:
The established children will help the new children to settle into our groups and routines. We will be learning how to consider the feelings of others through story and role play. The children will be excited to learn, explore and experiment. We will be sharing, turn taking and interacting with our peers and new friends. The children will be continuing to learn and develop their independence and confidence within the unit and older children will be encouraged to demonstrate games, songs and routines to help the new children in 'Blue Group'.

Physical Development:
We will develop our digging and building skills outdoors when hopefully we will be making snowmen and snowballs and tidying up our garden. Fine motor control will be developed when making ice sculptures. We will also be busy creating homes and igloos for our snow animals carefully building and balancing bricks, boxes and fabrics.

FIGURE 4.3 Planning example

1,2,3 You and Me

1,2,3

WHY?

Through traditional tales the children will be learning to order for size, position and media. They will explore repeated patterns and story structure as well as extending their imagination and vocabulary.

SMSC

The children will learn about 'Changes'' when looking at new growth in our garden and on the pond. Children will learn about different cultures through celebrating Jewish festival of Passover, Chinese New Year and Christian Easter traditions.

Communication and Language: The stories Goldilocks, 3 Billy Goats Gruff and the Three Pigs have repetitive structure and repeated phrases and the children will be encouraged to join in. Puppets and props will be used to retell the story or children to add their own storylines and use of words. Role play in Goldilocks Cottage will enable the children to use new words and understand the elements of the story. In small groups we will talk about our own ages and that of our friends or people in our families.

Mathematics: We enjoy learning about and practising numbers everyday. The children will be learning about 1 more and 1 less when counting the 'Billy Goats' on either side of the bridge. The children will discuss 1st 2nd and 3rd and positional language e.g. in-between, next to, under and over. When learning about Goldilocks and the Three Bears we will be looking at small, medium and large and working on 1-1 correspondence-bowls, spoons, chairs and beds. The children will use the large and small wooden blocks, boxes, duplo and other construction sets to build houses and dens and we will explore 3D shapes such as cube, cylinder and cone.

Literacy: We will be reading the stories The Three Pigs, The Three Billy Goats Gruff and Goldilocks and the Three Bears. The children will have opportunities to retell and sequence these stories through adult scribe, mark making, picture cards, puppets and use of books. We will write letters, invitations and lists for the characters. The children will begin to recognise repeated names and phrases that the adults will model reading, signs, and lists. We will 'read' recipes to make porridge and Easter biscuits and follow sequence cards to make Easter Nests.

Understanding of the World: We will be experimenting building houses with straw, sticks and bricks as well as exploring these in the sand and water and the outdoor environment. The children will have a go at growing grass for the Billy Goats and discovering the best conditions in which to help it grow. Everyone will experience making porridge for Goldilocks. We will also compare photographs of when we were 1,2 and 3 years old.

Expressive Art and Design: The children will bring in their own bears and attempt to paint pictures using powder paint and palettes to mix shades of brown, yellow, orange or any required colour. They will also choose from small, medium and large pieces of paper. The children will use bells to represent each goat trip-trapping over the bridge and will be encouraged to find an instrument to represent the troll. In small groups the children will 'perform' their use of percussion.

Personal, Social and Emotional Development: The established children will help the new children to settle into our groups and routines. We will talk about who is 3 years old and the things we enjoy in nursery. We will be learning how to consider the feelings of others through story and role play. The children will be excited to learn, explore and experiment. We will be sharing, turn taking and interacting with our peers. The children will be continuing to learn and develop their independence and confidence through 1,2,3 activities.

Physical Development: Large scale skills are developed when playing outdoors, making the 3 pigs dens or trip-trapping over the bridge. We practise these skills in our soft play area. We will be building houses using large bricks and play flats and large cardboard boxes. Small motor control is developed during a range of activities and by using a variety of tools, when building, cutting, painting, writing and stirring. Control will be developed when playing percussion instruments to the Three Little Pigs Rap and the 3 Billy Goats Gruff rhyme.

FIGURE 4.4 Planning example

Transition to reception and Year 1

It has been several years since the DfES first reported on the transition from EYFS to Year 1 (Sharp et al., 2006). The recommendations were very clear and summarised as:

- Transition to be seen as a process not an event.
- EYFS staff should meet with Key Stage 1 staff to discuss children's needs.
- Routines, expectations and activities to be similar in Year 1 to the Foundation Stage.
- Parents to be involved in the process.
- School managers to allocate resources to enable Year 1s to experience some play-based activities – sand, water, role play, construction and outdoor play.
- There should be additional support for children with learning difficulties, disabilities, English as an additional language and less able children.
- A reduction in the amount of listening and more encouragement of independent learning and learning through play.

A follow-up HMI survey (HMI, 2005) focused on how children developed social skills, attitudes, knowledge and learning in their transition from reception to Year 1. Their findings stated that:

- the literacy and numeracy strategies provided continuity;
- there was less continuity between the nursery and reception classes;
- less attention was given to improving standards through creative and expressive areas;
- leaders were not involved in planning for transition;
- teaching assistants were important;
- too much assessment was taking place.

Current preparation for transition

The Tickell review (Tickell, 2011) signalled a new dimension to transition quite strongly. This was the recommendation that when children are in the reception class, their experience should prepare them for the move to Year 1, both in terms of the level of development most children should have reached and in the knowledge that most children would be expected to have. The recommendation that arises from this is that the:

> EYFS requirement relating to delivery through play is clarified, including emphasising that this does not preclude more adult direction or teaching, and by setting out what playful adult-directed learning looks like.
>
> (Tickell, 2011: 35)

The recommendations of the Tickell review have not been adopted with regard to more able children working at National Curriculum levels in the reception class. The EYFS *Practice Guidance* (DfE: 2014) states clearly that there should be continuity between settings with the children's social, emotional and educational needs addressed appropriately. Transition is a process not an event, and should be planned for and discussed with children and parents. Settings should communicate information which will secure continuity of experience for the child between settings. Effective use should be made of the summative assessment of each child recorded in the EYFS profile to support planning for learning in Year 1. While this is no longer a requirement due to the introduction of baseline assessment on entry to reception, it is likely that teachers will continue with the EYFS profile to inform Year 1 teachers. A case study described by the National Strategies (DCSF, 2008) highlights the difficulties faced by children's transition to Year 1. The results being that the teacher spent too much time managing classroom behaviour and the children's learning suffered because they were not engaging in the decontextualised activities provided. Assessment records in the form of learning journals were not referred to. The school reorganised into a lower school comprising the Foundation Stage and Year 1 with continuity in experiences provided in the autumn term and a gradual move towards whole class sessions by the end of the year. The features of effective practices for those 5- and 6-year-old children identified the following features of good practice and less effective practice.

Recommended	Not recommended
■ Play-based	■ Work-based
■ Active	■ Static
■ Led by adults or children	■ Directed by adults
■ Thematic	■ Subject-based
■ Emphasises a range of skills	■ Emphasises listening and writing

A review of your current practices using the format above could be a useful starting point. It is all too familiar to hear Year 1 teachers blaming the independence and freedom of their children in EYFS as the reason for their inattention and misbehaviour in Year 1. Tickell is clearly inferring from her review that learning in a reception class is likely to be different in some ways and needs to prepare children for Key Stage 1. It is important that the whole school review the likely need to change some of the long-established routines and organisation in Year 1 classrooms. It is possible to create a lower school comprising EYFS and Year 1 as a unit. This possible finding is favoured following two reports – *The Independent Review of the Primary Curriculum* (Rose, J. 2009) and *The Cambridge Primary Review* (Alexander, R.2009) – both of which challenge the status quo with regard to Year 1. The latter review suggests that EYFS should be renamed and extended to age 6. A report entitled, 'Drying the tears of a tricky transition' in the TES (30 August, 2009) is unequivocal: 'More play-based lessons instead of sitting still in class could help end bad experiences for Year 1 pupils and staff.' Also, a gem of a comment by a Year 1 boy who said that being sat on the carpet, 'wastes your life' (NFER, 2006). *The Primary Curriculum Review* (DCSF, 2009) debates this issue in relation to 'summer-born' children. The issue for such very much younger children is that they are disadvantaged in several ways: lack of free pre-school education, less time in a play-orientated early years environment and continued lower achievement throughout the school system, the latter being most marked in the early stages of education. The summer-born children risk being treated as immature in comparison with their older classmates, giving rise to a lack of confidence and low self-regard and may limit expectations of them and their expectations of themselves. A recent announcement by government (DfE, 2014d) is that the parents of summer-born children could be allowed to let their child start school a year later. This is because summer-born children are likely to achieve less well than their older classmates. Parents can opt to let their children start school in reception a year later than their peers or join their own age group in Year 1.

Below is an example of an action plan for transition from EYFS to Year 1.

Action plan for transition from EYFS to Key Stage 1

Summer term

1   Review the progress of EYFS children to identify the proportion not likely to meet the ELGs.
2   Meet with Key Stage 1 leader and Year 1 teacher(s) to arrange transition strategies – teacher swap, children familiarised with Year 1.
3   Decide on the reorganisation needed in Year 1 classrooms (more play-based activities and access to outdoor learning if possible).
4   Arrange for Year 1 and EYFS teachers to swap roles to enable Y1 teachers to see the effectiveness of EYFS practice on children's behaviour and attitudes to learning.
5   Can teaching assistants move to Year 1 with children with EAL or learning difficulties?
6   Arrange a meeting with parents to inform them of the need for some continuation of EYFS practices in Year 1.

Autumn term

1   Monitor the learning and attitudes and behaviour of the Year 1 pupils.
2   Evaluate the impact of all the suggested changes and agree priorities for future practices.
3   Write a transition policy for EYFS to Year 1 to fit alongside transition from pre-school/nursery to reception (if children are not already in the school's EYFS).*

* There is an assumption made here that nursery and reception children in one school will already be working together; if not, then apply transition arrangements which are likely to be well established.

There are two strands to transition. First, there is the transition from pre-school to school and then from the reception class to Year 1. The early years report of HMCI (Ofsted, 2015a) suggests that more needs to be done to improve the development of disadvantaged children. It is suggested that it is the best interests of all children to have a strong partnership with all the education providers that the children in their reception classes are likely to attend. The Tickell review (Tickell, 2011) signalled a new dimension to transition quite strongly. That was the recommendation that when children are in the reception class, their experiences should prepare them for the move to Year 1, in terms of both the level of development most children should have reached and the knowledge that most children would be expected to have. The recommendation that arises from this is that the:

EYFS requirements relating to delivery through play is clarified, including emphasising that this does not preclude more adult direction or teaching, and by setting out what playful adult-directed learning looks like.

(Tickell, 2011: 35)

The above statement is reflected in the case study settings identified by Ofsted in their good practice publication *Parents as Partners in Teaching: Trimdon Grange Infant and Nursery School* (2015c). The thrust of their evidence is that the parents have a fundamental role in their children's education and that the most powerful learning takes place when more and less experienced learners work together to achieve a common goal. The philosophy that penetrates everything that takes place in this school is that everyone is an educator. So what then are the implications of this for expectations, teaching and learning in the reception class? The EYFS *Practice Guidance* states clearly that there should be continuity between settings with the children's social, emotional and educational needs addressed appropriately. Transition is a process not an event, and should be planned for and discussed with children and parents. Settings should communicate information which will secure continuity of experience for the child between settings. It is vital that there is the opportunity for reception classes and their pre-school providers to work together. There are suggestions in HMCI's annual report (2015a) that some schools do not engage with their provider pre-schools, nurseries or childminders. The transition from reception to Year 1 is the one with most potential to upset children through, for example:

- lack of access to free-flow indoor and outdoors;
- restrictions in the activities available in Year 1;
- more time spent in a whole class group together;
- daily assemblies with the rest of a school;
- less access to self-initiated learning.

Effective use should be made of the summative assessment of each child recorded in the EYFS profile to support planning for learning in Year 1. A case study described by the National Strategies highlights the difficulties faced by children's transition to Year 1. The results being that the teacher spent too much time managing classroom behaviour and the children's learning suffered because they were not engaging in the decontextualised activities provided. Assessment records in the form of learning journals were not referred either. The school reorganised into a lower school comprising the Foundation Stage and Year 1 with continuity in experiences provided in the autumn term and a gradual move towards whole class sessions by the end of the year. The features of effective practices for those 5- and 6-year-old children identified the following features of good practice and less effective practice. The Good Practice example published by Ofsted (2015c) focused on an open plan nursery and infant school where 2-, 3-, 4- and 5-year-olds can be seen working alongside each other at some point in the day. Older children helped the youngest as they responded to tricky problems encountered when making a crane, for example. An older child effectively models key language and less confident older children thrived on the responsibility given for helping the younger children. Less advantaged 2-year-old children are provided with many more opportunities and there is the start to 'narrow the gap' between less and more able children. Case study 4.1 describes exemplary early years practice in an area of disadvantage.

CASE STUDY 4.1 Laurel Avenue Infant and Nursery School

Based on their very low skills and ability when they start in the nursery, children make excellent progress by the time they leave the Foundation Stage unit in all areas of learning. They quickly settle into the routines. Home visits help to allay any parental concerns and begin to give children confidence. It is the view of parents that their 'children come on in leaps and bounds'. Children exceeded the level expected for their age by the time they started in Year 1. However, there is fluctuation year-by-year and not all children attending the nursery transfer to the school. Overall, most children reach the expected level and an increasing number reach beyond it. Achievement is outstanding because teaching is exemplary and fully engages children in everything they do. Not an opportunity is missed to encourage children to develop their literacy skills, whether it is reading their name when choosing a fruity snack, self-registering when they come into school or reading the instructions to make a cup of tea during outdoor playtime. Children enjoy learning because it is fun. An investigation into the range of everyday utensils and crockery very successfully helped to improve children's early language skills. Teapots, jugs, kettles and different kinds of tea generated a wealth of learning that helped to improve the speech and understanding of many children. Personal, social and emotional development is very well promoted too. Children grow in confidence and play calmly and productively at all times. Children delight in brushing their teeth as soon as they arrive into the unit. Assessment is exemplary and fulfils two main purposes excellently: to guide future learning for the children and to inform parents of their child's progress. Leadership of the unit is outstanding because of the excellent model of exemplary teaching and the impact of this talent on other staff.

The most recent findings of how transition arrangements are managed can be found on the websites of local authorities who provide packs of information to schools, as in Oxfordshire, for example. Not surprisingly, the most recent survey of arrangements for this by Ofsted was in 2004 and by NfER in 2006. Looking at the NfER research (Sharp et al., 2006) of a telephone survey of sixty English schools, one can see that children certainly felt this period was a milestone for them as it represented their transfer from 'play' to 'hard work', but also an indicator that the children 'were getting bigger' (2006: 21). Children stated they did not like spending time 'sitting still, and listening to the teacher during, carpet time'. The case study above describes an outstanding setting in a disadvantaged area of a city in the north east.

Topics for discussion

- Share your priorities for preparing children for the transitions from pre-school to school and from reception to Year 1.
- Discuss your views on advising parents to delay their young 4-year-old a year in the reception class and joining Year 1 a year later, admitting a younger 4-year-old a year later into the reception class or staying with the status quo.

Further reading

Fisher, J. (2010) *Moving on to Key Stage 1: Improving Transition from the Early Years Foundation Stage.* Buckingham: Open University Press.

Bruce, T. (2013) *Early Childhood: A Guide for Students.* London: Sage.

Wiltshire County Council (2013) *Early Years Foundation Stage Planning Examples Pack.* www.wiltshire. gov.uk/eyfs-planning-examples-pack.pdf

Assessing children's learning

Introduction

The aim of this chapter is to outline various assessment techniques used to gather a profile of the development of the children in a setting, to share the strategies used by practitioners with parents and to outline the current statutory requirements. The progress check at age 2, the Healthy Child programme and assessing children with special educational needs are included. Although the EYFS framework is common for all children in early years and childcare provision from birth to 5 years, there are differences in assessment practices depending on the age of the child. They are modified to engage with very young babies in a one-to-one situation, whereas assessment of a 4-year-old may be most effectively achieved via non-participant observation. It is important that children are seen as individuals and every child's journey is 'unique' to them. Actively listening to children and giving them time to express themselves, monitoring their progress, and sharing the findings with children and parents and planning next steps that will engage and motivate them are at the heart of effective planning for learning and development. The introduction of a baseline assessment for children as they start in reception class is the most recent development referred to later in this chapter. The following statement from the statutory EYFS is a key reminder to practitioners that the days of reams of planning and assessment records are not the priority when working in the early years. To quote the Department for Education's statutory guidance:

> Paperwork should be limited to that which is absolutely necessary to promote children's successful learning and development.
>
> (DfE, 2014a: 13)

Table 5.1 is an example of how assessments can be recorded. The key assessment method expected in settings is 'formative assessment'. This is the ongoing assessment that is an integral part of the learning and development process. It involves practitioners observing and playing with children to understand their level of achievement, interests and learning styles and knowing what the next steps are for each child. Key workers become adept at learning to know children's strengths and weaknesses, interests, aptitudes and attitudes relatively quickly. Observing practitioners working with 2-year-olds recently, it is clear that assessment is at the heart of interaction, guidance and encouragement to the children as they learn to play, to cooperate and communicate with adults and other children. Assessment is integral to all the activities observed as practitioners question, explain and challenge children to take the next

TABLE 5.1 Observing and assessing mark-making

Child's name	X		
Adult observer	Xx		
Area of provision	Mark-making		
Date:	**Time/duration**		30 minutes

What happens/happened

X was playing in the mark-making area. She is using the scissors to cut some paper to the specific size she required.

X then began to write small marks on the pieces of paper. I asked X what she was writing, and she replied, 'I'm write Daddy.' X said she would like to know how to write daddy 'for my letter'. I repeated back to her the word daddy, stretching put the sounds for her to hear, and asked her to listen carefully. I then demonstrated how to write 'daddy', saying the sounds in the word slowly as I modelled the writing. X then proceeded to imitate my writing.

X then began to write on one of the other pieces of paper. 'That letter for grandma and granddad.' X asked for envelopes to put her letters in, these were provided and X put her letters inside. X put lines on the back of the envelope. 'Those are my words' she said.

X then got the hole punch. 'I just got to do clicks,' she said. X put her envelope in to the hole punch and made one hole in each. 'Look, I made one hole.'

X then returned to making small lines on the backs of the envelopes. 'These are writes and this says to daddy.' X picked up both her envelopes. 'Now I'm need to post them.' X went to post the letters in the box.

PSED	CLL	PSRN	KUW	PD	CD
	Writing and handwriting			Using equipment and materials	

What was learned about the child's interest, abilities or needs?

Child: X understands that words can be written down, and that words have meaning when written down. X is interested in making marks.

Parent: X's parents tell us that when letters arrive, she asks for the envelopes to do her writing on.

Practitioner: X showed great interest in the party invitations and envelopes given out by another child.

Possible lines of development

Provide post office resources to develop X's interest in creating and sending letters. Encourage X to write other letters so we can take her to a real postbox and post the letter to her house.

step, or if not, to demonstrate how, for example, to match same colours on a board game or fix apparatus together to balance. There are moments when practitioners need to stand and observe. Can the children communicate? How do they share their gardening tools? It is vital that assessment takes place early to ensure that interactions with adults are appropriate, building on the child's understanding and creating the next steps in their learning. This type of assessment is also known as 'observational' assessment and is at the centre of the teaching and learning cycle. Observing what children are able to do (assessment) determines to a degree what children need to do next and thus is informing planning. A further purpose is to inform parents, carers and practitioners of children's progress and identify their needs. While an on-entry baseline assessment in reception classes is the latest government policy, I am sharing strategies used successfully by practitioners over many years as a basis for developing children's learning.

The principles and purposes of assessment

The early years sector has traditionally favoured formative rather than summative assessment (Nutbrown, 2006). There is some concern about the normative development view that what children should achieve by certain months may create a tension. Practitioners surveyed in the recent past have said that the EYFS profile generates a tension due to its summative nature. The findings of a recent survey indicate how settings tackle assessment on entry to pre-school. This, importantly, included frequent sharing of information between parents, other pre-school settings and health visitors (Ofsted, 2015a: 7). A more recent publication states quite categorically that 'assessment is at the heart of successful teaching and play' (Ofsted, 2015b: 23). The publication acknowledges the difficulty in assessing children's capabilities and, along with the views of practitioners, compiled a list of skills required by practitioners which included:

- high-quality skills of observation;
- in-depth understanding of child development;
- excellent subject knowledge across a range of areas to know the precise next steps to take;
- working quickly to secure an accurate assessment of children's starting points;
- considerable attention to the above where children have significant learning and/or developmental delays;
- liaison with parents and other providers, such as childminders;
- plan a home visit (or series of home visits) if possible.

A typical extension of the home visit is the start of a child's learning journey, where photographs, records of a child's achievements pre-school are collated. The ongoing liaison with parents was felt to be crucial by these early years practitioners. As to be expected, the range of ways in which settings record children's achievements are considerable but generally include paper-based systems of scrapbooks and journals with half of settings having electronic systems that enable collation of photographs, captions and comments. The most effective gave clear indications of children's gains in their learning, especially when a gap in their learning had been overcome. The assessment information gathered was used assiduously to inform teaching.

The combination of planning with assessment can help to provide the basis and match of activities most appropriate for the next steps in children's learning. This also acknowledges those practitioners who use a child's learning journey record to identify the next learning steps. A range of assessment techniques – for example, observational (formative), summative assessment and the learning journey – are frequently used in settings. The learning journey approach and assessment of learning through play are very typical for younger children in pre-schools with what the children enjoy and take part in being extended by a more knowledgeable adult to develop their learning and understanding (Vygotsky, 1978). It is likely too that the stimulus to extend learning is introduced by skilled practitioners to ensure children make appropriate progress together with a short description of their learning characteristics (DfE, 2014b). The example below demonstrates how the interests of a group of boys contributed excellently to their learning. A writing project for boys was initiated with boys being given a range of shared drawing and mark-making opportunities outside, linked to topics that interested them. Those boys developed a range of skills including:

- Working together in small groups
- Giving meaning to the marks they make
- Playing alongside others
- Forming recognisable letters
- Sharing and taking turns
- Developing concentration
- Using a range of mark-making tools.

(Ofsted, 2015b: 26)

The learning journey

Assessment of young children in other countries has had an impact on what assessment strategies are adopted in many settings in England. *Learning Stories* were developed in 2001 in New Zealand as an answer to the Te Whariki early childhood curriculum requirements. This is a holistic, transactional, formative assessment procedure. Learning stories describe 'significant learning moments in a child's day-to-day experiences'. Key information about individual children is gathered for each child covering any or all the following topics or magic moments that relate to each child's experiences and favourite things. Consultation with parents is encouraged. The ultimate aim is to gather evidence of a child's learning and development as they make progress towards the early learning goals at the end of time in pre-school and transfer to the reception class. This may then be continued in the reception class. I know that most children will have no problem identifying their own interests. The child is a central player in this form of assessment. It is important to date contributions to the learning journey or diary in order to keep track as to when statements are achieved. It is also possible to involve a variety of adults as well as the child's key person and parents. My own experience tends to suggest that a learning journey is more typical in a pre-school setting and less common in reception classes. Typical themes for a child's learning journey are:

- All about me
- My holidays
- My family
- My pets

- My toys
- My friends
- My favourite stories
- My favourite film (e.g. *Frozen*).

It is also common to find examples of early writing, stories read and numeracy activities in the booklets. Parents should have the opportunity to contribute to this assessment method.

Formative/observational assessment

Ongoing observational assessment (also known as formative assessment) is an integral part of the learning and development process (DfE, 2014b: 13). It involves practitioners observing children to understand their level of achievement, interests and learning styles, and to then shape learning experiences for each child reflecting those observations. Paperwork should be limited to that which is absolutely necessary to promote children's successful learning and development' (DfE, 2014b).

> 'Formative assessment will lie at the heart of providing a supporting and stimulating environment for every child'.
>
> (Evangelou et al., 2009: 5)

Formative/observational assessment informs planning and helps practitioners observing children to understand their level of achievement. Practitioners can observe children as they interact in their play. They take photographs, make and record observations, video events, save examples of children's activities and gather information from parents. It is important that practitioners share their observations with parents and carers. An example of how this is managed in some settings is through a weekly meeting of staff to share observations with each other. Each member of staff has overall responsibility for a number of children, thus the weekly meeting is used very effectively to capture magic moments and to share observations and update records.

Observational assessment is integral to effective early years provision and evidence shows that this type of assessment lies at the heart of providing a supporting and stimulating environment for every child (Evangelou et al., 2009). Table 5.2 is an example of recorded assessments following an observation. Tickell (2011) broached what has always been a major concern of my own when inspecting reception classes. This is the 80:20 rule. The reliability of the judgement on whether a child achieves as a result of a child-initiated activity or an adult-directed activity is much debated. This has caused dilemmas for practitioners and undermines their professionalism, so to read that Tickell does not think the 80:20 rule is helpful in practice and recommends that assessment should be based primarily on the observations of daily activities that illustrate children's embedded learning is reassuring. Now there is statutory EYFS guidance supporting the reduction in paperwork and only recording what is absolutely necessary to promote children's learning and development. Assessment should not entail prolonged breaks from children (DfE, 2014b: 13). Further actions required by practitioners to ensure the smooth introduction to assessment practices are:

- getting to know a child better and developing positive relationships with children and their parents/carers;
- planning appropriate play and learning experiences based on the children's interests and needs, and identifying any concerns about a child's development;
- developing your understanding of a child's development;
- developing a systematic and routine approach to using observations;
- making use of assessments to plan the next steps in a child's developmental progress and regularly review this approach.

Summative assessment

This is a summary of all the formative assessments gathered over a longer period and makes a statement about a child's achievement by the end of the EYFS, which is the end of reception year. Currently, the EYFS profile is the summative assessment used to review children's progress towards the early learning goals and to inform Year 1 of the levels children are achieving. However, there is some doubt about the future of the EYFS profile as there is no requirement to complete this if a baseline assessment is carried out in the first six weeks of the reception class year. There are certainly some schools that still plan to conduct an end of year assessment in the reception class to inform the subsequent class teacher. It is likely that an end of year assessment/profile for each child will continue. The key person plays a central role in collecting information/observations about their key children. It is suggested (DCSF, 2008) that the key person spend some one-to-one time with children working in an area they have identified from their own observations. This information may be recorded as professional notes of a child's learning journey (see Table 5.2, an uncompleted record and Table 5.3, a

TABLE 5.2 Professional notes (DCSF: 2008)

Name:		Photo
Age:		
Context		

We observed:	
We thought:	
We tried:	
We found out:	
We changed:	
Next we will:	

EYFS references

TABLE 5.3 Example professional notes

Name:	Erin	Photo
Age:	19 months	
Context:	Free exploration in the role-play area	

We observed:	■ Erin really likes to play in the role-play area. She keeps opening and shutting the doors to see what's inside and finding resources from other areas of the room to put in the washing machine.
We thought:	■ We should add some resources, which might encourage Erin's interest in filling and emptying and 'What's inside?'.
We tried:	■ Adding large pasta shapes, real fruit and vegetables, scarves and some bags.
We found out:	■ Erin was fascinated by the addition of the bags and began to place resources carefully inside them, picking up one object at a time. ■ Erin played for extended periods of time. She also transported the bags all around the room, showing practitioners the contents.
We changed:	■ We are going to leave these resources out for a few weeks and observe Erin's play before we change anything.
Next we will:	■ Consider what other areas of the learning environment could be used to support Erin's interest in filling and empting. Start a learning journey to document Erin's interest in this area more thoroughly.

Source: DCSF, 2008 – CD-ROM

completed assessment). It is vital to demonstrate complete openness about each child to their parents as well as other professionals. The implicit reduction in paperwork in the early years would appear to suggest that files of assessments may be less necessary unless they are a fully integrated aspect of children's learning.

Progress check at 2 and the integrated early years check

There is a statutory requirement to review the progress of a child between the age of 2 and 3 years and provide parents and/or carers with a short written summary of their child's development in the prime areas. This progress check must identify the child's strengths, and any areas where progress is less than expected. If there are significant emerging concerns, or an identified special educational need or disability, practitioners should develop a targeted plan to support the child's future learning and development, involving parents and/or carers and other professionals (e.g. the provider's special educational needs coordinator or health professional) as appropriate. Beyond the prime areas, it is for practitioners to decide what the written summary should include, reflecting the developmental level and needs of the

Some important things that I now do at home…		At my setting I like to play with Jake and Henry. We really love to dig with the soft soil in the low-level planters.
I have just moved house and I can sleep in my own bed without a stairgate at the door. I am going to my old nursery one day a week but will soon start to stay here for three days a week.	**All about me** Name: Zara Age: 22 months Date: April 2008 Key person: Maria	I can walk confidently around the room and I am able to climb the stairs putting one foot in front of the other. I can run quite quickly when we play music.
I really love books. I have lots of stories at home and I like to read at home and at nursery.		At my setting I love to play with the train set.

FIGURE 5.1 First assessments

individual child. The same requirements apply as for the prime areas with regard to areas in which the child is progressing well, areas in which some additional support may be needed, and focus on any area where there is concern that a child may have a developmental delay. The progress check should usually be undertaken by the setting where the child has spent most time. The information from this progress check is to be shared with other relevant professionals, including their health visitor and staff of any new provision the child may transfer to. Parents must be provided with a short written summary of their child's development in the three prime areas when the child is aged between 24 and 36 months. Parents and practitioners should reflect together on:

- what a child likes to do;
- what he/she has just mastered or has just learned;
- what new words/language structures are emerging;
- particular interests or patterns in play and exploration observed.

(DfE, 2012b: 3)

Figure 5.1 is an example of a first assessment carried out following observations of a younger child.

Expectations of Ofsted

This section looks at the ways in which Ofsted interprets the Progress Review and what settings are likely to need to provide during an inspection. Ofsted inspectors are required to judge children's progress and in order to do this they need to know what the children's starting points are. The expectations of providers will be to understand how well children are making progress. A major source of evidence/questions may be to establish when parents are asked for information about their child's progress. How often, for example, do practitioners share a good-quality summary of their observations of children with the children's parents, and their plans for reviewing children's progress at age 2? They will also wish to know the involvement of the SENCO and/or other partners where there are concerns about a child's development and learning. As an inspector tracks a particular child, they will need to gather evidence from the progress check at 2 years. How children make progress will only be able to be judged if there is the evidence of their starting points and/or capabilities.

What local authorities provide

Each local authority has developed a format for the progress check at age 2. They are very similar and provide a starting point for staff to develop a template to complete this. The example below is from the National Children's Bureau publication *A Know How Guide* (2012) on the progress check at age 2.

Key principles

- The check should be completed by a practitioner who knows the child well and works directly with them in the setting. This should normally be the child's key person;
- Arises from the ongoing observational assessments carried out as part of everyday practice in the setting;
- Is based on skills, knowledge, understanding and behaviour that the child demonstrates consistently and independently;
- Takes account of the views and contributions of parents;
- Takes into account the views of other practitioners and, where relevant, other professionals working with the child;
- Enables children to contribute actively to the process.

(National Children's Bureau, 2012)

What do parents want from the progress check? The most useful and valuable summaries will:

- be clear and easy to read;
- be easy to understand, avoiding unfamiliar jargon, acronyms or terminology (with interpretation and translation available where appropriate);
- present a truthful yet sensitive reflection of what the child can do and their achievements to date;
- identify areas where the child is progressing at a slower place than expected;
- recognise parents' in-depth knowledge of their child by incorporating their observations and comments;
- give parents an idea of how their child's development will be taken forward in the setting.

Assessing children with special educational needs

Some of your children may have additional needs that require involvement of other agencies. As a key worker for a child with additional needs, you may be involved in contributing to the

Common Assessment Framework (CAF). This is a standardised assessment which gives a full picture of a child's additional needs at any stage. Information from parents is included and it covers all aspects of the child's development including health, education and social development. It is important that children are seen as individuals and every child's journey is 'unique' to them. Actively listening to children and giving them time to express themselves, monitoring their progress, sharing the findings with children and parents, and planning next steps that will engage and motivate them are at the heart of effective planning for learning and development. Someone needs to analyse the progress children make and respond to the findings in terms of planning, resourcing and teaching. Generally, leaders and managers have a key role to play in improving quality through assessment by establishing systems, supporting staff and analysing information to:

- Track progress of individual children, and use that progress summary to identify next steps and communicate with others
- Involve parents and partner professionals in understanding and supporting children's progress
- Ensure the accuracy of evaluations of children's progress
- Use the information to support transitions as children move on to other settings
- Plan and implement changes to meet identified needs.

(DCSF, 2009)

Healthy Child Programme (HCP)

The report on a pilot integrating the EYFS progress check with the Healthy Child Programme has recommended the 'integrated review' is renamed to avoid confusion about how checks can be carried out. The HCP 2–2.5 year health and development review similarly looks into learning, social skills, and speech and language skills of children aged 24 months and 30 months and is carried out by health professionals. It is recommended that integrating health and early years is better for children and their parents as it gives parents a more complete picture of their child's development. This would appear to be a consensus view, as stated by Liz Bayram, chief executive of PACEY who says, 'It marks a big step forward in the changing status of childcare professionals and recognises their contribution to not only children's educational development but also their health and well-being' (www.pacey.org.uk). The pilot programme also concluded that integrating progress checks will successfully provide a more holistic and complete picture of a child's progress. An issue, as yet unresolved, is who will carry out the review and how nursery staff may be able to carry out the reviews alongside health visitors.

Reception baseline assessment

The use of a reception baseline assessment has not been made mandatory; schools may elect not to adopt an approved baseline scheme. However, there is a strong incentive to do so.

(DfE, 2015)

Reception class teachers lacked any great enthusiasm for baseline assessment as only 33 per cent of respondents to the consultation were in favour of this. The opening guidance from the DfE (2015) states that the aim of a baseline assessment in reception year is to improve how progress in local authority primary schools is measured. All the data gathered from baseline assessment will be used to measure progress against Key Stage 2 results in 2022. Independent schools are not required to carry out a baseline assessment, or to send their data to the DfE if they decide to do so. The completion of the EYFS profile will no longer be compulsory. The baseline assessment is planned to assess children starting in reception class from September 2016. Schools that do not use the baseline assessment in 2015 will only have their progress measured from Key Stage 1 to Key Stage 2. It is optional for settings to use the baseline assessment in 2015. The government has published a clear set of principles upon which the assessment reforms are based. The sample below is relevant to the early years. They are:

- ongoing teacher-led assessment is a crucial part of effective teaching;
- schools should have the freedom to decide how to teach their curriculum and how to track the progress that children make;
- both summative teacher assessment and external testing are important.

(DfE, 2014b: 4)

The government has identified that there will be national assessments at key points in children's primary education along with different approaches to assessment through a child's education and development, using the most appropriate approach for capturing children's learning at each stage. As far as the early years are concerned there will be:

- the existing statutory 2-year-old progress check undertaken in early years settings;
- a short reception baseline that will sit within the assessments that teachers make of children during reception.

The government claims that those responding to the consultation supported the principle of schools being accountable for the progress of their pupils, and that progress should be measured from the earliest point in school, hence the baseline assessment. Schools say they already make assessments of children when they start school. The response to the question 'Should we introduce a baseline check at the start of reception?' had almost half of the respondents saying that this was too early to assess children.

The early years sector have very mixed views on this development with about half of the consultation group against introducing a baseline check, 34 per cent in favour and 16 per cent not sure. Very few (19 per cent) felt the baseline should be optional. Practitioners have rightly raised concerns as to how this will be administered, but recognise that doing an assessment on entry is an essential part of pedagogy. A supportive claim by 4Children's head of early years Sue Robb said, '4Children is supportive of the principle of a reception baseline upon entry to school in order to help the early identification of need' (Robb, 2014). However, many early years organisations are very much against this development and see it as more to do with 'monitoring school performance than supporting children to have a strong foundation for future learning' (Liz Byram, chief executive of the Professional Association of Childcare and the early years). A very valid point made by Julian Grenier, the National Chair of Early Education, emphasised the difficulties of assessment at this age, citing the likely 11 month age gap and the stress and distress of starting school for many children. It is likely too that many children will have had their progress checked in pre-schools. In February 2015, the Association for Professional Development in the Early Years and (TACTYC) and the British Association for Early Education (Early Education) printed guidelines on baseline assessment to its members with recommendations not to opt into using a baseline assessment scheme, but recognising that some schools will do so and advising to choose one of the five models that most closely adheres to the principles of EYFS assessment. Three schemes have been accredited by the DfE as meeting their criteria, which include requirement to provide a single numerical score with the majority of the content related to communication, language and literacy and mathematics. The final score is not age-adjusted. It must be completed in the first six weeks of reception, or, depending on scheme used, in the first two weeks. Most of the approved scheme is scripted tests, with children answering a narrow range of closed questions. The government-approved providers are:

- Centre for Evaluation and Monitoring (CEM), Durham University;
- Early Excellence;
- National Foundation for Educational Research (NFER).

The views of the early years lobby are quite decisive: 'We must scrap the new baseline tests for primary school children' (Nutbrown, 2015). This is a view from a very experienced early years leader based on the reality that a baseline assessment as they first started primary school was introduced for children in 1997 and abandoned in 2002 because it was a damaging and ineffective policy. It can only be serving to provide national data for the government to compare school against school in terms of the rate of progress from a starting point to the end of the primary school in 2022. This is not helpful to the early years practitioner, the pupils they teach or their parents. This is a very young age to carry out a formal assessment. But much more damaging than these data is the time being wasted carrying out the assessment in place of the interaction between the children and teachers as they help the children to settle into another phase of their educational journey. Alongside this will be those schools that still require the EYFS profile to be completed at the end of the reception year. This is very likely to continue as Year 1 teachers need to have an understanding of the range of abilities and needs of their new intake of pupils. Observational assessment and interactions between adults and children are the current methods of assessing children in the context of their day-to-day activities. The information is used to take the child forward to their next stage of learning. Schools have chosen their option for the baseline assessment. It will be for the early years profession to report on the value of the baseline assessment in the future. It would appear that of the three providers of baseline assessment, more than half of England's primary schools have chosen Early Excellence to provide their baseline assessment. The likelihood is that Early Excellence as the preferred provider was chosen because its assessment methods are those most prevalent in reception classes, that is, through observations, interactions and daily activities. However, there are two other providers, including CEM, which are based on the same principles as PIPs – the assessment is available on a computer and likely also in tablet form in future. Children sit one-to-one with a teacher or teaching assistant at the computer. The assessment follows a story guided through by Milly the bug. It will be interesting to review if there are any advantages to children being assessed by the different schemes.

Personally, the idea of the computer-based assessment is likely to appeal to those children already very familiar with games on tablets.

National Portage Association

The National Portage Association was established in 1983 to offer support and information to parents and professionals and has been at the forefront of developments in support of young children and their families since then. The association aims to:

- work with families to help them develop a quality of life and experience for themselves and their young children in which they can learn together;
- play together, participate and be included in their community in their own right;
- play a part in minimising the disabling barriers that confront the young children and families receiving Portage services;
- support the national and local development of inclusive services for children.

Portage is named after a town in the United States where this type of early education programme was first provided. The programme was first introduced in Britain in the 1970s and was set up in Barking and Dagenham in 1978. Although under some threat of the withdrawal of government funding, Portage is still very much in place in several local authorities. It continues to provide home-based support to parents and their children with special educational needs. There is more information about Portage in Chapter 6.

Topics for discussion

- Discuss the ways in which you review your assessment procedures.
- What are your views on baseline assessment?
- What were your priorities if you selected a baseline assessment package?
- Share the strategies used to involve parents in assessing your children.

Further reading

Early Education (2015) *Guidance on Baseline Assessment in England.* www.early-education.org.uk/Baseline%Assessment%Guidance

TES Early Years Foundation Stage Observation Sheet (n.d.) www.tes.com/early-years-foundation-stage-observation-sheet

National Foundation for Educational Research (NFER) (n.d.) *Baseline Assessment.* www.nfer.ac.uk/schools/baseline-assessment/

Wiltshire Council (2013) *Early Years Foundation Stage Planning Examples Pack- Reception and Reception/Year.* www.wiltshire.gov.uk/-eyfs-planning-examples-pack.pdf

Wood, E. (2013) *Play, Learning and the Early Childhood Curriculum.* London: Sage.

Meeting the needs of 2-year-olds

Introduction

FIGURE 6.1 A 2-year-old

This chapter aims to cover recent research into the characteristics of 2-year-olds, their educational provision, support for children with special educational needs and the key roles played by all those involved in ensuring that this age group has the best start to their first educational experiences from key workers to early years leaders in various settings across the country. The debate as to the pros and cons of the inclusion of 2-year-olds in schools is reviewed along with a case study showing how this initiative operates in one small infant school. The lobby against 2-year-olds in school is discussed. Anne Longfield OBE, the chief executive of 4Children, states that the extension of free early learning to 40 per cent of the country's most disadvantaged 2-year-olds from September 2014 has huge potential to improve the life chances of millions of children for years to come. That is why we must prioritise rather than delay this crucial programme of work. The issues relating to quality childcare have become critical in the past ten years due, in part, to increases in provision provided by the private, voluntary and independent (PVI) sector across the country. The provision of government funding for some 2-year-olds to have free early education and childcare is one recent initiative. This is causing turmoil within the early years lobby following the statement by HMCI that rather than practitioners complaining that there are insufficient places for 2-year-olds in pre-schools, they can go to school. This chapter shares examples of how schools are integrating 2-year-olds (see Figure 6.1). The additional funding for 2-year-olds is restricted to parents who are in receipt of various benefits or to children who are looked after by the local authority, or have a statement of special educational need (see Table 6.1 for the conditions applying). Other 2-year-olds can attend a nursery or pre-school but they have to pay until they are 3 years old for the 15 hours a week they are currently entitled to. This will rise to 30 hours a week from 2016 and is an entitlement for the children of working parents based on the announcement in the budget by Conservative government in 2015. At last, it would appear that early years is being given a much higher profile across the country, although mostly for the wrong reasons according to a great many early years organisations. There is without doubt huge criticism of the 'schoolification' of 2-year-olds in what practitioners describe as extending formal schooling approaches down into the early years and insufficient provision available to take 2-year-olds into pre-school settings. A speech by Her Majesty's Chief Inspector of Schools (HMCI) raised the concerns of the early years lobby in 2014 in his suggestions that a school environment would be beneficial to 2-year-olds:

> What children facing serious disadvantage need is high quality early education from the age of two delivered by skilled practitioners, led by a teacher in a setting that parents can recognise and access.
>
> (HMCI Wilshaw, quoted in Ofsted, 2015a)

TABLE 6.1 Conditions attached to free childcare for 2-year-olds

Parents are able to apply for free childcare for a 2-year-old child if they are in receipt of one or more of the following:
■ Income Support
■ Job Seekers Allowance
■ Support for a 'looked after' child
■ Child Tax Credit – income below £16,190
■ Guaranteed Element of State Pension Credit
■ Support under the Immigration and Asylum Act 1999
■ Employment and Support Allowance – income related
■ Disability Living Allowance (child)
■ Working Tax Credit and earn no more than £16,190
■ Current Statement of Special Educational Needs or an Education, Health and Care Plan (child)
■ Left care through Special Guardianship, or an Adoption, or Residence Order

FIGURE 6.2 Integration of 2-year-olds?

I am opening this chapter with an account of what is happening in one small infant and nursery school in northeast England as they integrate 2-year-olds into their early years unit, comprising nursery- and reception-aged children. The huge success this is having on the eight 2-year-olds is immediately palpable both from the outcomes for the children concerned and their older siblings and friends to the impact the initiative is having on parents and the community. The most positive benefits of this initiative are shared and acknowledge the huge success and impact it is having on the 2-year-olds and also their siblings and families (as illustrated in Figure 6.2). This is directly attributable to the passion and commitment of the headteacher and her team to making it work for all children involved and not just the 2-year-olds.

CASE STUDY 6.1 2-year-olds in school

Trimdon Grange is a small infant school with about 125 pupils serving a small village in the centre of what was once a coalmining area. The early years unit is integrated with children from the ages of 2 to 5 learning to play and learn together. A key priority is given to supporting and engaging parents and families in their children's development. As the headteacher says, 'At this school everyone is an educator – children, staff, parents and grandparents are all considered partners in teaching.' The approaches to teaching and play meet the needs of the community, parents, children and staff. There is no direct instruction on what to do in the EYFS. The learning experiences are conceived in the mind of the adults as to what children need. Children have free exploration, have a go, and can walk away. There is a key meeting point between the children and adults. Children need to learn how to play. They learn how to master skills in their environment. When children play they are

---

learning. A close relationship between adult and child-led experiences takes place with the adults acting as facilitators for the children, thus extending their learning through their play. Quality play is the outcome of effective teaching, through reinforcement of language, praising children and supporting them. Everything an adult does is to promote children's learning. Teaching is observing, developing curiosity, communicating and modelling language, solving problems, demonstrating, explaining and forming attachments. Through adult–child interactions, staff are questioning, facilitating, encouraging, and developing independence and perseverance. As an example, a dragon hunt in the outdoor forest trail is central to learning, for example, 'Can you find a dragon in the tree?' 'I got 2' (2-year-old). Children are recalling, learning to cooperate, taking risks, encouraged to explain their ideas (see Figure 6.3). Staff take account of their interests, explain ideas and structure the routines of the day along with developing respect between adults and children. The ultimate goal is wanting children to learn. Displays are large and focus on the achievements of the children. Parents see that 'children's learning takes centre stage'. The headteacher recognises that 'parents and grandparents can be highly skilled and instinctive educators'.

FIGURE 6.3 Outdoor play

Research findings

There is plenty of criticism of HMCI's directive that the needs of 2-year-olds are not going to be met well in schools (Goddard, 2014). Goddard's claim is that he shows a 'woeful lack of understanding of how children develop, grow and learn, with directives being aimed at "teaching" children under five rather than providing an enriching environment in which they learn through exploration, discovery and trial and error about the world around them and their place in it'. The case study (6.1) and the two Ofsted reports (Ofsted, 2015b and Ofsted, 2015c) describe how the adults and older children are interacting with the 2-year-olds to provide the encouragement to have a go, to listen, to take part and to celebrate their achievements within a very playful context. In January 2014, in a report for the Sutton Trust charity, several early years experts – Kathy Sylva, Naomi Eisenstadt and Sandra Mathers – recommended that the government delay its expansion of free nursery places for disadvantaged 2-year-olds until it could guarantee access to good-quality places. The government did not take the advice of the early years experts, despite a significant lobby of academics critical of this development. Several early years organisations have vehemently criticised this development as one where quality is being sacrificed for the sake of quantity. The rise of university academics campaigning against this development via the 'Too much, too soon campaign' is strong evidence of the concern in academia. The consensus being that the problem will not be solved by putting children into a formal setting at an even younger age. More strong views against 2-year-olds are reflected in 'The Conversation' – an online forum for articles and comments. The general thrust of their views alongside those already quoted is that the government is encouraging parents to place their children in nurseries shortly after their second birthday. A convincing case for not having 2-year-olds in school is made by Pam Jarvis (May 1, 2015) and Caitlin Mclean (May 1, 2015). Newspaper headlines that the current provision for 2-year-olds is not fit for purpose due to lack of resources and staffing (*The Guardian*, 4 February 2014) is a recurring theme. Early years settings are not designed with the needs of 2-year-olds in mind. The comments by HMCI of Schools Sir Michael Wilshaw continues to ruffle the feathers of many early years specialists because of his assertion that schools can provide well-resourced provision for 2-year-olds.

The case for 2-year-olds in school

A useful question to ask is: 'Who are the adults supporting children's learning?'

There are proponents of this development which can be read about in the report *Parents as Partners in Teaching* (Ofsted, 2015c), which describes how three early years settings, including a small infant school, are integrating eight 2-year-olds into their early years unit with tremendous success. Each session in the setting I am familiar with has four 2-year-olds. The youngest children have a very small base room, but quickly integrate with nursery- and reception-aged children in the early years indoor and outdoor classroom for all their activities. Having seen this in operation, I am very confident that replicas of this practice have the potential to address the need to provide high-quality education to children under 3. The integration of the 2-year-olds in the early years unit is impressive due to the sharing of learning and experiences for all the children under 5, the close relationship with parents and the gains made by disadvantaged 2-year-olds evident once they start statutory schooling. Play is central to developing learning in all the children in the early years unit. Figure 6.4 demonstrates the successful integration of the children. I am aware that this is not the norm as frequently the 2 year-olds are kept apart from the older children in many settings.

It was reported in *The Guardian*, August 23, 2014, that thousands of middle-class nurseries were declining to accept 2-year-olds from poor backgrounds despite a £100 million government initiative to extend childcare to the most deprived families. One view held is that there is no doubt about the urgency in ensuring disadvantaged parents take up that nursery

FIGURE 6.4 Early mathematical learning

provision for their 2-year-olds. This initiative has the capacity to improve children's readiness for school and potentially break down their children's disadvantages in areas such as language development. Research commissioned in 2010 by the government (Roulstone et al., 2010) confirms the degree of disadvantage. The opportunity for 2-year-olds from disadvantaged backgrounds to access childcare provision is a step in the right direction, although the reality, as described in numerous news headlines at the time, was very different. The then education minister wrote to all local authorities asking them to encourage schools to take 2-year-olds into their onsite nurseries to combat the shortage in childcare. There is a strong justification provided by researchers for 2-year-olds from disadvantaged backgrounds to have access to early years provision (Mathers et al., 2012). The opinion that 2-year-old children from poor backgrounds are in danger of underachieving if they are not in some form of early years provision is one justification for this. What is critically important is that the provision for 2-year-olds is developmentally appropriate. That remains to be seen in some settings. Estelle Morris brings a good dose of reality to this issue, reminding us that early years provision matters for all children who do not learn at home: the toddlers who become the infants already lagging behind when they start school and find it difficult to ever catch up (*The Guardian*, 22 April 2014). The experiences related in this chapter are exceptional, but they show what is possible if the environment and emphasis on learning through play remains a high priority.

Two-year-olds in the community

A priority should to be given to the needs of the developing child and assurances that their well-being is prioritised over educational attainment. What is best for the children? The answer to this is linked to what sort of start all these disadvantaged 2-year-olds are getting in the home. How best can parents be supported to enable them to provide supportive and caring home lives for their children? Various charities and donations from Lottery funding are helping to provide support to parents with young children across the country following the closure of so many Sure Start Centres. An example of this is the Lottery-funded Better Start programme (2014). Naomi Eisenstadt, CB has been active in policy and practice in the field of early years for over thirty years. She is currently working with the DfE and the Social Policy Department to pursue her interests in children's services, poverty and its impact on children and family policy.

I would advise watching her discuss the Better Start programme on YouTube (www. youtube.com). Its aim is to give parents practical support along with what children are likely to need with the following three priorities for the children:

- diet and nutrition;
- social and emotional development;
- language development.

The three priorities are well justified. Parents are helped to prepare healthy meals in a weekly cooking class, which gives them greater confidence. It may sound unbelievable but some parents (usually the mother) had never cooked anything, due to lack of confidence and never having been taught at a younger age. All sorts of activities were set up for the 2-year-olds in 'stay and play' sessions, 'wriggle and play' for babies and access to a speech service for children with language difficulties. An immediate finding of this was the increase in the confidence of the mums. They asked questions and became confident to breastfeed their babies, and there was an opportunity for their 2-year-olds to play with other children. Another function of Better Start is the way key agencies work together to make sure that babies receive the early care and nurture they need for healthy development. Statistics suggest that 30 per cent of babies are born into poverty, with 30 per cent of mums smoking and only 56 per cent of babies being breastfed. Medway, Blackpool, Southend, Bradford and Gloucestershire are just some of the regions covered by Better Start. As an initiative to develop children's well-being, it is a vital service that may become more widespread. I would advise watching a YouTube extract from the Born in Bradford initiative where the focus is very much on providing parents with the necessary basic skills to enable them to help their young children develop and play in the security of their own homes.

Language development

Language development at the age of 2 years predicts children's performance on entry to primary school.

(Roulston et al., 2011)

The developmental window for developing neuro-motor and language skills is in the first three and a half years of life. If one accepts this premise, neuro-motor skills are developed in the context of free physical space, while language develops through social engagement, free play and imagination, all of which is vital for child development and can be provided in many early years settings. More recently reported in *The Guardian* in April 22, 2015 were the comments of Shadow Education Minister Tristram Hunt to the National Association of Headteachers annual conference in Liverpool. He stated that 4-year-old children are starting school unable to speak properly because their parents were not getting down on all fours and playing with them at home. Hunt said that he had been struck by the number of headteachers who had raised concerns about children arriving in reception classes with delayed speaking, listening and motor skills. Headteachers commented that this had got remarkably worse over the last decade, thus reinforcing the need to ensure the youngest children and their families are given all the support they need to help their children make better progress in language acquisition. Can this be resolved by the 2-year-olds going into a nursery environment geared to children almost twice their age? Several charities across the country are supporting families with young children such as Better Start and the Born in Bradford study, which provides the key to improving life chances for Bradford babies, funded by the Big Lottery Fund as outlined earlier. This is widespread in several other authorities with a high proportion of vulnerable children. Further details of these developments are included in Chapter 7, involving parents and carers. Professor Nutbrown and Anne Longfield, the then chief executive of the charity 4Children, claim that the status of the early years professional is being downgraded by government changes. For example, Cathy Nutbrown's conclusion that the early years profession is seen as 'low status, low-paid and low-skilled' and was a turn off for the brightest children. This situation arises due to the lack of qualifications needed to work with young children by many staff in the PVI sector. Settings may not even insist on basic numeracy and literacy skills in their staff and some staff looking after young children would struggle to read a story aloud. On top of all this is how early years staff compare with their European counterparts. English early years professionals are the lowest paid in Europe, with childcare workers being the lowest paid. In Europe, according to *Nursery World* (April 2015) a coalition of organisations concerned with early language development are calling for every nursery in England to be led by a graduate by 2020.

This section examines the developmental stages that 2-year-olds go through as their language develops. A wise statement that is very relevant to current times made by Margaret Donaldson in 1978 was that when children start school it is already too late or that nothing can be done without direct intervention in the homes of the underprivileged. Such a relevant comment from so many years ago! So what do early years practitioners do to plug the gap of disadvantage in so many very young children? The government have offered a solution in the provision of childcare and education for 2-year-olds from disadvantaged backgrounds. However, there is sufficient evidence from the evaluations of the Sure Start projects suggesting that out-of-home provision may not always be the best answer for some children. The rub here is that the out-of-home provision has not been good enough because of the lack of trained early years professionals to meet the needs of those children and families. Early years research corroborates this to some degree due to the inadequacies of some staff in the early years sector, particularly the PVI sector. The increased priority to an earlier attempt to eradicate the disadvantages many children have when it comes to their communication and language skills is further confirmed by the third of children who are not confident in communication, language and literacy by the end of EYFS. There can be many interpretations as why this is the case. The research by Roulstone et al. (2011) found that in spite of most children developing speech and language skills effortlessly, some are slow to develop these skills and then go on to struggle with literacy and academic skills throughout their schooling. It is the first few years of life that are critical to their subsequent development. Children's understanding, use of vocabulary and their use of two–three word sentences at 24 months was very strongly associated with their later performance, even when adjusted for social class. A child's language adds value to their development irrespective of their social background.

Listening to babies and children

This section has a focus on the ways in which the very youngest children learn to communicate and utter their first words. In order to talk with a child, it is necessary to listen and watch. A small child needs time and an opportunity to talk when an adult listens and they give the child space to speak. When an adult watches, they can see what a child might want to talk about, even if words are not easy to understand. This means that the child's attempts to communicate can make sense to an interested adult. Then the adult can talk with the child. A child engaged in this way will learn new words and want to talk, because they know that their attempts to talk are heard and understood. A view promoted by EYFS is that of a listening approach because it gives a child much more scope for learning to talk than does an adult reliant on naming objects, or asking a child to name objects.

Babies and young children learn to focus on adult speech very early in their lives. It helps if adults make the communication easy for the child to listen to and understand. Parents often do this. They adapt their own language levels to those of the child to help them to listen effectively. The focus is on giving the child a listening and speaking part in the conversation. This contrasts with an adult using a high proportion of directive commands, which do not allow the child a turn to speak. It is true that the more parents talk to their children, the more the children speak themselves. Practitioners can encourage conversation and extend the use of language through everyday situations such as changing routines, mealtimes, shopping and cooking. An effective open partnership with parents is vital, as they most easily understand their child's communications and can help overcome any barriers that may occur. As a practitioner, what is a typical expectation of a 12-month-old child? According to EYFS practice guidance and the review of the *Development Matters* statements by Early Education (2012), children should be starting to form words by the time they are a year old. To communicate effectively, children must understand what is being said to them and learn how to speak by forming the correct sounds within words, putting words together in short phrases and sentences and then learning to tell stories (Law and Harris, 2001: 7) (see Table 6.2 for terms used in speech and language). Possibly children with special needs will develop alternative systems for communicating such as sign language, gestures or picture symbols. Strategies to use when talking to very young children include:

- speak about the here and now
- use simple words
- use key words only
- use few word endings
- use sentences which are one or two words longer than child words are

- speak slowly and carefully
- repeat ideas.

The revised *Development Matters* statements are available on line at www.foundationyears.org. uk. Table 6.2 is indicative of the language and speech expectations of a 16–26-month-old child.

As shown in the research statistics mentioned earlier, boys from all social classes are likely to start school with lower language and communication skills. Parents must spend more time:

- singing nursery rhymes
- playing word games
- reading picture books
- making eye contact
- creating stories.

Parent time with young sons from birth in an effort to stop them failing once they start school is vital for language development. To quote Sue Palmer, author of the book *Toxic Childhood* (2007): 'the first three months are critical for speech and language development'. In order to talk with a child, it is necessary to listen and watch. A small child needs time and an opportunity to talk. When an adult listens, they give the child space to speak. When an adult watches, they can see what a child might want to talk about, even if words are not easy to understand. This means that the child's attempts to communicate can make sense to an interested adult. Then the adult can talk with the child. A child engaged in this way will learn new words and want to talk, because they know that their attempts to talk are heard and understood. A view promoted by the EYFS is that of a listening approach because it gives a child much more scope for learning to talk than does an adult reliant on naming objects, or asking a child to name objects.

TABLE 6.2 Terms used in speech and language development

Comprehension	The ability to understand words and sentences. A comprehension difficulty means that a child cannot understand what is said to him. Typically he cannot do as asked, or does only part of what is asked. (This may need to be distinguished from the case where the child can understand but will not cooperate!)
Expressive language	Using words and sentences. An expressive language difficulty means that a child might point or make noises instead of words; or that an older child uses only one word at a time instead of sentences.
Speech sounds	The accuracy of pronunciation. A speech sound difficulty means, for example, that a child says *tar* instead of *car*.

Source: Law and Harris, 2001: 7

TABLE 6.3 Communication and language: understanding

OBSERVING WHAT A CHILD IS LEARNING: UNDERSTANDING	
8–20 months	■ Developing the ability to follow others' body language, including pointing and gestures. ■ Responds to the different things said when in a familiar context with a special person, e.g. 'Where's Mummy?' 'Where's your nose?' ■ Understanding of single words in context is developing, e.g. 'cup', 'milk', 'daddy'.
16–26 months	■ Selects familiar objects by name and will go to find objects when asked, or identify objects from a group. ■ Understands simple sentences, e.g. 'Throw the ball'.

Source: Development Matters, 2010.

TABLE 6.4 Observing what a child is learning: speaking

OBSERVING WHAT A CHILD IS LEARNING: SPEAKING	
8–20 months	■ Uses sounds in play, e.g 'brrrm' for toy car. ■ Uses single words. ■ Frequently imitates words and sounds. ■ Enjoys babbling and increasingly experimenting with using sounds and words to communicate for a range of purposes, e.g. 'teddy', 'more', 'no', 'bye-bye'. ■ Uses pointing with eye gazes to make requests and to share an interest. ■ Creates personal words as they begin to develop language.
16–26 months	■ Copies familiar expressions, e.g. 'Oh dear!', 'All gone'. ■ Beginning to put two words together, e.g. 'want ball', 'more juice'. ■ Uses different types of everyday words – nouns, verbs and adjectives. ■ Beginning to ask simple questions. ■ Begining to talk about people and things that are not present.

Communication environment

> Language is the most powerful tool in the development of any human being. It is undeniably the greatest asset we possess. A good grasp of language is synonymous with a sound ability to think. In other words language and thought are inseparable.
>
> (Vygotsky, 1986)

In the early stages of language development, it is the particular aspects of a child's communication environment that are associated with the rate of language acquisition rather than the broader socio-economic context of the family. Previous research by Chomsky stated that children mastered the grammar of their first language at a very early age. Children will commonly say 'I bringed it', suggesting there is no imitation of adults in this situation. The use of communication and language is at the heart of all learning. Learning to speak initially emerges out of non-verbal communication. It is important that practitioners value children's talk and appreciate the importance of making time for conversation with young children, both on a one-to-one basis and within small groups. It is vital to reduce the number of children with speech and language problems requiring specialist intervention by the age of 4. Table 6.2 shows the aspects of speech and language development needing consideration.

Law and Harris (2001) identified five key themes to set the context for helping children's communication skills:

- The importance of adult–child interactions, especially parent–child interactions.
- The relationship between communication skills and other aspects of a child's general development.
- The potential for a local community environment to impact on a child's development.
- The importance of collaboration between the many people involved with a child's development.
- The potential for a child's (or parent's) resilience to reduce the impact of potentially stressful circumstances and the importance of enhancing that resilience.

In the early stages of language development, it is the particular aspects of a child's communication environment that are associated with the rate of language acquisition rather than the broader socio-economic context of the family. Previous research by an ongoing medical research study that has tracked the lives of 13,500 babies and their families since 2007 is the Better Start Bradford project funded by the a Big Lottery grant. The central aim of this study is to explore why some children stay healthy and others fall ill. Communication and language is one of the key themes along with nutrition, obesity and environmental changes. The funding granted for this is used to run projects and initiatives to support families and their children at key stages of their early years development.

Recent research findings reveal a mixed picture regarding the actions taken in some parts of the country to address the gap between those children showing concern as to their level of language understanding on starting school with other children who are fluent and articulate chatterers. Already we know that funded provision is due to increase for childcare once children are age 3, but all the most recent researchers are saying that this is too late. A key survey (Avon Longitudinal Study of Parents and Children (ALSPAC), 2007), although carried out some years ago, examined the characteristics of the environment in which children learned to communicate. The key findings of this survey are:

- There is a strong association between a child's social background and their readiness for school.
- Language development at the age of 2 predicts children's performance on entry to primary school.
- The child's communication environment influences language development (see below).
- The communication environment is a more dominant predictor of early language than social background.

A key feature of a child's communication environment includes mother's parenting score, which includes a range of activities and interactions, her perceived feelings of being supported (by family, partner and social systems generally) including access to childcare, the resources available to the mother and children's books and toys, as well as the environment at home, including the amount of time the TV is on in the home. Generally mothers' parenting activities match various teaching activities by teaching clapping games, naming body parts, colours, numbers, songs as well as childcare activities such as feeding, bathing, reading to a child, playing and walks.

Recent research by Roulstone et al. (2011) corroborates the ALSPAC findings:

- Mother with support by family, partners and by the social system generally. The perceived feeling that family, partner and social system are supporting the mother generally, including access to childcare.
- Resources – books, toys, the amount of time the TV is on, teaching activities, clapping games, names of body parts, colours and number song.

The list is endless. These tasks, too, should generally be undertaken by the mother as well as feeding, bathing, reading, playing and going for walks. The research further shows that attending a crèche/pre-school is associated with higher achievement. Scores on entry to school decrease in line with the amount of time TV is on in the home. Thus we can see that here are four key factors to successful language acquisition:

- mothers parenting
- toys
- home
- social support.

The research findings were relevant to all children irrespective of their social class. High social class does not necessarily equate with successful entry outcomes. An effective home communication environment has the following attributes:

- What the mother did.
- What the mother felt.
- What material they had at their disposal.

The key to the mother's parenting and social support are book ownership and trips to the local library, a home score and limited or controlled TV usage in the home. The research by Close (2004) shows that children under 2 years old are unlikely to benefit from children's TV other than for it to be visually stimulating, but would not contribute to new vocabulary.

Learning through play

Play is something we need to teach specific skills.

(Headteacher)

Two-year-olds are not the same as 3-year-olds. Athey (1990) maintains that the needs and priorities for the youngest children should reflect their behaviours. Children are curious, they notice what is going on around them. They have their own intrinsic motivation which must be facilitated by materials and support from adults, especially a key person. These patterns of behaviour are called schema. This is a pattern of repeatable behaviour into which experiences are assimilated and are gradually coordinated (Athey, 1990: 37). Schemas need to be enriched and supported. There are many schemas, some of the easily identifiable ones are:

- connection (joining) – a child may enjoy playing with train tracks, construction sets, string or sellotape;
- enveloping (covering and surrounding) – wrapping up, covering up and posting notes in envelopes to post;
- rotation (circles) – playing circle games, being fascinated by wheels, roundabouts, spinning tops or kaleidoscopes;
- trajectory (straight lines) – throwing games, woodwork, percussion, football or climbing and jumping off;
- transporting – carrying small items around in bags, buggies and pushing toys around in a pram or trailer;
- enclosure – filling and emptying boxes, climbing into boxes, making dens.

It is vital that practitioners allow the 2-year-olds time to repeat and be left alone to do so.

Play-based learning maintains a high status in the early years and especially for 2-year-olds. I will draw on the research findings of Garrick et al. (DfE, 2011b) whose brief was to investigate the experiences young children were having of the EYFS. In particular what the findings were in answer to the question, 'To what extent and in what manner are children's experiences in early years settings based around play and how enjoyable are these experiences?' The key findings for this question were:

- Children talked about the range of play, including 'pretend' play, construction, drawing and painting, computer games and football. Children's access to such experiences seemed to vary considerably from setting to setting.
- Play can be linked to all six areas of learning and development, but children conveyed most enjoyment of play linked to Creative Development, Knowledge and Understanding of the World, Physical Development and aspects of Communication, Language and Literacy.

An area that the children mention frequently is the regularity of their wish to play outside. The outdoor curriculum in recent years has been influenced by the Scandinavian model of early education, where it is common for kindergartens to provide extended, daily opportunities for physically active and challenging play in forest environments.

I make no apologies for giving this section something of a historical slant as I feel that it effectively demonstrates how far the early years profession has come in the past thirty years and more. Piaget (1926), Donaldson (1978), Bruner (1983), Vygotsky (1978) and Meadows (1993) have all studied young children to establish the workings of their minds and how and what children think about as they grow. What are the most favourable circumstances to promote early learning? How far do adults, as suggested by Vygotsky (1978), need to engage with children to ensure a steady rate of development? There are those who feel that given the correct environment children will make progress through their play and interaction with other children along with practitioners who believe that play constitutes a way for the child to make sense of his or her world. Some research says that children create knowledge when they play (Levin, 1990). Practitioners need to balance child-initiated learning alongside adult-led focused activities to meet the requirements of the EYFS (DfE, 2014a). However, more important is the development of practitioner understanding of the nature of learning in the early years. As will be shown, it is not a one-sided argument between those who preach learning through play and others who cite Vygotsky's theory that children learn most effectively with a more knowledgeable other involved in the learning. It is not a case of one or the other, as will be shown there needs to be an equal balance between freely chosen activities and practitioner-supported and extended interaction with children when you have 2- and 3-year-olds together in the same setting.

Play constitutes a way for the child to make sense of his or her world. Play with friends has a key role in social development. It allows children to exercise self-control and develop what they already know, take turns, cooperate and socialise with others (Glover, 1999). Play, inner motivation, self-control and starting from the child are central. A crucial aspect of learning for the young child is that the act of learning is far more focused than the objectives of learning. Children learn by:

- imitation
- doing
- talking
- experimenting
- trying and failing
- trying and succeeding
- reflection and communication
- playing.

All this is different from the objects of learning, which are what we as teachers understand so well. How then do we guide children to learn what we have prescribed for us to teach by the DfE (2014a)? A trawl through the statutory guidance provides ample support for a play-based curriculum.

> Play is essential for children's development, building their confidence as they learn to explore, to think about patterns, and relate to others. Children learn by leading their own play, and by taking part in play which is guided by adults. There is an ongoing judgement to be made by practitioners about the balance between activities led by children, and activities led or guided by adults.
>
> (DfE, 2014a: 9)

Interactions such as the above were found to be characteristic of high-quality settings. The Effective Provision for Pre-school Education project (EPPE, 2004) corroborates previous findings referring to the role of teachers and children in extending and supporting learning. It found that children whose thinking was developed alone or in the company of supportive adults would do better than children whose thinking was developed alone or in the company of their peers. This study very effectively corroborates the findings of Vygotsky that the educative relationship children have with 'more knowledgeable others' enables children to get what Vygotsky calls the 'higher ground' or the next level of cognitive functioning. In determining the impact of the environment on children's all-round development there are many factors to consider, especially the variation in the quality of children's home learning environment and their stage of development when they start pre-school at age 2 or 3 years. A major impact on the quality of provision for children under 5 is the ever-improving quality of training for aspiring early years practitioners and the diversity of routes to achieve a recognised qualification. The following dialogue occurred between an adult and a barely 3-year-old girl. The extent of the child's close relationship with her mother is evident in her ready use of adult language in an exchange with myself.

ADULT: Is that a tree trunk?
CHILD: A fallen down tree trunk.
ADULT: Let's make a garden.
CHILD: A colourful garden. Don't put the colourful garden away.
ADULT: What can I have for breakfast?
CHILD: Nothing, you are not hungry.
CHILD: You can actually wash them. We have one toilet and two washing (bathroom) rooms. After toilet wash my hands.

Portage for 2-year-olds

The National Portage Association was established in 1983 to offer support and information to parents and professionals and has been at the forefront of developments in support to young children and their families since then. The Association aims to:

- Work with families to help them develop a quality of life and experience for themselves and their young children in which they can learn together.
- Play together, participate and be included in their community in their own right.
- Play a part in minimising the disabling barriers that confront the young children and families receiving Portage services.
- Support the national and local development of inclusive services for children.

Generally Portage visitors work with preschool children with special educational needs in their own homes, helping them to develop learning techniques and improve communication. Parents place a high value on this service. Sadly as the funding for 3-year-olds to have free nursery education increases, some local authorities decided to reduce their funding for Portage, which will stand at a 37 per cent reduction by 2016. The reasoning for this is that the needs of 3-year-old children with disabilities and additional needs are now being met in early years settings (Goodhead, 2013). Despite pleas by Mencap's chief executive, Jan Tregelles, that the cutbacks were depriving children with a learning disability and their families of 'the best possible start in life', several local authorities have cut Portage services completely in the past five years. Independent supporters are now funded by government, to ensure every family that needs help with an education, health and welfare plan gets it. An injustice of this reduction in funding is that the support by Portage was given in the homes of children below the age of starting pre-school. For example, parents' comments reflect this very well:

> Portage has been an amazing support for my daughter. I feel strongly that this support will benefit the long term future of my child.
>
> (Mother of 8-month-old child with Downs Syndrome)

> Portage has helped us to understand our son's condition more. Also taught us how to engage with him. Could not have got here without this service
>
> (Mother of child with autism, aged 3 years)

The official website for the National Portage Association is www.portage.org.uk.

The Portage model of learning is characterised by the following attributes:

- Regular home visiting.
- Supporting the development of play, communication, relationships, and learning for young children within the family.
- Supporting the child and family's participation and inclusion in the community in their own right.
- Working together with parents within the family, with them taking the leading role in the partnership that is established.
- Helping parents to identify what is important to them and their child and plan goals for learning and participation.
- Keep a shared record of the child's progress and other issues raised by the family.
- Responding flexibly to the needs of the child and family when providing support.

The role of the key person

Each pre-school child must be assigned a key person. Their role is to help ensure that every child's care is tailored to meet their individual needs, to help the child become familiar with the setting, offer a settled relationship for the child and build a relationship with their parents. As well as involvement with parents in completing the progress check, a key person may also be involved in starting a record of a particular child's learning journey. Developing a close working relationship with parents is a vital part of the key person's role in order to establish a secure degree of trust and an effective communication channel between the key person and the parent (Elfer, 2012). As stated elsewhere, a key person has a crucial role to play in implementing a reflective practitioner approach. There are some differences in the views of practitioners regarding the 'key worker' role. Reception class teachers generally felt it was an unrealistic role to carry out given all their other responsibilities, whereas in other pre-school settings the 'key worker' system was felt to be valuable to support children's well-being, the norm being to have 'key children' (Brooker et al., 2010).

Two-year-olds at home or in school?

There is still some debate about where 2-year-olds are likely to receive the most effective support with an emerging consensus that their needs may be best met in the home with parents receiving support to know how to contribute to their children's emerging language skills and what conditions need to be in place to ensure this. The research is debateable when it comes to the most effective conditions which need to be in place in the home to ensure this happens. A lack of development of expected language skills is not only linked to poverty, as not all children from such backgrounds are necessarily lagging in their language acquisition. There is conflicting research on this claim however, with EPPE research in the late 1990s stating that children who received pre-school education then had better cognitive development. The key to success is linked to parental involvement in early learning, irrespective of social background. Summing up what research says, one can quote Margaret Donaldson's claim that by the time children start school it is too late, therefore good-quality EYFS provision may be the answer. What is vital is that the first two years are critical for children's development, although Sure Start evaluations, the work of Kathy Sylva and others raise concerns about the calibre of staff working with children under age 3. As stated earlier, high-quality early years provision can help to narrow the gap and successive governments have implemented policies designed to address these early inequalities. The current dilemma arises because of the increased numbers needing placements and lack of suitably qualified staff and provision. The development of the widespread activities in Bradford and Gloucestershire, for example, may be how this dilemma is resolved. Giving parents confidence, basic skills and praise to raise their self-esteem and skills levels has an impact on the whole family, but especially the children.

Good quality pedagogy for all children under age 3

The most recent review of the research evidence on quality in early childhood education and care for children under age 3 (Soukakou et al., 2014) outlines a review of the evidence on the quality of early childhood education and care for children under age 3. Particular account is taken of the governments programme for free early years provision for disadvantaged 2-year-olds. The key pedagogical findings being the need for:

- Stable relationships and interactions with sensitive and responsive adults.
- A focus on play-based activities and routines which allow children to take the lead in their learning.
- Support for communication and language.
- Opportunities to move and be physically active.

(Soukakou et al., 2014)

Look out for the five key conditions necessary for quality pedagogy cited below in the case study of 2-year-olds in school:

- Knowledgeable and capable practitioners, supported by strong leaders.
- Stable staff team and low turnover.
- Effective staff deployment (favourable ratios, staff continuity).

- Secure yet stimulating physical environment.
- Engaged and involved families.

The case study at the beginning of this chapter provides the answer to the two viewpoints stated above for 2-year-olds – at home or in school. Admittedly, the provision is exceptionally outstanding. What it does, though, is to show there needs to be an effective partnership between home and school to create the ideal conditions for successful learning for 2-year-olds. To possibly allay the wealth of criticism of this initiative, Ofsted's recent publication, *Good Practice Example* (Ofsted, 2015c) evaluates the provision for 2-year-olds in school and has produced several examples of good practice on YouTube (www.youtube/user/Ofsted).

In response to agitation by many early years practitioners as to the inappropriateness of 2-year-olds attending school rather than one of the many pre-schools there are available is the suggestion that a suitable answer may be that schools can provide this provision, initially raised by HMCI. The pedagogical practices required need to be play-based activities and routines which allow children to take the lead in their learning and support for language and communication through the use of narrative, shared reading, informal conversations and songs and rhymes. The example of the small school in northeast England successfully integrating a small number of 2-year-olds into an early years unit is a testimony to how this can work for all concerned, the 2-, 3- and 4 year-olds, their parents and the practitioners engaging with the children day by day.

Topics for discussion

- Discuss the pros and cons of 2-year-olds in school.
- What is the adult to child ratio achieved in your setting and is it sufficient?
- Is school or pre-school admittance the answer for 2-year-old children from disadvantaged backgrounds?

Further reading

Ofsted (2015b) *Teaching and Play in the Early Years: A Balancing Act.* London: Ofsted. www.gov.uk/government/organisation/ofsted

Morton, M. (2015) *Two-year-olds in Early Years Settings: Journeys of Discovery.* Buckingham: Open University Press.

Tassoni, P. (2014) *Getting it Right for Two-Year-Olds.* London: Hodder and Stoughton.

7

Involving parents and carers

Introduction

Good parenting and high-quality early learning together provide the foundation children need to make the most of their abilities and talents as they grow up (DfE, 2014a: 5).

No one doubts the key role played by parents as their child's first educator. The importance of the experiences children have in their early years can have a lasting impact on their learning and development in every respect. It is essential that all children, but particularly children from disadvantaged backgrounds, receive provision of the highest possible quality. This may be in the home but is increasingly likely to be in an early years setting. While this chapter is about how pre-school and school settings involve parents and carers, it is also about the ways in which organisations other than schools help and support disadvantaged families, with more information about this in Chapter 8. Sure Start Children's Centres were intended to be the solution to tackling disadvantage, but the regular evaluations (Melhuish et al., 2008, 2010) over several years raised concerns that the families most in need of the support of the Sure Start Centres were not accessing the provision as often as required. As a result, local authorities have closed many centres across the country or reallocated them to charities or voluntary groups. This chapter examines the revised roles of Children's Centres following the closure of many and the more explicit briefs they now have from government and local authorities. However, the disadvantaged children remain and schools and pre-schools continue to be encouraged to work with parents of all children but particularly with those parents who meet the criteria to have support for their 2-year-old children in a school or early years setting. A major focus of this chapter is the ways in which schools are encouraging parents to work with them and their children to support the children's development. The findings and examples described in recent Ofsted surveys (Ofsted, 2015b, 2015c) are included to illustrate examples of exemplary practice in a range of different types of setting across the country.

The role of schools that have allocated places to 2-year-olds features widely in this chapter. Chapter 6 addresses the conflicting views as to the wisdom of 2-year-olds in schools in the face of compelling support from Ofsted (2015b, 2015c) following the HMCI's speech in which he made the suggestion that to provide 2-year-olds with qualified staff in their settings going into a school would be a solution to the shortfall in spaces in early years settings. Typically, middle-class parents preparing their children for their first experiences of the education system join with other parents and their child/children in weekly parent and toddler groups or attending a pre-school with other same-aged children. However, the reality may not always suggest this ideal of the child's needs coming first. There are many children whose lives do not follow the ideal portrayed previously due to family circumstances such as poverty, illness or the need for a mother and father to work and leave their child in the care of others. The critical issue is the need for high-quality out-of-home provision for disadvantaged children. The research suggests that this is not always happening due to the quality of staff in some settings (Mathers et al., 2014). However, recent research has some interesting findings about the current position at a time when the birth rate is rising. This chapter aims to throw some light on what is going on today and, importantly, highlight how practitioners can encourage and support parents to be their child's first and foremost educator because this is so fundamentally vital for all children's future well-being. How practitioners need to relate to parents to share the progress of all children, especially very young children, is crucial. The statutory framework for the EYFS (DfE, 2014a) signals the overriding importance of a strong relationship between parents and early learning. There are further strong messages from the Marmot Review:

> Parents are the most important 'educators' of their children for both cognitive and non-cognitive skills. Parental involvement in their child's reading has been found to be the most important determinant of languages and emergent literacy.
>
> (2010: 4)

Statutory requirements

Good parenting and high-quality early learning together provide the foundation children need to make the most of their abilities and talents as they grow up, according to the opening statement in the introduction to the EYFS framework (DfE, 2014: 5). A key aim of the guidance is that the EYFS seeks to provide partnership working between practitioners and with parents and/or carers. This is reflected in the fundamental early years principle:

> Children learn and develop well in enabling environments in which their experiences respond to their individual needs and there is a strong partnership between practitioners and parents and/or carers.
>
> (DfE 2014a: 6)

This reminds me of my role as a home–pre-school teacher in Knowsley in the early 1980s where a team of qualified teachers were employed to work in the home with parents (usually the mother) to promote play and language development, at least once a week in each family with children under 3. A long lasting memory of this fulfilling and frustrating experience were the welcomes received in homes by children, especially if toys were provided for the children with opportunities to play with someone, and sadly, the number of toyless and bookless households visited. There were some toys, but often put away in the wardrobe upstairs. Parents at this time generally held very negative attitudes towards institutions, and schools in particular, to the extent there were those who were terrified at the prospect of even stepping over the threshold of a school building.

Parental involvement in early learning

> Parents are a child's first educator, therefore it is crucial that schools work with them at all times.
>
> (Headteacher Trimdon Grange Infant School)

The interactions that take place in the home environment have more influence on a child's future achievement than innate ability, material circumstances or the quality of early years or school provision. There is a growing body of evidence that theoretically sound parenting programmes, which are underpinned by strong research evidence, can provide positive gains for parents and children. Reviews have found that parent-training programmes can be successful in improving maternal psychosocial health, in improving emotional and behavioural adjustment of young children under 3 and in contributing to safer home environments and reduced unintentional injuries in children. However, there is older longitudinal research (Feinstein, 2003) suggesting that how well children achieve educationally is determined by class differences, measured by parents' occupational classification (Socio-Economic Status, SES) at the child's birth. It would be encouraging for us all to say that this research is somewhat dated and that the increase in early years provision in the past ten years is making a difference. However, the findings of Feinstein could not be more realistically brought home to myself as I read the information provided for parents in an affluent corner of England. Would parents struggling in the most disadvantaged areas cope with their clearly defined role as expressed in Box 7.1?

BOX 7.1 What can I do to support my child?

- Choose a special time and place to share and enjoy books, five to ten minutes each day will make a difference, but be flexible. Young children have a short attention span.
- Choose books that have lots of joining in – farmyard animal noises, counting or actions.
- Catch initial attention: tone of voice; create suspense: 'I wonder what this story is about?' 'What can you see at the front?' 'Can you guess what's inside?'
- Encourage your child to get involved – turn the pages, lift the flap, etc.
- Take time to let your child look through the pictures and relate it to their own experiences and interests.
- Draw attention to features in the book. Make comments, 'Look at that huge dinosaur', or ask questions, 'Can you see where the little mouse is hiding?'
- Using props such as a puppet or toy vehicle will encourage your child to retell the story.
- Take an interest in what your child is doing in nursery, you could link stories with themes they are covering in class, e.g. holidays, weather, etc.
- Books can be varied – cloth books, bath books, or even a catalogue.
- Most importantly have fun and enjoy the story together.

Regular information about what children are learning in school is sent to parents via emails. The examples provided in Box 7.2 illustrate in general terms what children in a reception class are learning about in the summer term with guidance on how parents can help their children at home. In Box 7.3 is an example of weekly information about children's learning displayed in school.

BOX 7.2 Weekly information displayed for reception class parents

This term our topic is celebrations. This week we are looking at birthdays and writing invitations.

We continue to look at our 5 senses and this week we are focusing on hearing and touch.

Sounds learned so far are: s, a, t, p, i, n, c, k, e, r, m, d, g, o, u, l, f, b.

Ai, j, ou, ie, ee, or, and z.

The children are coming home with their phonic books. If your child is not too tired, please can you practise writing these letter sounds. We will still be doing lots of handwriting practice in class. Please do not practise writing sounds that have not yet covered in class.

In numeracy we are looking at numbers 0–10 recognising them and writing them in order. We are also doing lots of 1 to 1 counting.

BOX 7.3 Communicating with parents and carers of reception children

Dear Parents

Tel:

Email:

Welcome to the Summer Term and hope you have all had a relaxing summer break. The children are particularly enjoying being outside, now the weather has started to warm up. Please remember to apply sun cream before the start of the school day and also send in a sun hat.

This half term our topic is Traditional Tales and we will be following on from the work of Adam Gullain in retelling and writing stories. Our focus will continue to be on writing simple sentences independently which can be read by the children themselves and others. Thank you for all the help you have given your child in writing their holiday diaries. I can see that the effort that has gone into these and they have been very enjoyable to read. I will be sending these home shortly. Please continue to help your child to write regularly at home in different genres, e.g. letter, cards, lists and stories. This work must be done independently, focusing on capital letters, finger spaces and full stops. When we write in class, children think of the idea, say the sentence out loud (check grammar), count how many words are in the sentence and then write the sentence. It is then important for the child to read back their work.

For children to reach the expected early learning goal in the Foundation Stage, they need to be able to use their phonic knowledge and write simple sentences where some words are spelt correctly and others are phonetically plausible. They are also expected to write some irregular common words.

In numeracy we will be looking at practical activities involving subtraction and addition, as well as solving problems including doubling, halving and sharing. We will be using everyday language to solve problems involving time, money, distance, weight and capacity. We will be also be reinforcing ordering numbers 0–20 and being able to say the number before and after a given number up to 20.

Next half term the children will get the opportunity to visit Year 1 on quite a few occasions and become familiar with the environment.

As always if you have any concerns please feel free to email me (xxx@xxx) or speak to me at the end of the school day. We are all really looking forward to our trip to Windsor Castle next week and hope the warm weather remains with us.

Kind regards

There is inevitably considerable variation in the ways in which children are raised by their parents. For many children in today's consumer rich society, toys, gadgets, technological devices and endless children's television dominate their lives at the expense of time to learn to talk in order to engage in conversations about what is going on around them. I am aware that research pinpoints failures in children's early language development to weaknesses in staffing in pre-school settings, particularly in the more disadvantaged areas. Personally, I think it goes beyond this and it may be unfair to totally blame the providers when one looks at what is going on in many of the homes of all children, and particularly disadvantaged children's families, as parents struggle to make ends meet, possibly being a lone parent or having other issues that leave them unable to provide the educational experiences their young children need. The recent news flash that a very young child was found wandering about the streets of Glasgow in his wellingtons at 6 a.m. one morning really brings home that there are vulnerable children everywhere as their parents struggle to cope with impending and real poverty, illness and mental issues. The closure of many Children's Centres is happening at a time when research by the charity 4Children, for example, identified an increase in families using centres in 2012.

Activities that parents engage in at home that support children's language and communication are likely to include touch screen devices as well as books. Results from the first annual Early Years Literacy survey (Formby, 2014) show that 99.7 per cent of children aged between 3 and 5 have access to books and 73 per cent have access to screen devices. The children need to look at print or read print-based stories, join a library or play educational games. The average family has eighty-nine books at home. The more books, the better the communication and language outcomes at age 5. It is important that children enjoy reading. A parent modelling reading has an impact on their children. Research shows there are benefits to sharing stories on a touch screen compared to looking at stories in print, particularly for children of low socio-economic status. Technology plays a large part in the lives of the under-5s. There is a view that it is a route to reading particularly for the disadvantaged 3- to 5-year-olds. There is more information about technology in Chapter 11, the specific areas of learning. Children are likely to enjoy reading more if they look at stories using a touch screen and books. Children enjoy the variety offered by the touch screen such as painting, drawing, playing games and using different apps.

The role of charities in supporting families with young children

To return to how charities and lottery funding are filling the gap for the most disadvantaged families, a 'Better Start'-funded project of £215 million was awarded to improve the life chances of children and families in five areas of England in 2014. The areas run a variety of programmes and initiatives to improve children's outcomes in three key areas of development:

- social and emotional development;
- communication and language;
- nutrition.

Local health, public services and the voluntary sector worked together. Each area is linked with a charitable organisation. Those involved include the Pre-School Learning Alliance, National Children's Bureau (NCB), National Society for the Prevention of Cruelty to

Children (NSPCC), Bradford Trident and the Nottingham City Care Partnership. Each area has focused on particular areas of development. In Bradford, for example, a medical research study has been in place since 2007 looking at why some children stay healthy and others fall ill by tracking the lives of 14,000 babies and families. An 'Eat Better, Start Better' programme is taking place in Gloucestershire to improve families' diets and reduce levels of obesity and overweight children. The overall aim is to support healthier food provision in early years settings and in families with young children aged between 1 and 5 years; and to increase the food, nutrition and healthy cooking knowledge, skills and confidence of early years and health practitioners and parents.

The National Childbirth Trust

The National Childbirth Trust (NCT) provides services tailored to the needs of young parents. There are approximately 6 per cent of live births to mothers under 20. These young mothers are greatly in need of support because teenage pregnancy and early parenthood are widely recognised to be associated with poor health and social exclusion. There are higher rates of infant mortality, lower birth weight and poor emotional health. These mothers are also less likely to access maternity care in early pregnancy. The NCT works to build confidence in these mothers via drop-in centres and help lines. Gingerbread is a charity that provides advice and practical support for single parent families.

Respecting diversity

All families are important and should be welcomed and valued in settings. Families are all different. Children may live with one or both parents, with other relatives or carers, with same-sex parents or in an extended family. Families may speak more than one language at home; they may be travellers, refugees or asylum seekers. All practitioners will benefit from professional development in diversity, equality and anti-discriminatory practice whatever the ethnic, cultural or social make-up of the setting. Parents and practitioners have a lot to learn from each other. This can help them to support and extend children's learning and development. Parents should review their children's progress regularly and contribute to their child's learning and development record. Parents can be helped to understand more about learning and teaching through workshops on important areas such as play, outdoor learning or early reading. Some parents may go to access further education at their own level. In true partnerships, parents understand and contribute to the policies. The areas of child development causing concern to professionals include:

- being able to listen to stories;
- paying attention;
- using the toilet;
- dressing themselves;
- starting to read and write;
- doing simple sums.

The answer to this by Marmot (2010) in *Fair Society Healthy Lives* is more action to improve the lives of families, supporting good parenting and improving access to good quality, affordable early years services. Parents are the most important 'educators' of their children for both cognitive and non-cognitive skills. Parental involvement in their children's reading has been found to be the most important determinant of language and emergent literacy.

The new face of Children's Centres

The impetus to include this update on how the central role of Sure Start Children's Centres has changed in recent years and how this impacts on families used to relying on their wide range of services for themselves and their children educationally, socially and medically is important. Many Sure Start centres have ceased to exist as they were. They used to offer home-based support, healthcare and advice, good-quality play and learning, childcare, and speech and language support. In addition, there were classes for parents: parents of babies, breastfeeding classes and a range of pre-parenting courses. Four hundred Sure Start centres closed between 2011 and 2013 with a £430 million cut in the Sure Start budget. In my own authority, as stated earlier, the Sure Start centres have reduced from forty-three to fifteen in the last couple of years. The remaining Children's Centres have transferred to other providers, charities and community groups amidst claims this is about improving services! An all-party group of MPs who met to set out the future for Sure Start centres in 2013–14 expressed the view that there was a lack of clarity about their purpose and what centres should offer. Coupled with questions raised by Ofsted as to their effectiveness and expected levels of accountability compared to schools, the government introduced a core purpose for Children's Centres. Local authorities would be expected to organise and commission services from the Children's Centres with much stronger accountability for how well they perform through their Children's Centres in improving outcomes for children. This was an expected action due to Ofsted data showing that approximately a third of Children's Centres were judged to require improvement following their inspections (Ofsted, 2015a). A discussion on what the core purpose of a Children's Centre should be, for children or parents, and what their priority should be was followed by the need to have links with a qualified teacher. More action is required in local authorities in identifying the most vulnerable children and in raising the awareness of these children for Children's Centres. A barrier to involving disadvantaged groups needs to be addressed in practical ways. It was further suggested that closing Children's Centres is unpopular and should only go ahead where there has been proper consultation and where alternatives to closure have been considered. The main premise of this seemingly drastic move nationally is based on research that shows Children's Centres are not as effective as they should be in 'narrowing the gap' of disadvantage. Primarily this is claimed to be due to the lack of qualified teachers or early years professionals working in the centres. However, many direct quotes from parents and via Ofsted reports found compelling evidence of the positive impact of the centres on the lives of individual children and families. The latest 4Children census found that 73 per cent of centres reported an increase in the number of families using centres over the past year, with more than one million families now accessing services, which suggests they are well used.

Involving parents and carers in pre-school and reception classes

The optimum engagement of parents with early years practitioners is where there is a great effort to establish a genuine partnership between home and school with parents and teachers equally sharing children's school-based experiences. This is a view endorsed by a recent Ofsted (2015a) report. Typically a meeting of parents is held prior to the transfer of 4-year-olds from pre-school to school. The school's approach to learning, the curriculum and routines are shared with parents. Parents have the opportunity to talk to staff about their children's home experiences. A useful starting point for parents is in the role they can play in compiling the learning journeys, diaries and photographs, all of which help practitioners get to know the new families. Parents are immediately involved in understanding the work of the school. Ease of access for parents to such assessment information is vital, as well as providing examples of learning in the home, thus giving parents a role in the assessment of their child and a greater understanding of their learning. A home visit may take place when there is a phased admission to a reception class. The displays of weekly planning for parents' benefit around the classroom/ setting helps to develop the partnership between home and school and possibly encourage parents to help in the classroom (see examples in Boxes 7.2 and 7.3). In *Practitioners Experience of the Foundation Stage* (Brooker et al., 2010), a range of successful systems for record-keeping to be shared with parents were identified by practitioners including:

- scrap books (used by childminders and nursery teachers);
- learning journeys (nursery teachers);
- all about me books (early years professionals);
- my unique child books (nursery staff);
- learning loops (reception teachers);
- contact books (nursery and reception teachers);
- portfolios (widely used).

Parents may have a better understanding of the EYFS now it has been in place for a few years, compared to the time when EYFS was a new educational jargon word as far as parents were concerned. The misunderstanding by some parents is in the role of play and the contribution it makes to learning. Familiarisation with the Development Matters (Early Education, 2012) statements was one way of highlighting learning through play and may still be used. The key to informing parents is to encourage their participation in early years settings. As the opening statement suggests, 'parents are their child's first and foremost educator'. How can you provide parents with information about what their children will be doing in school day by day? Early years settings need to be aware of children's home circumstances when setting up ways to keep them informed. Home visits, 'learning letters', contributions to children's learning stories and an open door policy to 'stay and play' with their children are fairly typical solutions. Outstanding settings take this a step further by planning away-day visits to places of interest in the local area so that children and parents have the opportunity to take part in activities they might not otherwise experience. In small communities it may be possible to organise family days in school where children, parents, grandparents and staff can work together as a family group on a project of common interest.

Such activities go beyond the typical parents' evening/after-school discussion with a child's named teacher or key person as they involve whole families in everyday events and contribute to promoting questioning, demonstrations and explanations of what has happened, what is currently happening and promotes children's curiosity and perseverance as they solve puzzles, construct paper lanterns, go-karts or totem poles.

Involving fathers

A 'light and dark' party planned in a small infant school provided an excellent encouragement to involve parents and grandparents.

The purpose of a light and dark party was with families, with plenty of scope for creativity involving the children and parents, including dads and grandparents. The fathers were challenged to work together to make paper lanterns for a night-time feast in the woods, and there was a 'go-cart workshop' where families built a vehicle from scratch in the school yard. It proved to be a great opportunity for raising children's expectations, challenging their thinking and demonstrating problem solving and perseverance. The children were fascinated by the topic, the building construction, exploring key concepts such as the world around them, variation in types of vehicles and the strategies mastered to make a vehicle from scratch.

Irrespective of the degree of involvement they have in the care of their child, fathers should be routinely offered the support and opportunities they need to engage in their parental role effectively. All settings can develop effective systems to gather information about fathers in all the families they are in contact with. Data collection sheets should include space to record information about fathers and other male carers, and agencies should be encouraged to provide this information at the point of referral. A parent link or community outreach worker with a specific remit to engage with fathers will be most effective, but all staff should be encouraged to engage proactively with fathers at initial contact. This will include inviting fathers to be present at initial home visits, which should be arranged at times they can make, and following up to gain contact with fathers who are not present to begin with – unless there is a clear child welfare reason not to do so. The Pre-School Learning Alliance makes several practical suggestions as to how fathers can be involved in early years settings. As a first step, an environment needs to be created in which fathers feel welcome and want to participate. This is less of an issue than it was in the past as fathers generally play a much greater role in the upbringing of their children. There may of course be social class differences, as can be seen from the example of the camera club in the following case study. However, middle-class fathers may be a regular feature in a pre-school in more affluent areas where both parents may be working, leading inevitably to fathers bringing their child to a childcare setting and possibly taking their turn as a parent helper. Examples of how settings ensure fathers are involved and well-informed are listed below:

- Address all communication to both the mother and father.
- Invite both parents by name to introductory sessions.
- Hold an annual fathers' week.
- Have a rocket-making session.
- Hold a running club for fathers.

The statutory EYFS guidance includes the principle that children learn and develop in enabling environments and there is a strong partnership between practitioners and parents. Research suggests that less than 20 per cent of dads read a bedroom story with their child. Children's Centres arrange weekend 'stay and play' sessions for dads. There are many examples of infant schools that target dads in their posters. For example, story sacks containing puppets and books to encourage dads to engage with their child's learning are available to take home. The setting up of a lending library for parents and their children to choose a book for home reading is also likely to capture dads collecting their children from school. The National Literacy Trust has designed a pack to encourage fathers to communicate more with children from birth to age 3. It appears obvious when written that when both parents engage, children tend to do better. There is a view that when dads are trained in infant communication, babies' intellectual development is greater than when only mums are trained. There is more information about this claim at www.talktoyourbaby.org.uk. There are possibly wider implications for addressing this issue given the number of children that do not have both parents living in the family home. It is important to ensure that registration forms include a place for the father's name and contact details (see literacytrust.org.uk/assets/0000/0808/ CommunicatingDads.pdf).

The case study below describes the strategies used to encourage the involvement of fathers in a disadvantaged inner city area with great success.

CASE STUDY 7.1: Involving dads in the Children's Centre

A partnership was established between home and the Children's Centre with a focus on a topic guaranteed to capture the interests of the fathers. Five sessions were allocated for parents and staff to work together preparing, evaluating previous experiences and documenting significant learning taking place. Fathers were trained (if required) to use a digital camera and download photographs of their visits and activities with their children. The head of the Children's Centre spoke with passion of her success in getting a group of fathers from a very disadvantaged area to join the project. It was a case of, 'You will do this' rather than 'Would you like to.' Several visits were made to the coast focusing on rock pools and collections, to the coast focusing on building and creating with sand or pushes and pulleys (moving sand), to a Sealife Centre and to a venue selected and researched by parents. The sequence was to run as listed below over the half term period.

- Week 1
  Introduce project and intentions. Introduce equipment and expected usage. Evaluate current knowledge and attitudes through activities to examine possible learning opportunities. Prepare for next week's visit to the coast and learning opportunties.

- Week 2
  Visit the coast, examining rock pools, discussing wildlife and environmental issues, collecting natural items. Parents to take some collections home to work with the children creatively and take photos of the process. Staff expected to do the same in school, using dictaphones for stories.

- Week 3
  Feedback from the visit and subsequent activities, examining learning opportunities, sharing experiences and initiating documentation took place. Preparation for sealife centre visit.

- Week 4
  Sealife centre visit to investigate creatures found in the sea, take photos of creatures, draw and record observations.

- Week 5
  Feedback from sealife centre and checking ongoing documentation. Preparation for coast visit, using planned and reclaimed resources to play creatively, solve problems and have fun or build with sand or 'moving sand'.

- Weeks 6 and 7
  Visit the coast/beach for above purposes and take photographs. Feedback from beach visit and documentation of learning takes place. Planning parents' choice of visit for next week took place.

- Weeks 8, 9 and 10
  Parents' choice of visit, feedback from this and working with a technician to create a presentation for a wider audience. Planning a party and a final session of celebration of events involving the wider community and other parents took place culminating in a vibrant display in the centre including a clear statement of the aims of the project for parents, practitioners and children.

The case study above exemplifies how an early years setting embarked on reaching out to fathers to get them involved with the setting based on their own interests, then taking this a step further by developing closer links with their children's learning and interests. For newly graduating practitioners, the first step to engaging with parents may be daunting, but it is a very worthwhile means of breaking down barriers and getting to know the children you are working with. Find out what your setting's policy is for meeting parents. In the examples cited in this book, it was typical for informal chats with reception class parents to take place each morning in the playground. In other schools, and always in pre-schools, parents drop in with their children and chat with a member of staff on a daily basis or make an appointment to talk at a more convenient time. However, to make provision for parents to help in the classroom or unit by signing a rota to help is an excellent ice-breaker for many parents.

Topics for discussion

- Share strategies to involve fathers in your setting.
- What are the main barriers to involving parents and how have you overcome them?

Further reading

Ofsted, (2015c) *Parents as Partners in Teaching: Trimdon Grange Infant and Nursery School.* London: Ofsted.
Pugh, G. and Duffy, B. (eds) (2014) *Contemporary Issues in the Early Years.* London: Sage.
Whalley, M. (2007) *Involving Parents in their Children's Learning.* London: Sage.

Vulnerable children

Introduction

There are increasingly disturbing statistics relating to the number of vulnerable children in our society. Many of these children will become a priority for early years professionals in the ways in which they support them and their families in their early years. It ought to be a given that the most disadvantaged children need the best qualified and most experience teachers and checks on a child's learning should sit alongside the widely accepted checks on their health according to Estelle Morris (*The Guardian*, 22 April 2015). Social workers warn that the current benefit cuts will hit the most vulnerable children. This is likely to be in addition to the many difficulties faced by children such as abuse and neglect at home or problems at school. A major change will be the reduction in help to working parents through changes to tax credits. A less advertised change outlined by the independent Institute of Fiscal Studies is the report that the poorest families have paid the heaviest penalty under the coalition cuts and tax changes, and on current trends Britain, one the richest countries in the world, will see a steep rise in children living in poverty. Almost one in three children, most of them living with parents in work, experience conditions that blight their life chances, according to the Child Poverty Action Group, and that costs the public purse £329 billion a year (Longfield, 2015). The Marmot Review, *Fair Society Healthy Lives* (2010), was undertaken as a strategic review of health inequalities in England post-2010. It portrayed a further disturbing picture of the degree of inequality across the country and highlighted the importance of good-quality childcare for children and their families from disadvantaged backgrounds. There continues to be concerns nationally that the number of vulnerable children across the country is on the increase. The rise in terms linked to poverty such as 'austerity' and 'food banks' are becoming all too well known for many families and the impact this can have on their children. According to research (Reed, 2012) commissioned by three leading children's charities – Action for Children, the Children's Society and the National Society for the Prevention of Cruelty to Children (NSPCC) – families will be affected over the next few years by changes to the tax and benefits, changes to public services and the ongoing effects of the post-2008 downturn. The protection of children from the impact of austerity is a key need. One cannot only measure the vulnerability of children without considering the contexts in which they live. In 2010 all the political parties signed up to the target of reducing child poverty to less than 5 per cent by 2020. Instead, the figure is nearing 33 per cent with four years still to go. From a health perspective, there are some woeful physical characteristics of children in these families such as low birth weight, poor health and behavioural and educational difficulties

(Dixon-Woods et al., 2006; Woodman et al., 2012). The recent appointment of Anne Longfield as the children's commissioner for England to promote and protect children's rights working to the UN convention on the rights of the child is a positive move in enabling the voice of this worrying and hidden situation to be more widely shared and improved. Her role now allows her to report to parliament and to be able to order a 'robust' investigation where she feels fit. This chapter aims to alert readers to the organisations that are able to help with vulnerable children, to what actions you need to take where you have identified concerns about children in your care and to share the findings on the Marmot Review *Fair Society Healthy Lives* (2010).

Defining vulnerable children

For too many children, the foundations for a successful start to their education are weak. In 2014 around two-fifths of children did not have the essential skills needed to reach a good level of development by the age of 5. In the most deprived communities, the outcomes were much worse. There are a range of characteristics that may be attributable to vulnerable children and families as defined by Howard Reed (2012). The range of circumstances is wide, but it is worth noting that not all children will fall into the 'vulnerable child' category. The measures of vulnerability are:

1 Worklessness – no parent in the family is at work.
2 Housing – the family lives in poor quality and/or overcrowded housing.
3 Qualifications – no parent in the family has any academic or vocational qualifications.
4 Mental health – the mother has mental health problems.
5 Illness/disability – at least one parent has a limiting long-standing illness, disability or infirmity.
6 Low income – the family has low income (below 60 per cent of the median).
7 Material deprivation – the family cannot afford a number of food and clothing items.

Between 2003 and 2008 the number of families with five or more vulnerability measures reached a peak of around 160,000 in 2004 and fell to just over 130,000 in 2008. Just to look at children specifically, by 2008, 900,000 families had three or more vulnerabilities and 1.87 million had two or more vulnerabilities. By 2008, there were nearly three times as many children (885,000) living in families with four or more vulnerabilities, nearly two million children living in families with three or more vulnerabilities and 3.9 million with two or more. This is a clear indication of the need to provide support to many of these families. The creation of Sure Start centres should have been how this would happen. Case studies in other chapters suggest some of the outstanding ways in which parents are active participants in the education of 2-year-olds in school (Chapter 6). How other schools and pre-schools engage with parents is reported in the Sure Start Evaluations (Melhuish et al., 2010). This survey found that generally the quality of information was poorer where there is most deprivation. The findings from the *National Evaluation of Sure Start* (Melhuish et al, 2008, 2010) focused on impact of programmes on children and families. Through a series of themed studies promoting speech and language development, early learning, play and childcare services, family and parent support, outreach and home-visiting, empowering parents and children and parents with special needs, the impact of Sure Start Local Programmes (SSLPs) were evaluated. The findings in 2005 for 3-year-olds revealed that among non-teenage mothers there was greater child social competence, fewer child behaviour problems and less negative parenting. However, the findings among teenage mothers showed less child social competence, more child behaviour problems and poorer child verbal ability in SSLP areas. The evaluation then set out to find out why some SSLPs were more effective in achieving outcomes than others. Three factors were considered in measuring proficiency. These were governance and management, the informal but professional ethos of the centre and the empowerment of service providers and users. At this time, several challenges for children's centres and training emerged. They were:

- higher reach needed (especially overcoming barriers for 'hard to reach');
- better multi-agency working;
- sustainable shared systems for monitoring service use/treatments;
- more rigour in measuring the impact of treatments;
- grasp of the cost of effective deployment of specialist/generalist staff;
- co-ordinating outreach and centre-based services.

The Department for Education (DfE, 2011a) reported the final evaluation of the impact of the SSLPs commissioned by the previous UK government and before the new UK government took office in May 2010. Melhuish (2011) completed a further evaluation of Sure Start with a focus on the impact of SSLP on 7-year-olds and their families. It is important to bear in mind the key aim of the SSLP to enhance the life chances for young children growing up in disadvantaged neighbourhoods. The reasons behind this are very clear. Children in this type of neighbourhood are at risk of doing poorly at school and having trouble with peers and agents of authority (i.e., parents and teachers), which leads to compromised life chances such as early school leaving, unemployment and limited longevity. These children are all also likely to have low cognitive and language development. All the SSLPs were placed in areas of high deprivation with all children under 5 serving as the 'targets of intervention'. All the centres were under the control of local authorities, which led to some variation among the local authorities. The positive impact of SSLP, according to the most recent research, found that mothers in the SSLP engaged in less harsh discipline, provided a more stimulating home environment for the their children and created a less chaotic home environment for boys and for parents (lone and workless households only) to have a better level of life satisfaction. Overall it could be seen that SSLPs were successful in affecting hard to reach groups but there were no consistent SSLP effects for child development at age 7. Many reasons were put forward as to why this was the case, one being that by the age of 3 parenting effects were too little and too late. A key to child development is the impact of the home learning environment (HLE) and its importance in the first three years because of the importance of language development. SSLPs are generally now replaced with Sure Start Children's Centres and Children's Centres with a greater level of communication with local communities and a further recognition of the need to emphasise the importance of language development in the first three years. However, in recent years there has been a 50 per cent reduction in the number of Children's Centres.

One can speculate that changes to the tax and benefits system will on average have an impact on every type of vulnerable household analysed in Reed's (2012) report. While the

Universal Credit will result in a gain in income for some of the most vulnerable families, this is not large enough to offset the losses resulting from other changes to the benefits system, such as changes to housing and disability benefits. The negative impact is greatest for families with more vulnerability. These families will lose 8 per cent of net income from the changes compared to 5 per cent for families with no vulnerabilities. Sadly, the possible impact of budget cuts have become a reality in 2015.

Caring for vulnerable children

Contact with vulnerable families is an everyday aspect of general practice (GP) in deprived areas. The GP has access to extensive privileged information about families and almost universal contact with children and their families. GPs may be familiar with the Vulnerable Child Syndrome. This is a child who has an unusual susceptibility to disease or disorder. The characteristics of a vulnerable child match those stated earlier. However, GPs regard poverty as a critical contributing factor, sometimes there being neglectful poverty whereby the parent causes the poverty through their selfishness and irresponsibility by putting their own indulgences before the needs of their children. Disadvantage and social class can show adverse effects on child health particularly in the first ten years of life. This is described as the 'toxic effects of poverty' on child health (McNeill, 2010). This generally persists into adulthood, reflected in early morbidity caused by conditions such as CVS (cardio vascular) disease and diabetes to name just two conditions. There needs to be a proportionate state response to ameliorate the effects of poverty on adverse childhood outcomes. The implication here being that contact with GPs may be a crucial first step in concerns raised in Children's Centres for example. The UK scores particularly poorly across health and education despite its national wealth in comparison with other countries (Bradshaw and Richardson, 2009). In terms of child well-being, the UK emerges as a serious contender for the title of the worst place in Europe to be a child. Child poverty is an issue of concern in Scotland, but the issue facing all political parties is how great is the cost of poverty in the anticipated 4.2 million children living in poverty in the UK in 2020 (Brewer et al., 2011).

Many vulnerable children will access early years provision. Research has been carried out to evaluate the impact of the free entitlement to childcare and/or early education for children from lower social classes. It looked at the impact of the provision on children at age 5, the end of Key Stage 1 (age 7) and Key Stage 2 tests at 11. The main findings of this research were that there was only a small impact on the outcomes of children assessed at age 5, which gets even smaller by age 7, and disappears completely by age 11. This sounds worrying and questionable about the quality of the early education or childcare, but the small positive impact came mostly from children who would not have attended early education without the free entitlement. These children did almost fifteen points better on the Foundation Stage Profile (FSP) than they would have done. The most common form of vulnerability faced by these children is abuse in the home. The setting may be able to identify the particular needs of a child as long as providers are fully aware of the characteristics of vulnerable children through liaison with social and health services. The term used by Ofsted to describe vulnerable children is 'target groups with additional needs'. The target groups refer to the groups and families the centre identifies as having needs or circumstances that require particularly perceptive intervention and/or additional support. They may be:

- lone parents, teenage mothers and pregnant teenagers;
- children from low-income backgrounds;
- children living with domestic abuse, adult mental health issues and substance abuse;
- children 'in need' or with a child protection plan;
- children of offenders or those in custody;
- fathers, particularly those with any other identified need, for example, teenage fathers or those in custody;
- those with protected characteristics as defined by the Quality Act 2010;
- children who are in the care of local authorities (looked after children);
- children who are cared for by members of their extended family;
- families identified by the LA as 'troubled families' who have children under 5;
- families who move into and out of the area relatively quickly (transient families) such as asylum seekers or armed forces personnel;
- any other vulnerable groups.

Observations of such children will help practitioners to identify their particular needs. The case study below highlights how the home corner in a Liverpool nursery helped a 4-year-old come to terms with the death of his mother.

CASE STUDY 8.1: Jamie's home corner

Jamie enjoyed nursery school. He loved the home corner and spent most of his time playing out the same routine time after time, setting the table, putting out four plates and cups and then putting them away again. He preferred to be on his own because he could set out the dolls and teddies as he wanted. He talked to them all the time. Jamie had just returned to the nursery school after several weeks of absence. His home was destroyed in a house fire some months earlier, along with the death of his two younger sisters and his mother. During his time away from the nursery he was with foster parents and had now returned to the area to live with an aunt. He spoke very little on his return but appeared to be enjoying the security and stability of the home corner as often as he could. How do you help children like this come to terms with such emotional turmoil? The home corner was the turning point in the nursery for Jamie. Slowly, he began to regain his confidence and welcome playmates into his substitute home. A 4-year-old fostered boy attending a reception class in a Salford primary school also exhibited a great attachment to the cushioned reading corner in his classroom until one day he just did not come back because he was placed with a different family. I am sure this would not happen today, but what it shows is the security and comfort that little boy demonstrated on a daily basis in his classroom.

There are several charities that work to help the most vulnerable and neglected children. Action for Children to name but one has some worrying statistics related to neglect which is reported to be the most common form of child abuse in the UK today. It is the most frequent reason for a child protection referral, and it features in 60 per cent of serious case reviews into the death or serious injury of a child. This charity campaigns for change to raise awareness of government as to what is needed to reduce the level of child neglect. Although the Sure Start Local Programmes may not have had an impact on children's cognitive development by the age of 7, they did make a difference to the upbringing of children within their families, who were less chaotic as a result of parents' involvement with the Sure Start Centres. The need to improve parenting skills is apparent for many families. What needs to happen?

- Children seek and accept help.
- Parents seek and accept help.
- The public reports concerns about child neglect.
- Professionals are able to identify neglect and help children at the earliest possible stage.
- Local authorities know the scale of neglect in their areas and commission effective services to tackle it.
- National legislation, guidance and regulations enable a joined-up, long-term approach to helping neglected children.

A further finding by the Marmot Review (2010) was that children from deprived areas are more likely than those from affluent families to fall short of the developmental and educational milestones set down by the DfE. An indicator of vulnerability in the early years sector is whether or not a child is eligible for a free school meal, although this is more difficult to quantify once free school meals were made available to all early years children. Across the country, white British children still constitute the majority (65 per cent) of the free school meals (FSM) group. The attainment gap between FSM and non-FSM exists in pre-school, and is larger for white children by the age of 5 than for other ethnicities

Despite the cuts to local authorities' education budgets, links with a range of charitable or Lottery-funded projects or establishments have developed across the country to help to improve the life chances for the most deprived families in parts of England. The areas that have successfully achieved Big Lottery Fund awards include the Born in Bradford medical research study that tracks the lives of 13,500 babies and their families since 2007. Although having a medical aim to explore why some children stay healthy and others fall ill, communication and language development is one of the key themes along with nutrition, obesity and environmental changes. The Lottery funding granted for this is used to run projects and initiatives to support families and children at key stages of their early years development.

Safeguarding and welfare requirements in early years settings

The statutory requirements (DfE, 2014a) regarding safeguarding and welfare requirements are considerable and comprise more than half of the EYFS framework document. There are several websites that provide interpretations of these for settings. Local authorities may provide you with a protocol of procedures to follow for alerting outside agencies to concerns raised about a child in your care. Box 8.1 provides an example from an authority relating to how to deal with signs of physical abuse and what Ofsted recommends. It is imperative that checks are made with your managers/headteachers before carrying out any of the examples given in Box 8.1.

> **BOX 8.1** Actions to Protect Children (Barnsley)
>
> ### What to do if you are worried about a child?
>
> - Don't ignore it.
> - Do something about it.
> - You might just save a (their) life.
> - Is the child at risk from immediate harm?
> - Call the police.
>
> (www.safeguardingchildrenbarnsley.com)

The statutory guidance states that providers must take all necessary steps to keep children safe and well. They have a responsibility to:

- safeguard children;
- ensure the suitability of adults who have contact with children;
- promote good health;
- manage behaviour;
- maintain records, policies and procedures.

(DfE, 2014a)

There are variations in requirements for childminders and EYFS in schools provided the requirements are already met through existing procedures. You can expect to find a practitioner designated to take a lead responsibility for safeguarding children in every setting. As well as being trained themselves, they must train all staff and ensure that they all have an updated knowledge of safeguarding issues. It is particularly important that providers must enable staff to recognise signs of abuse and neglect at the earliest opportunity. Staff should look out for:

- significant changes to a child's behaviour;
- unexplained bruising, marks or signs of possible abuse or neglect;
- children's comments that give cause for concern;
- any reasons to suspect neglect or abuse outside the setting – for example in the child's home;
- inappropriate behaviour display by other members of staff or any other person working with the children – for example, inappropriate sexual comments; excessive one-to-one attention beyond the requirements of their usual role and responsibilities; or inappropriate sharing of images.

(DfE, 2014a: 18)

It will be important too that all practitioners and those who have regular contact with children are suitable. All those who have already had a criminal records check before 2005 will be deemed to be suitable.

All children have an absolute right to be safe from harm. Early years practitioners need to know the signs of physical, behavioural, emotional and neurotic abuse and neglect:

- Physical abuse signs
  Unexplained bruising, marks or injuries on any part of the body, bruises that might reflect hand marks or fingertips, cigarette burns, bite marks, broken bones or scalds.
- Behavioural indicators
  Fear of parents being approached for explanations, aggressive behaviour, severe temper outbursts, flinching when approached or touched, reluctance to get changed and withdrawn behaviour.
- Emotional abuse
  The physical signs are failure to thrive or grow, sudden speech disorders, developmental delay and physical or emotional progress.
- Neurotic behaviour
  Unable to play, fear of making mistakes, self-harm or fear of parent being approached.
- Neglect
  Constant hunger and stealing food, constantly dirty or smelly and loss of weight indicate neglect. The child may complain of being tired, have few friends or mentioning that the child is on his own sometimes.

Each child has to be assigned a key person whose role is to ensure their safety, to help the children become familiar with the setting and involve parents where appropriate. Children must always be within sight or hearing of staff at all times. There are further details of staffing ratios in different settings, class sizes for reception classes and reminders that in schools 'school teachers' do not include teaching assistants, higher level teaching assistants or other support staff. Groups of children in reception classes are taught in groups of no more than thirty.

Maintaining the good health of children and staff

The requirements covered with regard to health include:

- medicines
- food and drink
- accident or injury
- managing behaviour.

Medicines

Providers need to ensure that all necessary steps are taken to promote the good health of the children, to prevent the spread of infection and to take appropriate action if children are ill. There has to be a policy and procedure for administering medicines and keeping this information up to date for individual children. There are caveats regarding medicine which must be prescribed for a child by a doctor, dentist, nurse or pharmacist and written permission provided to the school by the parent to administer medicine to their child. A first aid box should be accessible at all times with child-friendly content. Providers must keep a written record of accident, injuries and first aid treatment. Parents/carers must be informed on the first day of any first aid treatment given.

Managing behaviour

Behaviour is the responsibility of the provider who must not give corporal punishment to any child. Failure to meet these requirements is an offence. If there is physical offence to protect another child or member of staff, it is not regarded as an offence. Again parents should be informed if such situations arise.

Other areas

The other areas the statutory guidance (DfE, 2014a) addresses are: the safety and suitability of premises, environment and equipment; smoking not allowed in or on the premises; specific measurements for spaces for children of different ages; and a requirement to have an outdoor space. In connection with the organisation of space and equipment, there is a need to carry out risk assessments on areas of the environment that need to be checked on a regular basis – for example, equipment in and outdoors and trips and visits. Children with special educational needs must have appropriate support and the setting must have regard for the Special Educational Needs (SEN) Code of Practic (DfE, 2015b). Nursery schools must have a SEN coordinator and other providers are expected to identify a SENCO.

> The best schools focus on every child, encouraging aspiration on an individual basis; we must make it a priority to safeguard the futures of all children, ensuring those from impoverished backgrounds, with health challenges, special educational needs and disabilities no longer remain part of what is becoming a 'hidden generation' of pupils.
>
> (Dr Hilary Emery, chief executive of National Children's Bureau)

Research

Research tells us that gaps in achievement between the poorest children and their better off counterparts are well established by the age of 5. High-quality early years education and care has a big impact on outcomes for disadvantaged children. The rub is that children from low-income families are less likely to attend high-quality early education and care programmes than their more advantaged peers. Parents and carers can play a major role in their child's early development and learning. As stated elsewhere in this book, 'parenting style' and the home learning environment strongly influence children's development and school readiness. However, children from poor backgrounds are much less likely to experience a rich home learning environment. The answer then is that children from poor backgrounds need to access high-quality early years provision led by appropriately qualified early years professionals. The reality is that many of the early settings in the PVI sector do not have trained early years professionals. Until the government address this dilemma, poor children will continue to be disadvantaged before they even start statutory education. Cathy Nutbrown was commissioned by the government in 2012 to review the qualifications of staff working in early education and childcare with a view to there being the opportunity and expectation that early years practitioners will have a higher level of education based on the research which clearly indentifies the positive impact, for example, graduates have when working in early years settings. Many organisations responded to a report from Ofsted (2013b), *Unseen Children: Access and Achievement 20 Years On.* These children are the invisible minority of children who slip though the net at 16 years old, by leaving school without the qualifications they need for employment. A range of factors are attributed to this by differing interest groups, especially the group of charities concerned with protecting and supporting disadvantaged young children. The response by the chief executive of the National Children's Bureau (NCB) pinpoints the need to make changes to early years teaching that would make the biggest difference to the lowest performing 20 per cent in terms of achievement. It is vital, she says, to recognise that changes to assessment do not hold the key; indeed, the reforms to measures for 4-year-olds run a real risk of damaging those children, especially the most disadvantaged; knocking the confidence and self-esteem for those already badly served. It is the quality of those working with children that should be the main focus. The best results come from high-quality nursery schools and foundation stages in primary schools which have well-trained teachers who really understand what matters at this age – which sadly the majority of 3- and 4-year-olds do not attend. It must be recognised for early years – as it has across other sectors – that good teachers and a focus on education are necessary in order to raise achievement.

Topics for discussion

- Share examples of vulnerable children with colleagues to show how you dealt with their particular needs.
- Share the guidance for concerns about children provided by your setting with colleagues to confirm there is a shared understanding actions to be taken.

Further reading

Horwath, J. (ed.) (2009) *The Child's World: The Comprehensive Guide to Assessing Children in Need.* London: Jessica Kingsley.

Wosu, H. and Tait, A. (2012) *Direct Work with Vulnerable Children: Playful Activities and Strategies for Communication.* London: Jessica Kingsley, Kindle edition.

The prime areas of learning

Introduction

FIGURE 9.1 Spider display

'The three prime areas reflect the key skills and capacities all children need to develop and learn effectively; and become ready for school' (DfE, 2014a: 9). Although the statutory guidance appears to give priority to the three prime areas of learning (communication and language, physical development and personal, social and emotional development), the overall learning and development requirements comprise all seven areas of learning including the four specific areas, which are literacy, mathematics, understanding the world and expressive arts and design. The three prime areas of learning are strengthened and applied through the specific areas of learning. Children under 3 are assessed on the prime areas only. The prime areas are deemed a priority in terms of sharing with parents should there be any issues surrounding their child's progress in one of those areas. This chapter aims to provide aspiring practitioners with an outline of what is required of the prime areas of learning and examples of how practitioners are interpreting this requirement in their day-to-day teaching. The prime areas are particularly important for developing children's curiosity and enthusiasm for learning and for building their capacity to learn and forming relationships. They are essential foundations for children's life, learning and success because they are connected to each other. Research suggests that physical development supports personal, social and emotional development as increasing physical control provides experiences of self as an active agent in the environment, promoting growth in confidence and awareness of control; it supports communication and language because a child who can effectively use large movements, gestures and the fine movements involved in speech is able to convey messages to others. Children do not learn compartmentally, it being very likely that one activity/experience may cover several areas of learning. This learning may be taking place irrespective of any planning or focused adult-led activities. Hence the decreased emphasis on planning in the statutory guidance, just as a reminder of an earlier quote in Chapter 3, 'The inspector should not routinely expect to see detailed written plans for the activities they observe.' The revised EYFS framework recognises this in paragraph 1.8 where it is stated:

> that each area of learning must be implemented through planned purposeful play and through a mix of adult-led and child-initiated activity. Play is essential for children's development, building their confidences as they learn to explore, to think about problems, and relate to others.
>
> (DfE, 2014a: 9)

A typical long-term written plan may look like the one in Figure 9.2. This is one of a comprehensive range of examples to download from the internet. The early learning goals for each prime area of learning head each of the prime area sections in this chapter along with the *Development Matters* statements indicating the typical learning expectations for children between birth and 5 years of age. These are useful guides for practitioners who must bear in mind that children develop at very different rates.

The case study of effective learning in a reception classroom, in an inner-city Manchester school below shows the children *playing and exploring* the books in the cave and they are engaging in *active self-initiated learning*. There is good evidence of concentration and persistence in their sharing of the books. They are *creating and thinking critically* as they develop their ideas in the cave, experimenting with the torches and enjoying the range of creatures hanging there.

Magic Beans & Plenty of Peas

Why?
The children will experience where some of foods come from and get great pleasure from growing, tending and tasting. They will also broaden their understanding by linking real life experiences to story and tales.

Communication and Language:
The children will have a chance to extend and practice new vocabulary when playing in the Garden Centre using language modelled by adults 'Can I help you?' "That will be 50p." We will encourage the children to re-tell the story of Jack and the Beanstalk to their friends and the adults will record the children's re-tell of the story. The children will be excited and motivated to talk about growing, picking, shelling cooking and tasting the peas and beans.

Mathematics:
The children will be learning that 10 x 1p = 10p and will be using this concept when working in the Garden Centre Shop. Over a week we will create a Giant Beanstalk, adding a metre of length and 1 leaf to the stalk each day. By using a height chart the children can measure each other and make their own simple beanstalk height chart. On a visit to the school allotment, the children will count the different sorts of garden tools we find and then make a simple graph to show how many of each we found. We will walk in Giant strides and Jack strides across the playground finding out how many steps it takes to reach the other side.

Literacy:
The child will attempt to write and record whilst role playing in the Garden Centre by writing lists, receipts,.. and labels. We will look at non-fiction books on gardening and compare them to the fictional book of Jack and the Beanstalk, looking at the differences of the two types of books. The children will be following recipes attempting to read the ingredients required to make soup. We will look at initial letter sound of the word and blend sound together using 'Fred Talk' (Read Write Inc). In groups we will identify the day of the week and attempt to write this in our 'Bean Diary' where we note changes each day to the bean.

Understanding of the World:
The children will be growing peas, beans and other fruits and vegetables. We will taste a variety of fruits and make fruit jellies similarly we will taste vegetables and will make our own soup. We will explore the best conditions to grow peas/beans and we will take photographs of each stage of growing. The children will be looking closely at the root system of beans grown in a jar. We will explore and taste different peas, mange tout, mushy, garden, cooked and raw.

Expressive Art and Design:
We will use puppets, props, and drapes to set the scene and retell the story of Jack and the Beanstalk. The children will listen to music and decide if they should be making giant steps, or tip toeing. We will make a collection of garden tools and the children will make observational drawings/paintings to be displayed in our Garden Shop. We will also take photographs to learn about the beanstalk developing, twisting and turning and changing shape and colour and try to replicate this is dance and other media.

Personal, Social and Emotional Development:
Whilst working in the Garden Centre the children will continue to learn how to share, take turns and interact with their peers. They will enjoy planting, growing and tasting being proud of their efforts and achievements. We will encourage parents, carers or staff to talk about their gardens or allotments and encourage the children to talk about theirs.

Physical Development:
Fine motor skills will be developed when using trowels, rakes, dibbers, hands and fingers to garden, plant and weed. When making soup and jelly we will be cutting, chopping, pulling, stirring and pouring. We will practise with scissors and cut out beanstalks and leaves for our role-play. Outdoors we will develop large motor skills in digging, planting and picking with large equipment or strong actions.

SMSC
The children will be learning about "Going for Goals" and being proud of our own and others' achievements. We will explore a selection of Christian and Jewish artefacts and explore the bible story of Noah and the Ark.

FIGURE 9.2 Planning example: Magic Beans and Plenty of Peas

CASE STUDY 9.1: Exploring Light and Dark

In a reception classroom, the structured play area was developed to provide opportunities to extend the topic 'Light and Dark' by setting up as a bear's cave. The space to do this in the classroom was very restricted, but as it turned out this was a bonus because of the security and intimacy provided for children in the cave. Ingeniously designed walls and flaps over the entrance ensured there was a high degree of privacy and authenticity for the two children able to play together. The stimulus for the story was *Can't You Sleep, Little Bear?*, copies of which displayed inside the cave along with other stories familiar to the children. Creatures suspended from the ceiling and cushions on the floor provided a comfortable, concealed environment away from the hustle and bustle of the classroom. Torches of various sizes and colours were available to see the pictures in the book. A clipboard with outlines of 'Mr Blobbie' was available for the children's use. The class teacher routinely targeted pairs of children with EAL to explore and work in the cave. Her intentions went beyond allowing the children to construct their own literacy and play experiences. Her curriculum plans identified the ways in which this environment was planned to support children's learning. She encouraged the children to share a story, always pairing a linguistically capable child with a less confident one. Children who spoke the same home language were encouraged to work together, thus providing support and encouragement for the less fluent speaker of English and also to enable the children to share the story in their home language.

Source: Rodger, 1998: 127

Communication and language

> Less than half of all disadvantaged children have the skills needed to secure a positive start to school; around one quarter still struggled to speak, listen or interact socially to support better learning overall.
>
> (Ofsted, 2015a: 4)

The statistics in the quotation above are alarming, but what is also concerning are statistics from University College London (UCL) saying that boys lag far behind girls when they start school and continue to do so over the course of their school careers. A quarter of boys from wealthier families start school with inadequate speech and language skills compared to just 15 per cent of girls. The gap is even larger among children from poorer families, with 42 per cent of boys lacking the language skills expected at the start of school compared with 27 per cent of girls. The statutory framework for EYFS states that the educational programme for communication and language must involve activities and experiences that involve giving children opportunities to experience a rich language environment, to develop their confidence and skills in expressing themselves, and to speak and listen in a range of situations. The fundamental role that play takes in all aspects of children's learning has a much higher status in the revised EYFS. The early learning goal against which children are assessed has three strands (Table 9.1).

Outstanding providers focus relentlessly on developing children's communication skills, language and vocabulary. They provide frequent opportunities for children to practise their speaking and listening skills by providing purposeful contexts in which they can interact with others. This can readily happen outdoors when children are planting seeds, watering the flowers, building a camp or sharing a large painting task for example. Communication and

TABLE 9.1 Early learning goals for communication and language

Listening and attention	■ Children listen attentively in a range of situations. ■ Children listen to stories, accurately anticipating key events and respond to what they hear with relevant comments, questions and actions. ■ Children give their attention to what others say and respond appropriately, while engaging in another event.
Understanding	■ Children follow instructions, involving several ideas of actions. ■ Children answer 'how' and 'why' questions about their experiences and in response to stories or events.
Speaking	■ Children express themselves effectively, showing awareness of listeners' needs. ■ Children use past, present and future forms accurately when speaking about events that have happened or are to happen in the future. ■ Children develop their own narratives and explanations by connecting ideas or events.

language should be a very high priority for all children, but particularly disadvantaged children. The key to their language development is being able to spend a high proportion of their time with an adult, particularly important for 2-year-olds who, when observed, tend to be quiet observers of their surroundings. The following steps need to be taken by newly qualified teachers and early years professionals to equip themselves with the key skills needed to support the development of language and literacy in the early years. At times, especially in reception classes, children will learn to sit and listen to a story, engage in discussion with their teacher and each other.

Recent research findings

Research has never been clearer – a child's early education lasts a lifetime. Securing a successful start for our youngest children, and particularly those from disadvantaged backgrounds, is crucial. It can mean the difference between gaining seven Bs at GCSE compared with seven Cs and is estimated to be worth £27,000 more in an individual's salary over the course of a career.

(DfE, 2014c)

The priority to promoting effective communication and language in the early years is vital. The role of the parent is paramount in supporting and communicating with their children under 2 years of age and makes a difference in their later language and communication development. Recent research confirms this. A significant project by the Nuffield Foundation (Mathers and Smee, 2014) illustrates very clearly that good language skills during the early years are one of the strongest predictors of later success.

This is also highlighted in figures from Ofsted (2015a) that the 19 percentage gap between disadvantaged children and their better-off counterparts has remained unacceptably wide for too long. This is once again corroborated by the latest release of the Early Years Foundation Stage Profile (EYFSP) results, which show that literacy is the area in which the greatest proportion of children in England failed to reach the expected stage of development by age 5 (DfE, 2013), with just 61 per cent reaching the expected level of development in all literacy early learning goals. There are suggestions from Ofsted (2015a) that the key to tackling the continuing failure of the most disadvantaged children rests with getting these children into school earlier. There is further information about this in Chapter 6. The research also claims that children most in need of good-quality support for language and literacy are least likely to receive it, at least, within the private, voluntary and independent (PVI) sector. The strong message here is that children living in disadvantaged areas, attending settings in disadvantaged areas, and attending settings alongside other disadvantaged children are the least likely to experience high-quality early years provision. The key to tackling this problem lies with the need to ensure that there is a graduate member of staff in place and a high proportion of staff qualified to Level 3 (A-level). The other need is to improve engagement with families to encourage how important their role is in developing early language acquisition. It was evident that the one issue that concerns headteachers is delayed and under-developed speaking, listening and motor skills. Headteachers say this has got markedly worse over the past decade. Mathers and Smee (2014: 3) described the reasons for lower quality in PVI settings as lower quality of interactions between children and carers, lack of support for learning language and literacy and lack of provision for diversity and individual needs. A reasonable explanation for this situation is that children growing up in difficult circumstances may be more at risk of language delays and behaviour problems, and more likely to speak English as a second language. As these are generally in areas of disadvantage, parents are unlikely to be able to afford to pay for more time for their child to attend more frequently than their free sessions. This situation may be massively accelerated when settings are funded for the children of working parents for 30 hours a week in 2016.

One needs to exercise caution in interpreting the research data as described above. Obviously, the most disadvantaged children have the furthest to climb from their low starting points compared to their middle-class counterparts. Therefore, rate of progress is the most reliable indicator of quality of provision. A higher level of qualification may not make tackling unruly behaviour or limited language use any easier to deal with. Research by Gamboro et al. (2013) compares the evidence from England and lessons from other countries in Chapter 1. In the early stages of language development, it is the particular aspects of a child's communication environment that are associated with the rate of language acquisition rather than the broader socio-economic context of the family.

Ofsted survey

In 2011, Ofsted carried out a survey to evaluate the impact of EYFS on the quality of provision and developmental outcomes for young children from birth to 5 years with a focus on communication, language and literacy (CLL). They found that maintained schools sustained a high quality of early years provision which confirmed an overall improvement since 2008. However, outcomes for CLL were only good or better in less than half of the settings. There were two reasons given for this:

- There was a difference in childcare providers and schools.
- The childcare providers relied heavily on daily routines, rather than planning activities to promote children's learning.

The development of children's use of language for thinking was not as well developed as their use of language for communication. They found that children were not encouraged to explain and extend their thinking or allowed time to think. At times assessment was underdeveloped with a focus on welfare and interests rather than their learning. This finding is reinforced to some extent again in the outcomes of another Ofsted (2012) evaluation which sought to identify how well trainee teachers are prepared to teach early language skills, reading and writing effectively. The sample group of fifty teachers were found to vary greatly in the quality of their initial teacher education and induction with considerable differences in their depth of knowledge and level of skills. The findings of this evaluation are important for all aspiring young teachers and others who feel they struggle with the demands of the revised EYFS. Conditions need to be in place to ensure that trainees and new teachers have the best possible chance of developing the necessary knowledge and expertise for teaching language and literacy well. A major advantage was for a trainee to have an initial degree in English or other language-based subject. On leaving training, newly qualified teachers were not always sufficiently skilled in adapting teaching to meet the needs of children at an early stage of learning English as an additional language, of disabled pupils and of those with special educational needs. Effective teaching includes a deep understanding of children's language development and of the links between language and literacy skills. Good questioning skills help children develop their thinking skills, through talking and listening. A good knowledge and understanding of phonics and how this supports reading and spelling is necessary to understand how to help children to use their skills learnt through the curriculum. The positive characteristics of teaching identified by Ofsted were:

- creating interesting experiences and activities that promotes the use of language and children's listening skills (see Table 9.2);
- being able to assess learning in language and literacy accurately and understand what to teach next to enable children to progress quickly;
- providing good models of spoken as well as written language;
- using accurate and precise pronunciation;
- blending and segmenting words when teaching phonics;
- using a wide range of resources to help extend vocabulary and create enthusiasm for writing;
- assessing children throughout lessons and targeting their questioning, providing sufficient challenge and support for different children;
- understanding how to support children with special educational needs and those who are at an early stage of acquiring English;
- being highly reflective practitioners (see Chapter 1).

Ofsted also indentified barriers facing trainee and new teachers, which as a reader you may wish to keep in mind as you reflect on your preparation to teach or wrestle with a teaching issue in the classroom. Look for opportunities to teach all aspects of language and literacy across other areas of learning and be able to teach children of different ages and those with different needs. Ask to have your teaching of specific areas of language and literacy observed, including phonics and get feedback. Sadly, it would appear, according to Ofsted many schools do not have an accurate enough view of the quality of their own provision or of the skills of different staff. Possibly, some of the examples in this book may help to resolve this for teachers

TABLE 9.2 Half-termly communication and language plan

Communication and language
■ We will be reading stories which the children can re-enact and extend their use of new vocabulary.
■ We will listen to the story of Kipper's monster and repeat the sound effects throughout the story.
■ The children will use puppets and props to explore 'Owl Babies'. And add their own thoughts and storylines.
■ Role play will be experienced in our candle shop.
■ During Circle Time we will be talking about Bonfire Night, sharing their experiences and describing the sounds and colours.

and trainees. Check too that your course includes the following and if not research into these elements:

■ Knowledge of the key skills needed by children of different ages.

■ Understanding of how to teach all elements of language and literacy, including developing effective communication and systematic synthetic phonics.

■ Understanding of the importance of reinforcing language and literacy skills consistently across all curriculum areas.

A more recent good practice survey by Ofsted (2015b), while having a focus on the youngest children in early years settings, has some very direct suggestions as to the effectiveness of the quality of the adult–child relationship. A very positive outcome of the survey was the very high priority given to communication and language in all the settings visited. The settings focused relentlessly on developing children's communication, language and vocabulary. Purposeful contexts were provided in which the children could interact with others. The key to this was that the schools/early years settings did not see teaching as separate from play. The list below indicates some of the basics in developing language in young children as cited in the survey:

■ Gentle reminders to say please and thank you.

■ To recognise and name colours and textures when unloading the washing machine when helping teachers.

■ For children to articulate items they are playing with.

■ To describe events with support.

■ To link topics to their interests.

The role of the adult, particularly in supporting communication and language development in 2-year-olds is critical. Older children too are generally taught in a formal and structured way. Teaching in this situation focused on the letters and the sounds they make (phonics). Leaders and staff in these settings had set up a daily programme of short, targeted teaching to enable the youngest children to secure the fundamental skills for speaking, listening and understanding and, when appropriate, the foundations of early reading. Adults pre-planned these short, sharp sessions with a specific goal in mind. (Ofsted, 2015b: 15). There are examples where schools employ an early reading specialist to support those children who

FIGURE 9.3 Collaboration

were identified as having a specific weakness. The sessions could often be repeated through the week, especially for 2-year-olds. They involved:

- playing memory games, to develop the prerequisite short-term memory needed when learning to read
- singing well-known songs to develop the familiarity with rhythm and rhyme
- using interesting and colourful pictures to support children's vocabulary development and the ability to create and maintain a narrative
- listening and making sounds to support auditory discrimination and raise awareness of concepts such as loud and quiet, fast and slow.

(Ofsted, 2015b: 15)

Older children formulated questions about the characters or actions in the illustrations in story books. They drew simple maps of the events in their favourite stories to help them remember the sequence of events and acquired at least three or four new sounds and representative letters each week. This systematic approach ensured that all children rapidly developed the step-by-step skills needed to read.

So how are language and communication developed in the very early years? Figure 9.4 shows a record of assessments made of children under 3.

We are starting to talk

Ethan 14 months

Points and makes his views known by squealing. Sits and plays with his voice by blowing and babbling. Sometimes calls for Dadda.

Begins to understand what he cannot do.

Enjoys listening to stories and a favourite programme *In the night garden.*

Can turn pages in a favourite book.

Bethany 12 months

Slightly reserved, watches but is not communicating verbally.
Begins to listen to others.

Lacks curiosity in things around her and is very tearful at times.

Possible practises

- Be physically close and make eye contact, use touch and voice to converse with babies.
- Learn and use key words in home language.
- Share stories and rhymes.
- Tune in to messages children try to convey.
- Wait and watch before responding.
- Use non-verbal communication.
- Talk to babies about what you are doing, to link words with actions.
- Watch for their understanding.
- Use talk to describe what children are doing.

Development Matters

- Make sounds with their voices in social interaction.
- Take pleasure in making and listening to a wide variety of sounds.
- Use single word and two word utterances.
- Understand simple sentences.
- Create personal words as they begin to develop language.
- Are intrigued by novelty and events and actions around them.
- Understand simple meanings conveyed in speech.
- Respond to the different things said to them when in a familiar context with a special person.
- Are able to respond to simple requests and grasp meaning from the context.

Ella 16 months

Listens to others and enjoys musical sounds.

Understands simple requests, wash your hands and hold the spoon.

Begins to talk to dolls in role play and mimics what she may have heard.

Begins to share and talk to others.

Mat 17 months

Chatters to others and makes his views clear. Curious and keen to talk about interests in the nursery – train set and small world play. Knows several nursery rhymes .

Assam 19 months (EAL)

We are not making headway with Assam. He does not appear to respond to verbal commands. Chat with colleague raises a possible hearing issue as he shows elation when signs are made – wave, gestures etc. – but otherwise is not engaging in play.

FIGURE 9.4 Language development, planning and assessment for under threes

TABLE 9.3 Development Matters statements for communication and language

Age band	Development Matters (Language for communication)
Birth–11 months	■ Communicate in a variety of ways including crying, gurgling, babbling and squealing. ■ Make sounds with their voices in social interaction.
8–20 months	■ Take pleasure in making and listening to a wide variety of sounds. ■ Create personal words as they begin to develop language.
16–26 months	■ Use single-word and two-word utterances to convey simple and more complex messages. ■ Understand simple sentences.
22–36 months	■ Learn new words very rapidly and are able to use them in communicating about matters which interest them.
30–50 months	■ Use simple statements and gestures often linked to gestures. ■ Use intonation, rhythm and phrasing to make their meaning clear to others. ■ Join in with repeated refrains and anticipate key events and phrases in rhymes and stories. ■ Listen to stories with increasing attention and recall. ■ Describe main story settings, events and principal characters. ■ Listen to others in one-to one or small groups when conversation interests them. ■ Respond to simple instructions. ■ Question why things happen and give explanations. ■ Use vocabulary focused on objects and people that are of particular importance to them. ■ Begin to experiment with language describing possession. ■ Build up vocabulary that reflects the breadth of their experiences. ■ Begin to use more complex sentences. ■ Use a widening range of words to express or elaborate on ideas.
40–60 months	■ Have confidence to speak to others about their own wants and interests. ■ Use talk to gain attention and sometimes use action rather than talk to demonstrate or explain to others. ■ Initiate conversation, attend to and take account of what others say. ■ Extend vocabulary especially by grouping or naming. ■ Use vocabulary and forms of speech that are increasingly influenced by their experiences of books. ■ Link statements and stick to a main theme or intention. ■ Consistently develop a simple story, explanation or line of questioning. ■ Use language for an increasing range of purposes. ■ Use simple grammatical structures.
Early Learning Goals	■ Interact with others, negotiating plans and activities and taking turns in conversation. ■ Enjoy listening to and using spoken and written language, and readily turn to it in their play and learning.

Source: DCSF, 2008

The Development Matters statements for communication and language provide a useful framework on what it is reasonable to expect children to be saying from birth to 5 years (Table 9.3).

Time for talking

It is vital that children are encouraged to talk, so how do practitioners go about creating a 'communication-friendly setting'? It is important that attention is given to 'the uniqueness of every child', the need to create 'an enabling environment' in which to learn and develop and

FIGURE 9.5 Solitary play

an understanding that 'children develop and learn in different ways'. A typical pattern in reception classes is for all the class to assemble together around the teacher at certain times of the day. Sometimes this is replicated in a pre-school nursery class because this is what happens once children start school in a reception class. All too often, especially in reception classes, there is the expectation that children are beginning to get ready for the next stage when it may not always be appropriate because daily sessions such as these have the potential to cause unrest and inattention by several children. Do not have thirty children sitting as a whole group too often or until you feel the children can cope with this and be fully engaged, listening and answering questions enthusiastically when requested. I would go as far to say that whole class carpet sessions are not communication-friendly enough and need to be phased into reception classes and generally be with smaller groups in pre-school settings. In outstanding nursery provision, large groups of children on the carpet is very unusual. Children talk as they play because they immediately have a context on which to base their conversation with each other or a nearby adult. All staff need to be encouraged to talk with children to extend their language development, provide a listening ear and encouragement to engage in conversation. This may be as they help children to get ready to go outside, naming items of clothing, explaining what they are going to do outside or, importantly, joining in with a play situation. Eventually, children will be ready for talking in small group time and learn to take turns as they grow in confidence. Let children know verbally what the daily routines are, especially when there are changes and why. List all the areas in your setting and create a list of questions, comments and activities to be displayed for staff, parents and visitors. Call these prompt cards. Add mirrors safely and strategically so small children can observe themselves as they talk, shout, sing or just watch themselves. Make sure there are plenty of props to support favourite stories. Begin to make links between spoken and written language as children develop. Audit each area of your setting to seek ways of enriching the communication environment. You are likely to have the following areas:

- Sound creating environment – push button, squeakers, music makers, radios.
- At least one comfortable story area with a wide variety of simple books, including board books, flap-books, musical books, fabric books and busy people books.
- Mark-making area.
- Sand and water.
- Home corner and role-play area, create a literary environment with newspapers, magazines, posters, recipes, dressing up clothes.
- A covered area such as a tent or blanket over a table for quiet moments.
- Café corner for help yourself snack time, preferably with an adult there when possible to encourage chat.
- Area for small world toys and layouts.
- Replicate indoors outside where possible, especially in the summer with tents, awnings, rugs, planting and gardening area.

In conclusion, this section perhaps covers the most vital area of learning and is certainly the cornerstone for children's learning and development. Discuss your routines with others and work towards what you believe to be the most effective from the children's point of view. A previous section has outlined what you need to know but what is useful to complete this section is a further reiteration of the value of play and teaching working together. Taking the play experience as the context for learning is a prime aim in which to develop children's learning in the prime area:

> Play provides the natural, imaginative and motivating contexts for children to learn about themselves, one another and the world around them. A single moment of sustained play can afford children many developmental experiences at once, covering multiple areas of learning.
>
> (Ofsted, 2015b: 8)

Physical development

> Physical development involves providing opportunities for young children to be active and interactive; and to develop their co-ordination, control and movement. Children must also be helped to understand the importance of physical activity, and to make healthy choices in relation to food.
>
> (DfE, 2014a: 8)

This section provides some indicators of what might be expected of children when they start pre-school education. The overwhelming message is that physical activity is central to young children's health and well-being. It is rightly identified as a prime area of learning. A fundamental priority for physical development in early years settings must be access to outdoor

FIGURE 9.6 Outdoor play

play. The priority needed to be given to this is so much more evident now than twenty years ago when a colleague and I were asked to lead an outdoor play training session for nursery headteachers in a rural northwest authority. Horror and considerable scepticism greeted our suggestions for equipment and areas for the indoor curriculum to be outside when weather permitted and to manage staffing accordingly. I am afraid we did not win them over immediately due to their concerns about safety and supervision. Times have certainly changed. One headteacher has described the learning environment as 'the best teaching tool we have. It allows us to provide children with direct access to resources and experiences, both real and imaginary, that they may not otherwise receive at home. The constant changes made to the environment allow children to solve problems, interact with each other and develop their imaginations'.

The two early learning goals for this area of learning (Table 9.4) are discussed below.

Moving and handling

Physical development is also about how babies and young children gain control of their bodies and how children learn to be active and healthy and how they learn to use equipment and materials successfully and safely. Children need to learn not to bump into things, how to pick up something and put it down. It is important that they become confident in their use of toys, such as how to push a care, ride a scooter and ride a bicycle. Fine motor control will develop as they learn to handle scissors, pens, pencils and paint brushes independently.

TABLE 9.4 Early learning goals for physical development

PHYSICAL DEVELOPMENT	
Moving and handling	■ Children show good control and coordination in large and small movements. ■ Children move confidently in a range of ways, safely negotiating space. ■ Children handle equipment and tools effectively. ■ Children handle a pencil for writing.
Health and self-care	■ Children know the importance for good health of physical exercise and a healthy diet. ■ Children talk about ways to keep healthy and safe. ■ Children manage their own basic hygiene and personal needs successfully, including dressing and going to the toilet.

Source: DfE, 2014a

Health and self-care

This may all seem rather vague for aspiring early years practitioners. It becomes important then to research further afield to give an indication of what children might be expected to do with regard to physical development at different ages. The reality is that the revised EYFS framework recognises the holistic approach to early learning, thus negating to some extent the compartmentalising that has characterised planning and assessment over the years. Many of you will wish this were really the case, but given assessment requirements it is important that practitioners understand and can break down learning activities into the areas of learning to enable assessments to take place as required. To provide examples of what children could be expected to be doing in this area of learning, I have turned to the website www.kidspot. com.au. I would also advise looking back at the Development Matters framework to support physical development expectations for different age groups. For example, what can be expected at 24–36 months, 36–48 months and then the early learning goals as cited in a previous edition. Table 9.5 shows what children should be able to do at different stages between birth and 5 years.

Indoor and outdoor play

Helen Bilton (2010) has written extensively on the value of outdoor play and has devised a useful set of outdoor play principles:

- Indoors and outdoors need to be viewed as one combined and integrated environment.
- Outdoors is an equal player to indoors and should receive planning, management, evaluation, resourcing, staffing and adult interaction on a par with indoors.
- Outdoors is both a teaching and learning environment.
- Outdoors design needs and layout needs careful consideration.
- Outdoor play is central to young children's learning, possibly more to some children than others.

- The outdoor classroom offers children the opportunity to utilise effective modes of learning – play, movement and sensory experience.
- Children need versatile equipment and environments.
- Children need to be able to control, change and modify their environment.
- Staff have to be supportive toward outdoor play.

The characteristics of effective teaching and learning are set out very clearly in the statutory guidance as: playing and exploring; active learning; and creating and thinking critically. What could be more appropriate for young children other than the outdoor environment? The case study below describes a problem-solving task set for a group of children in an early years unit.

TABLE 9.5 Physical development at 24–36 months

Aspect	24–36 Months	36–48 Months	Early learning goals
■ Moving and handling	■ Children gain increasing control of their whole bodies and are becoming aware of how to negotiate the space and objects around them.	■ Children maintain balance when they concentrate. ■ They negotiate space successfully when playing racing and chasing games, adjusting speed or changing direction to avoid obstacles. They handle tools effectively for the purpose, including mark-making.	■ Children show good control and coordination in small and large movements. They move confidently in a range of ways, safely negotiating space. They handle equipment and tools effectively, including pencils for writing.
■ Health and self-care	■ Children can communicate their physical needs for things such as food and drink and can let adults know when they are uncomfortable. They are beginning to be independent in self-care, e.g. pulling off their socks or shoes or getting a tissue when necessary but still often need adult support for putting socks and shoes back on or blowing their nose.	■ Children can recognise and express their own need for food, exercise, the toilet, rest and sleep. They can put on a jumper or coat with little assistance and can fasten big buttons. ■ They usually have bladder and bowel control and can attend to most toileting needs most of the time themselves.	■ Children know the importance for good health of physical exercise and a healthy diet and talk about ways to keep healthy and safe. They can mange their own basic hygiene and personal needs successfully, including dressing and going to the toilet independently.

TABLE 9.6 Continuous Curriculum weekly spaces for play plan (Indoors/Outdoors) EY Unit

Goldilocks and the Three Bears	Learning intention/emphasis	Indoors	Outdoors	Observe children's interests	Possible next steps
Book/listening	To know that print carries meaning and understand the story To listen to the story To retell the story	Books about bears, listening centre	Books about bears		
Construction	To build using different materials		Blocks, crates and cardboard boxes		
Creative	To use creative materials to represent features		Represent bears using plates and materials		
Physical/movement	To handle equipment and tools To use pencils for writing (HA)		Write names/mark for name on bear models Use paste spreaders		
Investigation	Children interested in why things happen and how things work To listen to instructions		Making meal in Goldilock's cottage		
Malleable	Children create simple representations Use what they have learned about media (HA)		Paintings of bears, models of bears using found materials		
Mark-making	Children give meaning to marks they make		Letters to Goldilocks, self-initiated activities		
Music	Children explore sounds Children listen and talk about the story of Goldilocks		Listen and begin to sing 'when Goldilocks went to the house of...'		
Role Play	Children engage in imaginative role play based on their experiences To retell story of Goldilocks				
Water					
Small World	Children talk about the characters and what they do				

CASE STUDY 9.2 Outdoor learning

Following external building works to the main building of a small rural infant school, the curiosity of the children became aroused as various equipment came and went into the cordoned off playground. As a result, the children were set a challenge to make a brick wall to stop the Big Bad Wolf from taking their toys. Children worked together with their peers and parents (sometimes Dads came to the rescue as the wall building progressed). The challenge of getting the wall built provided the opportunity to develop language and communication skills and physical development as they assembled tools and learned how to control the wheelbarrow. Counting the bricks reinforced one-to-one correspondence. Children learned to cooperate as they took turns to wheel the empty wheelbarrow and load it with carefully counted bricks as the wall was built. Concentration and perseverance with the task in hand was palpable as the children met their goal.

Research

A survey commissioned by the DfE, *Children's Experiences of the Early Years Foundation Stage* (Garrick et al., 2011), aimed at gathering children's views on their experiences in a range of early years settings sought to find out the extent to which children engaged in physical activity indoors and outdoors and what they enjoyed. The survey found that most, not all, children talked about their enjoyment of physical activities, particularly outdoors. They talked about cycling, climbing, chasing, jumping and balancing hoops and balls. The extent of these opportunities varied from setting to setting. Some children commented positively on being free to choose when to play outside, several children described feeling unhappy about waiting for a particular time of the day for outdoor activity. In a few settings, children described enjoyment of indoor physical activities. This included hall games in a reception class, large-scale construction play in a Steiner setting and dancing in two childminding settings. It is not untypical to find the indoor curriculum available outside at suitable times of the year, but not always with a physical development focus. Writing from experience and a recent report, I find my younger grandson Ethan being an outdoor boy as much as he can. This is in a one-form entry village school with its own dedicated outdoor play area for the reception class. I am sure the days of pre-schools without an outdoor area for the children to play are long gone. This too was not uncommon in the late 1990s. The research review (Evangelou et al., 2009: 92) describes children's fundamental development in interconnected domains with children primed to encounter their environment through relating to and communicating with others, and engaging physically in their experiences. The evidence gathered for the review found that physical development was cited by 40 per cent of respondents as the third most important assessment area. Many thought that physical development was under emphasised particularly for children from birth to 22 months, and was important because of the health aspect. As young children begin to develop concepts, they define these in terms of touch, movement and senses, they develop schema to repeat and test ideas. The ability to practice skills and develop control as Ethan moved around the garden learning how to manipulate a bucket and stirrer is a typical example of using schema to repeat and test ideas (Athey, 1990). As the observer of this activity, it was very apparent that it would have been impossible to replicate this experience indoors. Many aspects of *moving and handling* were evident. It was a classic example of the way in which the physical environment enabled exploration, control and confidence in a child who was an active agent in the environment. The work of Maude (2006) is cited in the evidence review as it links children's physical development to daily practices in early years environments. Suggestions made by Maude are that children's physical development curriculum needs to include:

- Physical development to stimulate growth, enhance physical development and to provide healthy exercise.
- Movement development to build on existing movement vocabulary, to develop coordination and body tension and to extend movement vocabulary.
- Movement skill acquisition to develop fundamental motor skills to the mature stage, to introduce the dynamics of movement, to develop coordination and teach accuracy in movement.
- Movement confidence development to teach movement observational skills, to develop movement experimentation and expression, to enhance self-expression and to enhance self-confidence, self-image and self-esteem.
- General education to teach movement observation, to teach appropriate vocabulary for discussing and explaining movement, to stimulate thought processes, to encourage independence and ownership of learning, to sustain periods of enjoyment.

(Maude, 2006: 194)

The importance of play in developing a movement curriculum for young children should be a high priority according to Maude, and indeed is fully reinforced in the EYFS. The value of outdoor learning is firmly acknowledged in the EYFS framework and its profile further developed by creating physical development as a 'prime' area of learning. A concern for all those working in the early years is to ensure that all children are able to engage in physical activity from a healthy lifestyle point of view as well as the great enjoyment that children get from playing outside and being physically active. However, despite research findings corroborating all the former comments, there is an issue with regard to the number of children who are categorised as obese or overweight. The pre-school years are considered critical for establishing healthy lifestyle behaviours such as physical activity. Studies of physical activity tracked through childhood into adulthood and establishing habitual physical activity early in life is therefore vital. The time spent outdoors is associated with greater physical activity in school-age children. A report published by the UK's Chief Medical Officer (CMO) (Davies, 2013) highlighted the need for intervention to promote movement in the early years 0–5 years. The Born in Bradford initiative, known as Preschoolers in the Playground or PiP was set up to offer families the opportunity to attend a 30 minute session with their children aged between 18 months and 4 years in a school playground for up to six times a week throughout the year. This started off well but retention fell back in the autumn and winter terms, leading to a consideration of other ways of encouraging parents to be physically active with their children. The impact of this study has yet to be published but certainly the take up by parents, particularly in the summer term, with an overall take up of 80+ per cent. Children cared for during the day by childminders may be the ones who relish the chance to play outside in a well-resourced garden. Examples such as access to a grassy area, skittles, logs for jumping, castle and fairy glen for imaginative play are all from one childminder's garden. Another view on the degree of exercise taken by pre-school children claimed by the editor of daynurseries.co.uk is that pre-school children have poorer physical and motor skills than twenty years ago (Learner, 2014). This she claims is because children are more fearful of hurting themselves and less confident in their physical abilities than they used to be two decades ago. This statement can be justified because generally children do not have the same amount of freedom to roam as they had in the past, all their exercise is determined by parents, usually the mother. Guidelines from the British Heart Foundation suggest that children should spend three hours a day involved in moderate/vigorous physical activity. The lure of sedentary pursuits such as playing games on a tablet, watching TV or playing sedentary games with an educational focus serve to assuage the guilt of parents. However, there is another valid reason. Many outdoor physical activities are available at a considerable cost and parents may not have the time or the money to afford these options. As a consequence, the time for outdoor play and learning in pre-school settings is important. What children should be able to do by the time they start pre-school aged 3 is listed below relating to gross motor and locomotor skills, fine motor skills and hand–eye and foot–eye coordination skills. Although not recent, the activities cited provide examples of the movements children are likely to enjoy as they move around in group. An Australian sample too provides examples of outdoor activities for the youngest children.

Gross motor and locomotor skills
- Walk forward backwards and sideways
- Walk on tiptoe
- Show a basic running style
- Climb up steps or a ladder with one foot leading, maximum step depth 21 cms
- Climb down a ladder with one foot leading, with hand support
- Pivot round and round on feet
- Walk up and down mounds
- Jump up and down on the spot on two feet
- Jump a distance of 36 cms
- Jump down from one foot to two feet from a height of 45 cms
- Balance walk along a plank at a height of 18 cms from the ground
- Balance on one leg for 4 seconds
- Crawl through a barrel or drainpipe
- Climb through the lowest rungs of a climbing frame

Fine motor skills
- Place three blocks on top of each other
- Make a straight road with ten building blocks, having been shown an exact replica
- Affix a piece of construction apparatus to a hole in another
- Assemble a six-piece jigsaw
- Paint a person with a head and two other body parts identifiable
- Grip and make marks on paper with a thick soft pencil
- Hammer shapes into a pegboard
- Make a ball with clay or playdough
- Pour water from a jug with a spout into a large container
- Thread beads onto a lace

Hand–eye and foot–eye coordination skills

- Catch a large ball thrown by an adult between their extended arms
- Catch a small ball thrown by an adult between extended arms
- Kick a standing ball with force
- Pedal a tricycle along a wide chalked or painted line
- Push a ball way from self across the floor surface
- Pull an empty truck around obstacles.

(Wetton, 1997)

Expectations of Australian children (Brooks, 2011)

Developmentally there are certain physical milestones such as gross motor skills, fine motor skills, vision, hearing and emotional and social behaviour which impacts on a child's ability to learn and interact with others. Taking a child at six monthly intervals the expectations of physical development are:

- *Physical development by 6 months*
  A child will show basic distinctions in vision, hearing, smelling, tasting, touching, temperature and perceiving pain. A child's head may lift up when on the stomach and possibly show squeals of delight as well as grasp objects and roll over.
- *Physical development by 12 months*
  Control of torso and hands, sit without support, crawl and has growing control of legs and feet. Standing or creeping across the floor may occur.
- *Physical development by 18 months*
  Can creep or crawl upstairs, possibly walk, draw lines on paper with crayon and show growing physical independence.
- *Physical development by age 2*
  Can go up and down stairs, run, sit self on chair, use a spoon and fork, turn single pages in a book, kick a ball, attempt to dress oneself, build a tower of six blocks, has bowel and bladder control, though may not show it.
- *Physical development by age 3*
  Can run well, march, stand on one foot briefly, ride tricycle, feed oneself (with a bit of a mess), put on own shoes and socks, unbutton and button.

Australia's Department of Health and Ageing has two recommendations for parents to encourage optimal physical development:

1   Children and young people should participate in at least 60 minutes of moderate to vigorous intensity physical activity every day.
2   Children and young people should not spend more than two hours a day using electronic media for entertainment.

The joy of outdoor play is that it is generally self-chosen, creative, imaginative and exploratory. Games may be led by adults, especially for the younger children, and the impact of outdoor play for helping to cement friendships where more than one child is required to play frequently is a high priority.

Personal, social and emotional development

> The best way to prepare children for their adult life is to give them what they need as children.

> (Bruce, 1996)

The principle stated above is a reminder to all readers not to lose sight of the children in the range of settings they are likely to be working as they wrestle with the demands of a statutory framework for EYFS curriculum, assessment requirements and their own professional development. This section shares a range of ways in which practitioners provide opportunities to support the personal, social and emotional development of the children in their care. Central to this will be a consideration of the role of a supportive adult, the impact of the quality of the relationships children have with parents in the home and how different settings plan to ensure children's social and emotional development progresses. An interesting question to ponder as the chapter develops is how adults assist children to become personally and socially competent in a planned way. Are social and communicative skills taught in a systematic way? Do they need to be? Another important thread of the chapter is the relationship between the context in which personal, social and emotional development (PSED) occurs and other areas of learning. Can attitudes to learning be taught? Is it possible to work with the child in isolation from his or her family to create effective relationships in a nursery setting? How is successful behaviour management achieved? How does the PSED of birth to 3 years old differ from that of older children? The recent elevation of the PSED area of learning to a 'prime' area of learning is to be welcomed. As stated in other chapters, PSED is at the heart of learning whatever the title of an activity. For very young children it is the foundation of learning. The poem below reminds us of the important role model offered by adults to the children in their care.

> Children live what they learn
> If children live with criticism,
> They learn to condemn.
> If children live with hostility,
> They learn to fight.
> If children live with ridicule,
> They learn to be shy.
> If children live with shame,
> They learn to feel guilty.
> If children live with encouragement,
> They learn confidence.
> If children live with praise,
> They learn to appreciate.
> If children live with fairness,
> They learn justice.
> If children live with security,
> They learn to have faith.
> If children live with approval,
> They learn to like themselves.

If children live with acceptance and friendship,
They learn to find love in the world.

(Excerpt from *Children Learn What They Live* by Dorothy Law Nolte, 1972, 1998.
Reproduced by permission of Workman Publishing Co. Inc.,
New York. All Rights Reserved)

Research findings

The development of PSED is central to learning in early years settings. A recent survey by Ofsted (2015b) found that 2-year-old children spent four-fifths of their time in activities that address PSED along with other areas of learning. Visits encouraged children to interact socially with different people and to learn how the world works. The revised definition of personal, social and emotional development covers every facet of children's relationships with others and with themselves. For all 5-year-olds to have acquired this level of relationship and attitudes is a great achievement, and when in place lays a firm foundation for their future lives. Do we as educators in England give enough attention to this area of learning in our day-to-day work? Is the attention intuitive? What needs to be remembered is that children's development is holistic in nature. Emotional and social behaviours all impact on cognition. There are differences in how babies and older children respond to adult attention. Babies can discriminate human faces and voices from another sensory stimulus. The security of the mother–baby attachment is crucial. The key for children attending pre-school is the quality of adult–child relationships. The positive caregiving of staff who were 'more educated' and 'held more child-centres beliefs about childrearing' was a definite indicator of quality in the EPPE research. The allocation of a 'key person' to each child (Elfer et al., 2012) has emotional implications for children and staff due to the forging of close emotional ties. All of which have implications for professional development of staff. As children get older, there is the need for them to accept the rules of acceptable behaviour and behave accordingly. The success of this in children is closely linked to the mutually responsive relationships between mother and child which promotes the development of committed compliance by children and ultimately the development of conscience (Kochanska et al., 2005). Children in high negative emotion ability need to have sensitive interaction between themselves and their caregiver. Harsh parenting tends to increase the risk of anti-social and aggressive behaviours in such children. A strong sense of mastery in children between the ages of 2 and 3 helps children to develop a more secure sense of self (Bandura, 1997). The ways in which adults talk to children may help to develop children's self-esteem in 5- and 6-year-olds (Reese and Newcombe, 2007). Children need to be active participants in their social world from birth. As a child's ability to use language and to symbiotically represent things emerges between 1 and 3 years of age, so does the capacity to develop a more extended understanding of the mind. This may lead to engagement in pretend play, whereby the child creates a safe arena in which to explore potential feelings and intentions of others.

'The 0–3 age range is a vital period when the right social and emotional inputs must be made to build the human foundations of a healthy, functioning society. The key agents to provide these inputs for 0–3 children are parents' (Allen and Duncan Smith, 2008: 4). An early education pilot (DCSF, 2009) for disadvantaged 2-year-old children providing free early years education to over 13,500 disadvantaged 2-year-olds between 2006 and 2009 confirms this view. The key findings from this evaluation were that the pilot did not significantly improve children's social development, the parent–child relationship or the home learning environment relative to the matched comparison group. However, where children attended higher quality settings, there was a positive impact on language ability and the parent–child relationship. Parents were the ones who benefitted from involvement in the pilot study because they felt that the setting had positively affected their ability to parent, their physical health and mental well-being. An outcome of the pilot was a recommendation that 2-year-olds should only be able to access free provision in 'good' settings based on Ofsted judgements. A more recent report published by the Centre for Social Justice (Allen and Duncan Smith, 2008) made a case for there to be early intervention for children aged 0–3. It quoted figures from the United State's WAVE TRUST research that highlights the very young brain's enormous capability for change, and how this rapidly diminishes well before children start school. There is absolute support for the claim that 'children's experiences in their earliest years of life are laying the foundations for their futures – for good or ill' (Allen and Smith, 2008: 46). This leads to two very simple conclusions:

- What parents do at this very early stage appears to be absolutely decisive in terms of child outcomes.
- What we do to prepare at-risk parents and potential parents to be effective is the most important social policy issue for modern society.

A further truism in this report is the claim that very young children need a high level of emotional responsiveness and engagement to ensure the reduction in the statistic that 30 to 40 per cent of abused or neglected children go on to abuse or neglect their own children. The report recommends SEAL (Social and Emotional Aspects of Learning; DCSF, 2007) and Roots of Empathy (Gordon, 2005). The latter Canadian programme helps children to learn compassion and caring. Emotional intelligence skills are learned by showing children how to learn from the bond between babies and parents. This is achieved with the use of parents with very young babies spending time in the setting on a weekly basis. The programme claims that this develops empathy in the children observing the mother–child relationship and enables them to engage in more pro-social behaviour, such as helping, sharing and including. Children also learn about empathy by being treated in an empathetic, caring way by their parents at home. This approach is seen to have an unforeseen effect on bullying. It is used extensively in New Zealand, United States and the Isle of Man. A further study in New Zealand known as the Dunedin study (1972) monitored the development of a thousand children from birth. When the children were age 3, nurses assessed them by watching them play for 90 minutes to identify those they judged to be at risk. At follow-up at age 21, it was found that the 'at risk' boys had two and a half times as many criminal convictions as the group deemed not to be at risk. *The Effective Provision of Pre-School Education (EPPE) Project* (Sylva et al., 2004) in England found that high-quality pre-schooling was related to better social/behavioural development and in line with evidence from the WAVE Trust; the quality of the home learning environment is more important for social development than parental occupation, education or income. What parents do is more important than who parents are. There is also research that has impacted on the organisation of staffing to provide maximum benefit for children. The key person system, with a small number of individually designated practitioners relating to particular children, enables responsiveness and sensitivity to individual children (Elfer et al., 2012).

The key person

As mentioned earlier, the key person is paramount for all children in the birth to age 5 range, but particularly for babies who need to develop an attachment to a significant person to feel that personal relationship developing through smiles, gurgles, long stares and pre-verbal exchanges of sound (Lindon, 2005). Although not applicable now, the National Standards describe key persons as 'providing a link with parents and carers and crucial in settling children into the setting' (Ofsted, 2006). However, checking the *Principles into Practice* cards (DCSF, 2008: 2.4) the same definition remains in their description of a key person as someone who has *special responsibilities* for working with a small number of children, giving them the reassurance to feel *safe* and cared for and building relationships with their parents. The requirement for this is in group settings. I know from experience that this does not take place in many reception classes because there is a different ratio of staff to children required for reception-aged children. The fundamental role of the key person ensures children and their families feel secure and trusting in the care of their child. Ideally, each family has a key person who gets to know them well, and this helps everyone feel safe. A baby knows that this key person is special and will do the same things as a parent will do. Peace of mind for a mother as she leaves her baby in day care is paramount to give her confidence in sharing worries with a familiar face each time she brings her child into the setting.

It is important to distinguish between the term 'key person' and 'key worker'. These two terms are often used interchangeably in nurseries. There is a clear distinction between the two terms. A 'key worker' is often used to describe the role that is about liaison or coordinating between different professionals or between different disciplines, making sure that services work in a coordinated way. This is very different from the 'key person' as defined earlier. The term 'key worker' is also used to describe how staff work strategically in nurseries to enhance smooth organisation and record keeping. This is part of the 'key person' role but it is also an emotional relationship as well as an organisational one (Elfer et al., 2012).

There is some rather disturbing recent research (Marmot Review, 2010) suggesting that 60 per cent of 5-year-olds in some of Britain's poorest areas do not reach a good level of behaviour and understanding. This is double that found in wealthier suburban parts of England. An earlier edition said that in effective settings, there is planned promotion of positive behaviour which takes account of the needs of the parents as well as children. While this is still true, there is a further imperative today to work with parents to demonstrate the effective ways in which to develop in children the understanding of what is right, what is wrong, and why. Are we involving children well enough in identifying issues and finding solutions? The EPPE research (Sylva et al., 2004) found that the most effective settings adopted discipline/behaviour policies in which staff supported children in rationalising and talking through their conflicts. Where settings were less effective there was often no follow-up on children's misbehaviour and, on many occasions, children were distracted or simply told to stop. *The Practice Guidance for the Early Years Foundation Stage* (DCSF, 2008: 35) provides some good examples of effective practice in Appendix 2: Areas of Learning and Development. Starting at birth and going through to 5 years old, these are:

- Find out as much as you can from parents about young babies before they join the setting, so that routines you follow are familiar and comforting.
- Demonstrate clear and consistent boundaries and reasonable yet challenging expectations.
- Reduce incidents of frustration and conflict by keeping routines flexible so that young children can pursue their interests.
- Help children to understand their rights to be kept safe by others, and encourage them to talk about ways to avoid harming or hurting others.
- Share with parents the rationale of boundaries and expectations to maintain a joint approach.
- Demonstrate concern and respect for others, living things and the environment.
- Be alert to injustices and let children see that they are addressed and resolved.
- Ensure that children have opportunities to identify and discuss boundaries, so that they understand why they are there and what they are intended to achieve.
- Help children's understanding of what is right and wrong by explaining why it is wrong to hurt somebody, or why it is acceptable to take a second piece of fruit after everybody else has had some.
- Involve children in identifying issues and finding solutions.

Research into to how to manage behaviours in pre-school provision has reported that the typical strategies used were exclusion, explanation or distraction. Staff prepared to raise with parents their concerns about problematic behaviours that endangered a child's safety were out of character. A similar example read on the Mumsnet blog suggests that there are settings that still revert to the somewhat old-fashioned methods of control, such as time out for a 3-year-old, which was applauded by the large majority of other parent members! Do you agree with this? How should a refusal to do something be reprimanded in a 3-year-old? Surely, you do not agree that time out away from the other children is a satisfactory remedy? As an early years practitioner, you need to be ready to tackle questions such as this. Parents, especially those with their first child are more likely to turn to staff in early years settings to discuss issues relating to what they consider to be bad behaviour in their child. They are very likely to ask what your strategies are for dealing with tantrums and incidents of hitting other children or not wanting to share the toys. The suggestions below are generally typical in most early years settings.

Temper tantrums in 2-year-olds

It may seem unnecessary to cover the management of the behaviours of very young children. However, given large number of web pages on the 'terrible twos' tantrum scenario, it is worth looking at strategies to deal with such a situation. Tantrums are a typical stage of child development. Toddlers are keen to do things as their mental and motor skills tend to develop more quickly than their ability to communicate. This can lead to frustration because as they do not have the verbal skills to express their frustration they do so by throwing tantrums. In the case of a frustration tantrum, the practitioner needs to send a clear message by walking away from a child using a tantrum to get his/her own way. By walking away, the child is taught that tantrums are not acceptable, which is part of toddler discipline. Frustration tantrums require empathy. Use the opportunity to bond with a child by helping out if they are struggling with a task, such as putting on a sock. Tantrums may be triggered by being over-tired, hungry, unwell or other reasons. Keeping a record of their frequency and what may be triggering the tantrum is a useful step into discovering what is causing the tantrum.

Managing feelings and behaviour

Children talk about how they and others show feelings, and the consequences, and how some behaviour is unacceptable. They work as part of a group or class, and understand and follow the rules. They adjust their behaviour to different situations, and take changes of routine in their stride.

Making relationships

Children play cooperatively, taking turns with others. They take account of one another's ideas about how to organise their activity. They show sensitivity to other's needs and feelings, and form positive relationships with adults and other children. The social dimension to PSED is important. Initially children learn to understand who they are and what they can do. Once children come to understand themselves, they do so in relation to others, how they make friends, understand the rules of society and behave towards others. Following on from this is children's emotional development and how children understand their own and others' feelings and develop their ability to be empathetic.

Topics for discussion

- Share how you have adapted your planning methods to meet the statutory requirements for the prime areas of learning.
- What are your key priorities for children's learning in your setting?
- Share the ways in which you manage free flow indoor/outdoor learning.

Further reading

Ephgrave, A. (2012) *The Reception Year in Action, Revised and Updates edition: A Month by Month Guide to Success in the Classroom.* London: Routledge.

Ephgrave, A. (2015) *The Nursery Year in Action: Following Children's Interests through the Year.* London: Routledge.

10

The specific areas of learning

Introduction

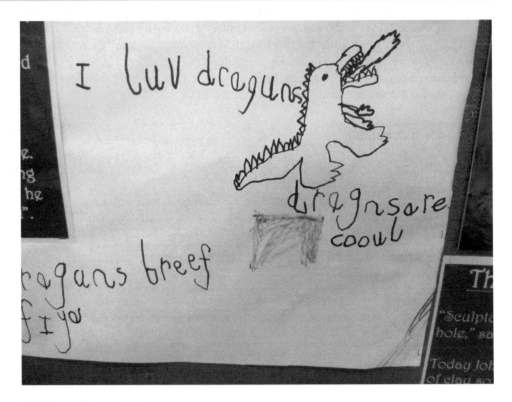

FIGURE 10.1 Dragon paintings

This chapter takes each specific area of learning individually in order to share the findings of recent research and to provide examples of the ways in which practitioners are interpreting and applying the statutory guidance in their day-to-day practice. There is no intention of implying that children learn, or are taught each area of learning discretely. The findings of Ofsted surveys are shared where appropriate. Literacy and technology have a high priority. It is claimed that mathematical learning receives less attention due to some of the insecurities held by staff based on their own school experiences according to Ofsted (2015b). This is despite it being just as important an area for children's development, particularly in the longer term. The specific areas of learning provide the support through which the prime areas are applied to meet the statutory framework for the EYFS. The statutory guidance states that prime and specific areas of learning are to be part of the educational programmes. Seemingly, this is very likely to be interpreted by practitioners as including all areas of learning equally as the revised and recently introduced baseline assessment assesses all areas of learning.

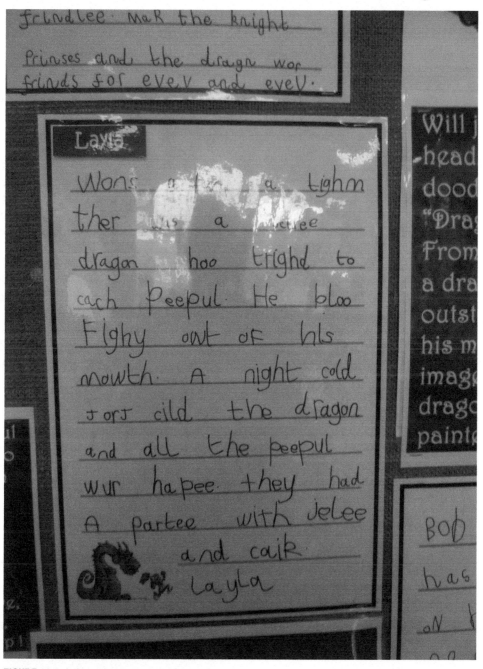

FIGURE 10.2 Independent reception writing

Literacy

> Literacy development involves encouraging children to link sounds and to begin to read and write. Children must be given access to a wide range of reading materials (books, poems, and other written material) to ignite their interest.
>
> (DfE, 2014a: 8)

There is national concern that young children, many of them from disadvantaged backgrounds or with English as their second language, are being left behind in their reading. The reasons for this are often linked to lack of attention to communication and language development in the very early years. The ways in which parents and practitioners encourage children to enjoy reading to enable them to become fluent and regular readers by age 11 is equally crucial. Table 10.1 outlines the expectations of children by the time they are age 5.

The priorities and methods used to teach young children to read have gone through several best methods in the past twenty years. There is no need to remind those about to enter the early years profession of these scenarios because they will learn for themselves that all children are different and will acquire the ability to read well in different ways. The early learning goals for reading in Table 10.1 are indicators of what children are expected to do by the time they are age 5. The Development Matters statements from 2012 show what it is reasonable to expect of children as they progress in their first five years of development as shown in the *Development Matters Statements* in Table 10.2. The current statutory requirement to teach young children to read is through using their phonic knowledge to decode regular words and read them aloud accurately. I find myself unable to leave learning to read by the phonic approach entirely based on my teaching experience and how my own three children learned to read. A presentation at a European conference by Henrietta Dombey (2013) suggesting that synthetic phonics is not enough will ring true to many practitioners. Based on UKLA's 2012 survey of teachers and headteachers the following comments were made. A significant majority of teachers and headteachers considered that the nonsense words were very confusing for children undergoing the *Phonics Screening Check* which:

■ undermines children's confidence as readers;
■ impedes successful readers and has failed a cohort of the most fluent readers;
■ misidentifies pupils who are beyond this stage of development as readers and favours less developed/emergent readers;
■ has negative implication for relationships with parents;
■ has negative implications for school organisation.

TABLE 10.1 EYFS reading early learning goals

Reading
■ Children read and understand simple sentences. ■ Children use phonic knowledge to decode regular words and read them aloud accurately. ■ Children also read some common irregular words. ■ Children demonstrate understanding when talking with others about what they have read.

TABLE 10.2 Development Matters statements for reading and linking sounds and letters

Age band	Development Matters (reading)	Development Matters (linking sounds and letters)
Birth–11 months	■ Listen to familiar sounds, words or finger plays.	■ Listen to, distinguish and respond to intonations and the sounds of voices.
8–20 months	■ Responds to words and interactive rhymes, such as 'clap hands'.	■ Enjoy babbling and increasingly experiment with using sounds and words to represent objects around them.
16–26 months	■ Show interest in stories, songs and rhymes.	■ Listen to and enjoy rhythmic patterns in rhymes and stories.
22–36 months	■ Have some favourite stories, rhymes, songs, poems or jingles.	■ Distinguish one sound from another. ■ Show interest in play with sounds, songs and rhymes. ■ Repeat words and phrases from familiar stories.
30–50 months	■ Listen to and join in with stories and poems one-to-one and also in small groups. ■ Begin to be aware of the way stories are structured. ■ Suggest how the story might end. ■ Show interest in illustrations and print in books and print in the environment. ■ Handle books carefully. ■ Hold books the correct way up and turn the pages. ■ Understand the concept of a word.	■ Enjoy rhyming and rhythmic activities. ■ Show awareness of rhyme and alliteration. ■ Recognise rhythm in spoken words.
40–60 months	■ Enjoy an increasing range of books. ■ Know that information can be retrieved from books and computers. ■ Explore and experiment with sounds, words and texts. ■ Retell narratives in the correct sequence, drawing in language patters of stories. ■ Read a range of familiar and common words and simple sentences independently. ■ Know that print carries meaning and, in English, is read from left to right and top to bottom. ■ Show an understanding of the elements of stories, such as main character, sequence of events and openings, and how information can be found in non-fiction texts to answer questions about where, who, why and how.	■ Continue a rhyming string. ■ Hear and say initial sounds in words and know which letters represent some of the sounds. ■ Hear and say sounds in the order in which they occur. ■ Link sounds to letters, naming and sounding the letters of the alphabet. ■ Use their phonic knowledge to write simple regular words and make phonetically plausible attempts at more complex words.

The findings of the interim evaluation of the phonics screening test, *The Year 1 Evaluation of the Phonics Screening Check: First Interim Report* had the following key findings:

- Teachers were overwhelmingly positive about phonics as an approach to teaching reading and its contribution towards early reading development.
- In the majority of schools, however, other strategies alongside phonics were also supported, suggesting there were no benefits to the check at all.
- More than half (53 per cent) of teachers reported they taught systematic phonics 'first and last' (i.e. they used a systematic synthetic phonics approach as the prime approach to decode print), although the teachers' responses regarding the use of other methods to teach children to decode words were not wholly consistent with these data.
- More than 90 per cent of teachers taught phonics to all children in reception, more often than not using Letters and Sounds as their core programme.

The key message emerging from the evaluation so far appears to be that many schools believe that a phonic approach to teaching reading should be taught alongside other methods. One needs to look closely at what children are discouraged to do when taught to read by the phonic method. Learning to read is not a one-way only strategy, however successful this is because children are different and may approach learning to read in several ways. The example guidance given to parents of reception-aged children as to what learning to read involves sums up very well what the all-embracing elements to the reading process are. This is well illustrated in the examples in Chapter 7.

In order to elaborate further on the tried and tested reading methods, here is a breakdown of some of the more common methods used by practitioners along side the phonological approach.

Routes to reading

There are ranges of ways in which children learn to read (Meadows, 1993: 17). These are the 'routes' into extracting meaning from a written word. There is the phonic route, currently used and promoted in the statutory guidance for EYFS, the lexical route and dual route approach. Children will also use visual recognition and the shape of a word, especially those with which they are familiar in their environment such as their name, words such as 'stop', 'go', 'McDonalds', 'Burger King', 'Aldi', 'Lego', 'Tesco' or 'Sainsbury's'. In educational settings, children engage in games with flashcards. They may pronounce an unknown word using their familiar phonemic word production system. Once they start to read, how often do they misread 'horse' for 'house', and vice versa? Contextual information and visual processing as well as phonological analysis all play a part. How then do the various components of skilled reading co-occur and interact as a child progresses from pre-school innocence of literacy to advanced reading skills (Meadows, 1993: 10)? We have learned that the reading process starts shortly after birth. A key activity for parents is to engage with reading to their child, however young they are. Another necessary activity is to sing and chant to your child. Familiarity with stories allows children to begin to predict when they read. Bruce (1997: 134) reminds us that reading is largely prediction. Children need to understand about grapho-phonics, syntax and semantics in order to read. 'Cracking the language code' will enable children to tackle syntax in a text. All of which is predicated with endless modelling of reading by an adult or older child using alphabet books or busy books with lots of events and familiar characters. It may not be emphasised in the EYFS statutory guidance but it is vital that children are surrounded by texts in books, on posters, on labels, or what they have said recorded in some way in print. The earlier photograph of a 4-year-old's writing of 'Dragans breef fiyu' demonstrates how he is learning to read and write based on his grapho-phonic knowledge (see Figure 10.1). Seen much less frequently in early years settings is the use of big books to share with a group. All of which helps children grasp that, for example, 'a' is pronounced one way in some words and another way in others. Create listening corners for children to listen to stories. Make use of technology to deal with the basics of learning to read. So far we have just raised issues relating to 'reading' words. There are many homophones, that is, words that have the same sound but different meanings such as 'wood' and 'would', 'witch' and 'which', 'to' and 'two'. It is with hesitation that I cite the statement in Meadows, that 'phonemic analysis is quite hard to learn, and young children and illiterate adults find it almost impossible to segment words correctly into phonemes, though relatively easy to segment them into syllables' (Luberman, 1977). Many may be familiar with terms such as 'onset and rhyme'. To help children understand the different sounds made by the symbols in our alphabetic system, children need to be able to distinguish separate sounds within the stream of language they hear when people talk and read aloud. Phonological awareness is decoding alphabetic letters which represent sounds, and strings of letters, by representing a sequence of sounds, can signify spoken words. According to Goswami and Bryant (1990: 3), children may recognise the word as a visual pattern without paying much attention to the individual letters or to the sounds that they represent, the assumption being therefore that children's awareness of sounds plays an important part when they learn to read and write. Children demonstrate different kinds of phonological awareness because there are different ways in which words can be divided up into smaller unit sounds (Figure 10.3).

As practitioners you will learn from interactions with children that they learn to read in different ways. Some children master this very quickly without any phonological awareness and others will struggle to sound out short words even after being drilled on the daily phonic treadmill. The examples of practitioners in reception classes putting the reading process centre stage in many physical activities and expecting children to want to use their whiteboards to recall what they said in words is a joy to see and works very effectively. The writing and reading process is centre stage. Prior to this is the need to ensure that all children have mastered developing speech, language and vocabulary. Are children encouraged to listen to each other, share their stories with others and use more adventurous vocabulary when describing an event? The key to success, however, is in the central role play takes as a means of engaging and interesting the children and the adults simultaneously in a shared activity that has links with reading and writing. The findings of a recent Ofsted survey corroborates this

	Syllable	Onset and rhyme	Phoneme
'cat'	cat	C - at	c-a-t
'string'	string	str- ing	s-t-r-i-n-g

FIGURE 10.3 Three ways to divide words into component sounds

approach that is well reflected in the title of the report *Teaching and Play in the Early Years* (Ofsted, 2015b). The role parents play in the early reading process is vital. An example of the information provided for the parents of reception children in a small rural primary in South Oxfordshire is given in Chapter 7.

The lexical route to reading

This reading method is the process whereby skilled readers can recognise known words by sight alone. Every word a reader has learned is represented in a mental database of words and their pronunciations that resembles a 'dictionary' or internal lexicon. It is likely that in time young children will internalise the word into their memory and recognise it and know what it means the next time they see it. It is likely that subconsciously a child's knowledge of phonemes (the sounds of letters and graphemes (the sounds of groups of letters) is used to decode the word. As adults, this is what we are likely to do when reading unknown words.

The dual-route to reading

This approach (Jackson and Colheart, 2001) uses the terms 'lexical' and 'non-lexical' to describe the two ways in which words can be read aloud. Essentially this is a combination of a route where the word is familiar and recognition prompts direct access to a pre-existing representation of the word name that is then produced in speech. Non-lexical refers to a route used for a novel or unfamiliar word. As these words are not represented in the brain's lexicon, they cannot be read directly. They have to be decoded using knowledge of phoneme and grapheme (letter-sound) conversion rules. An understanding of the routes is important when needing to discover what are the triggers for those children who cannot read in order to identify the strategies they use to attempt to read; for example, in diagnosing dyslexia.

Synthetic phonics

Prior to schools adopting the synthetic phonics approach to helping children learn to read, the National Literacy Strategy (NLS) recommended teachers to teach children to use four searchlights for reading: 'knowledge of context', 'phonics (sounds and spelling)', 'grammatical knowledge' and 'word recognition and graphic knowledge'. However, these approaches were short lived as too many children aged 11 were failing to meet national standards. As a result, and following an analysis of the Clackmannanshire method of using the 'simple view of reading' (i.e. that readers decode and then comprehend the word) and the recommendations of the Rose Report, 'synthetic phonics' became the way English pupils are taught to read and is currently the statutory way this happens. In this method, all letters and sounds are taught very rapidly, with an emphasis on blending the sounds. Teachers, generally, follow a phonics-based programme with scope to embed this approach into a 'language rich' environment and the use of 'real books'. Hopefully, the access to 'real' books is a major priority to allow those children using other strategies to read and especially children who do not speak English as their first language. Suggestions for creating a stimulating literacy environment are suggested in Figure 10.4.

Resource areas and resources

- Domestic role-play area.
- Imaginative role play-area.
- Cosy story telling area – undercover?
- Library corners in several areas with books displayed with front cover visible.
- Comfortable seating, such as throws, rugs, cushions.
- Mark-making materials in the domestic play area.
- Magazines and newspapers.
- Materials for writing stories – well-resourced with paper, crayons and pencils, etc.
- Headsets and tapes of stories.
- Magnetic boards with alphabet letters.
- Puppets linked to stories.
- Use of children's labels and captions.
- Alphabet at child eye height.
- Interactive whiteboard at child height if possible, but create a platform if not (boys love this).
- Pencils attached to painting easel to encourage children to write their name.
- Self-registration board with forename first, before adding surname too.
- Checklist displayed for children to record snack taken.
- Computers, desk and laptops in technology area.
- Signs on everything to recreate the richness of the visual literacy environment outdoors.
- An area for parents to read with their children.

Try to replicate as much of the above as possible outside.

FIGURE 10.4 Creating a literacy environment

Organising your literacy environment

Generally, practitioners are planning separately for Sounds and Letters which tends to be taught in small groups according to the children's understanding and age, especially in an EYFS unit comprising 3- and 4-year-olds. A successful approach to sharing books in small groups too tends to work more effectively when children are grouped by similar readiness to listen to stories and contribute. Very young children may find it very hard to join a large group and find it stressful. This may show itself in what appears to be disruptive behaviour, and indeed it often is. The answer may lie in a gradual approach to large group work. It is rarely ideal for 3-year-olds to be grouped in a large group for a story. Preferably continuous provision should give a high priority to promoting literacy skills by ensuring there is always an adult to encourage children to share books, role play in the puppet theatres and making use of listening devices to hear favourite stories. As a start practitioners may wish to audit their provision to ensure there is a high priority to literacy development and learning.

Characteristics of effective literacy teaching in a reception class

The findings of an Ofsted (2012) survey to identify the characteristics of effective literacy teaching suggests that the best new teachers are well supported and consequently have:

- a deep understanding of children's language development and understanding of the links between language skills and literacy skills;

- sufficient knowledge of language and literacy skills across the age groups, so that they were able to adapt their teaching for different age groups as well as pupils with a range of abilities and attainment;
- good questioning skills which helped pupils develop their thinking skills through talking and listening;
- a good knowledge and understanding of phonics and how this supports reading and spelling; they understood how to help pupils use their skills learnt throughout the curriculum;
- a good understanding of how to help pupils use the skills they have learnt throughout the curriculum.

They also have the ability to:

- create interesting experiences and activities that promoted the use of language and children's listening skills;
- assess learning in language and literacy accurately and understand what to teach next to enable pupils to progress quickly;
- provide good models of spoken as well as written language;
- use accurate and precise pronunciation;
- blend and segment words when teaching phonics;
- use a wide range of well-considered resources to help extend vocabulary and create an enthusiasm for writing;
- assess pupils throughout lessons and target their questioning, providing sufficient challenge and support for different pupils;
- understand how to support pupils with special educational needs and those who are at an early stage of acquiring English;
- be proficient in teaching language and literacy skills across the curriculum;
- be highly reflective practitioners.

The following case study reflects how successfully children make progress based on their very low skills and ability when they start in the nursery. The highlighted area shows very clearly the range of activities that take place to promote language and literacy development.

CASE STUDY 10.1 Promoting effective early learning in a nursery class

Children make excellent progress by the time they leave the Foundation Stage unit in all areas of learning. They quickly settle into the routines. Home visits help to allay any parental concerns and begin to give children confidence. It is the view of parents that their 'children come on in leaps and bounds'. The year 2007 was exceptional and children exceeded the level expected for their age by the time they started in Year 1. However, there is fluctuation year by year and not all children attending the nursery transfer to the school. Overall, most children reach the expected level and an increasing number reach beyond it. Achievement is outstanding because teaching is exemplary and fully engages children in everything they do. Not an opportunity is missed to encourage children to develop their literacy skills, whether it is reading their name when choosing a fruity snack, self-registering when they come into school or reading the instructions to make a cup of tea during outdoor play. Children enjoy learning because it is fun. An investigation into the range of everyday utensils

---

and crockery very successfully helped to improve children's early language skills. Teapots, jugs, kettles and different kinds of tea generated a wealth of learning that helped to improve the speech and understanding of many children. Personal, social and emotional development is very well promoted too. Children grow in confidence and play calmly and productively at all times. Children delight in brushing their teeth as soon as they arrive into the unit. Assessment is exemplary and fulfils two main purposes excellently: to guide future learning for the children and to inform parents of their child's progress. Leadership of the unit is outstanding because of the excellent model of exemplary teaching and the impact of this talent on other staff.

Research findings

The world of early literacy has exercised early years practitioners over time. There are experienced practitioners who will find the phonic route difficult to come to terms with given the wealth of research carried out over the past twenty to thirty years into how children begin to read and what needs to have happened in children's first two years of life. Do we know if reading standards are improving? Do all children learn to read via the same route? Observe children when you can to discuss with colleagues what you find. It is vital that practitioners explore beyond the DfE definition of literacy outlined at the beginning of this section. There is confirmation from a recent Ofsted survey (2015a) which looked at teaching and play in the early years. The findings were that approaches to early reading were viewed as the most formal approach to learning with dedicated time each day to teaching communication, language and literacy. Short, sharply focused teaching sessions together with frequent opportunities to apply learning across all other activities, allowed the rapid development of literacy skills. Close links were made too between all practical learning and play and the expectation that children will apply their phonic knowledge from reading to first sentences written to describe what the children have learned or as an explanatory label on a photograph or model. A word of caution needs to be exercised here and it is imperative that practitioners recognise that not all children will benefit from the phonological approach to early reading. In discussion, the president of the UK Literacy Association stated that, 'more attention needs to be paid to the other elements of what it means to become a reader as well as the phonic element. Phonics is necessary but it is not sufficient to become a reader in the rounded sense' (Scott, 2010). This view is supported by a Scottish academic saying that:

> In England you have a very centralized curriculum where the government, the policymakers, have to be seen to be doing something, but are often quite distant from the people who have to make their decision work. In Scotland there is a much more devolved system where decisions are made much closer to those who will have to implement them. Most current research shows that children need literacy teaching that is tailored to the individual.
>
> (Ellis, 2010)

The article cites the West Bartonshire phonics experiment which was launched in 1997, with the aim of eradicating pupil illiteracy within a decade. At the time the area had one of the poorest literacy rates in the UK with 28 per cent of children leaving primary school at 12 as functionally illiterate. In 2007, the council reached its target of full literacy, the first education authority in the world to do so. Synthetic phonics were at the core of the scheme, but only one strand in a ten-step programme that included extra time in the curriculum for reading, home support for parents and the fostering of a literacy environment in the community. In a study of sixteen Head Start settings, including 128 children in the USA, Yeh and Connell (2008) found that instruction emphasising phoneme segmentation blending and letter sound relationships was more likely to promote progress in reading than vocabulary instruction and, particularly, rhyming instruction. This was found to be true for highly disadvantaged children as young as 4 years old. The *Read on. Get on* campaign (Save the Children, 2014) cites new research showing that the UK has the strongest link among developed nations between poor literacy and unemployment. Their mission was to tackle the case for practical action to get every child reading well at age 11. To achieve this goal, headteachers and teachers along with parents and carers need to mobilise people on social media and educational evaluators according to Dame Julia Cleverdon, chair of the *Read on. Get on* campaign. It is widely recognised that children need to have strong early language skills as a first step and the foundations on which reading well at primary schools is based. The core definition of 'reading well' in this campaign is as follows:

> 'Reading well' by age eleven means that children should not only be able to read the words that are written down, but they should have a wider understanding of the meaning behind stories and information and are able to talk about them and comment on them… they should also be able to read a range of different materials, including magazines and newspapers, relevant websites, letters and dictionaries.
>
> (Save the Children, 2014)

Learning to write

The statutory guidance is quite explicit in directing practitioners to what children are expected to be able to do by the end of EYFS in writing. They are expected to use their phonic knowledge to write words in ways which match their spoken sounds (see Table 10.3). The example in Figure 10.5 is the first writing attempts of a nursery-aged child of 3 years linked to ongoing topics in the setting. The key to successful progress in writing is the ways in which practitioners integrate reading and writing so a writing activity is integral to everything that is going on in a setting. From a very early stage and once children have a grasp of the rudiments of phonics, they can apply this to their first attempts at writing. As stated earlier, a range of tools to encourage independent writing needs to be available around a classroom. There needs to be individual whiteboards and pens, paper and large sheets for less confident writers. The case below shows the development well. However, this is from a school where a high proportion of children exceed age-related expectations by the time they leave the reception class. It provides clues as to the children's success as writers.

TABLE 10.3 Early learning goals for writing

Writing
■ Children use their phonic knowledge to write words in ways which match their spoken sounds.
■ Children also write some irregular common words.
■ Children write simple sentences which can be read by themselves and others.
■ Some words are spelt correctly and others are phonetically plausible.

FIGURE 10.5 News from the garden

CASE STUDY 10.2 A literacy experience in a nursery unit

Learning to write permeates everything the children do inside and outside because it is linked to everything the children do. Children are grouped by ability for their short phonic sessions but are primarily encouraged to apply their literacy skills in the exciting range of activities. Everyone writes. Learning to read and write in this school happens because it is always a 'contextualised activity'. Children very confidently sound out unfamiliar words before they put pencil to paper. Writing materials are available everywhere – whiteboards and felt pens, screens, paper – examples of children's writing boldly displayed as captions within sight of the children as they play and learn. Phonological understanding in this school is an integral part of writing. There is a very strong 'I can' culture that is encouraged by all staff and parents. Children are encouraged to blend sounds and write words as they apply their phonic knowledge as they read captions or instructions. Key words such as 'farmyard' are available for them to copy. Children choose a word to use in their own sentence. A teacher may add to a sentence and encourage children to sound out a word before writing it down – for example, 'br'- ow- n – and praised for correct phonemes used. Figure 10.6 shows what is happening day by day in this exemplary early years environment leading to 60 per cent of children achieving above age-related expectations at the end of Key Stage 1.

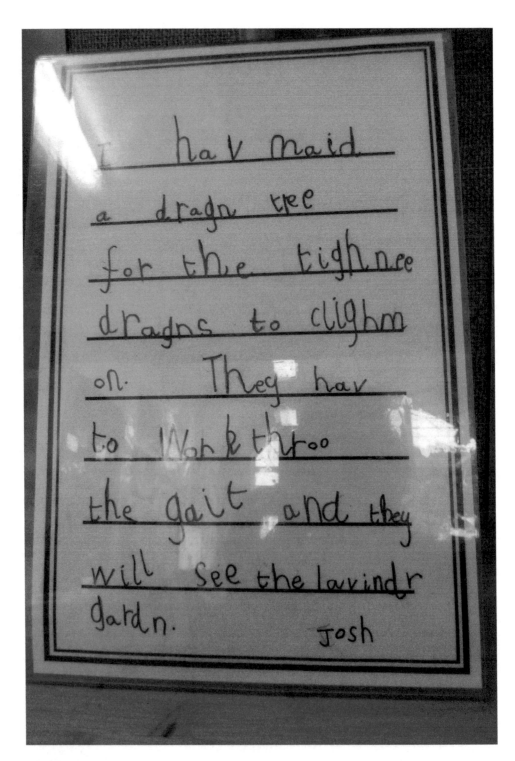

FIGURE 10.6 Contextual writing

The expectations of what is expected of children at different stages of writing are contained in the Development Matters statements (Table 10.4). They are only a guide but a useful aid for recently qualified practitioners along with the examples of children's writing.

TABLE 10.4 Development Matters statements for writing and handwriting

Age band	Development Matters (writing)	Development Matters (handwriting)
Birth–11 months	■ Use arms and legs and increasingly use them to reach for, grasp and manipulate things.	■ Play with own fingers and toes and objects around them.
8–20 months	■ Begin to make marks.	■ Begin to bring together hand and eye movements to fix on and make contact with objects.
16–26 months	■ Examine the marks they and others make.	■ Make random marks using their fingers and some tools.
22–36 months	■ Distinguish between different marks they make.	■ Begin to show some control in their use of tools and equipment.
30–50 months	■ Sometimes give meaning to marks as they draw and paint. ■ Ascribe meanings to marks that they see in different places.	■ Use one-handed tools and equipment. ■ Draw lines and circles using gross motor movements. ■ Manipulate objects with increasing control.
40–60 months	■ Begin to break the flow of speech into words. ■ Use writing as a means of recording and communicating.	■ Begin to use anti-clockwise movement and retrace vertical lines. ■ Begin to form recognisable letters.
Early Learning Goals	■ Use their phonic knowledge to write simple regular words and make phonetically plausible attempts at more complex words. ■ Attempt writing for different purposes, using features of different forms such as lists, stories and instructions. ■ Write their own name and other things such as labels and captions, and begin to form simple sentences using punctuation.	■ Use a pencil and hold it effectively to form recognisable letters, most of which are correctly formed. (Model holding a pencil between the thumb and forefinger and encourage this in children, but observe to see whether they are ready for this.)

Mathematics

> The time devoted to mathematical development is not as frequent or as systematic, especially for two-, three- and four-year-olds.
>
> (Ofsted, 2015a: 16)

The expectation for children's mathematical learning are clearly outlined in the early learning goals (Table 10.5). Research and Ofsted reports suggest that less attention is given to mathematical learning in the early years. The case study below describes the range of mathematical learning taking place in a nursery classroom.

An Ofsted survey found that the time devoted to mathematical development was not as frequent or as systematic in pre-schools with 2- to 4-year-olds.

CASE STUDY 10.3 Mathematical learning in a nursery classroom (Ofsted, 2015a)

The most effective ways develop mathematical learning is to extend any activity that calls for counting objects. This is important to help children understand that the last number when counting tells the child how many flowers they picked. Can the children record their numbers in a play situation? The setting up a shoe shop works excellently for developing counting and an understanding of the words 'pair' and 'same' when sorting shoes in the 'shop'. Settings do not need numeracy corners as numbers need to be spread around the setting to act as prompts to support counting activities. Displays of shapes too act as a preparation for indentifying shapes in the environment, in construction sets and as children build. Mathematical understanding develops from the context in which the skills are taught. Play provides a context; for example, building a tower, then building the tallest tower, looking at the shapes of the blocks, introducing the language of shape as it applies to this playful activity. How many blocks are there for each tower? Which tower is the tallest, the smallest? How many more are needed to make the towers the same size? Mathematical language acquisition in this activity alone is extensive – higher, taller, shorter, straight, flat. This is a child-generated activity with the involvement of a more knowledgeable adult taking the learning to the next level (Vygotsky, 1978).

TABLE 10.5 Early learning goals for mathematics

The statutory requirements for mathematics are:

- *Numbers*: children can count reliably with numbers from 1 to 20, place them in order and say which number is one more or one less than a given number. Using quantities and objects, they add and subtract two single-digit numbers and count on and back to find the answer. They solve problems, including doubling, halving and sharing.
- *Shape, space and measures*: children use every day language to talk about size, weight, capacity, position, distance, time and money to compare quantities and objects and to solve problems. They recognise, create and describe patterns. They explore characteristics of everyday objects and shapes and use mathematical language to describe them.

Source: DfE, 2014a

FIGURE 10.7 Logan counting

Reflect on the ways you can mirror this activity with different resources, inside and outside. Teaching is the key in extending learning through play and maintaining motivation in the children. Pre-schools do not need mathematical areas as numeracy is understood always in the context of an activity. Construction and building kits can help children conceptualise shapes and understand that a group of objects can be counted and the last number is the total. There is a considerable potential for overlap with understanding the world for mathematical understanding. Visits outdoors – ideally there will be an outdoor learning environment where children can collect and count. Shape displays act as a preparation for identifying shapes in the environment. Table 10.6 indicates the stages children go through in their numeracy understanding in the Foundation Stage.

TABLE 10.6 Development Matters statements for numeracy

Age band	Development Matters (numbers as labels and for counting)
Birth–11 months	■ Respond to people and objects in their environment. ■ Notice changes in groupings of objects, images or sounds.
8–20 months	■ Develop an awareness of number rhymes through their enjoyment of action rhymes and songs that relate to their experience of numbers. ■ Enjoy finding their nose, eyes or tummy as part of naming games.
16–26 months	■ Say some counting words randomly. ■ Distinguish between quantities, recognising that a group of objects is more than one. ■ Gain an awareness of one-to-one correspondence through categorising belongings, starting with 'mine' or 'mummy's'.
22–36 months	■ Have some understanding of 1 and 2, especially when the number is important for them. ■ Create and experiment with symbols and marks. ■ Use some number language such as 'more' and 'lot'. ■ Recite some number names in sequence.
30–50 months	■ Use some number names and number language spontaneously. ■ Show curiosity about numbers by offering comments or asking questions. ■ Use some number names accurately in play. ■ Sometimes match number and quantity correctly. ■ Recognise groups with one, two or three objects. ■ *Continue to create and experiment with written numbers.* *
40–60 months	■ Recognise some numerals of personal significance. ■ Count up to three or four objects by saying one number name for each item. ■ Count up to six objects from a larger group. ■ Count actions or objects that cannot be moved. ■ Begin to count beyond 10. ■ Begin to represent numbers using fingers, marks on paper or pictures. ■ Select the correct numeral to represent 1 to 5, then 1 to 9 objects. ■ Recognise numerals 1 to 9. ■ Count an irregular arrangement of up to ten objects.

Age band	Development Matters (numbers as labels and for counting)
	■ Estimate how many objects they can see and check by counting them. ■ Count aloud in ones, twos or tens. ■ Know that numbers identify how many objects there are in a set. ■ Use ordinal numbers in different contexts. ■ Match then compare the number of objects in two sets.
Early Learning Goals	■ Say and use number names in order in familiar contexts. ■ Count reliably up to ten everyday objects. ■ Recognise numbers 1 to 9. ■ Use developing mathematical ideas and methods to solve practical problems. ■ *Attempt to record using numbers.**

★ Added by author

Mathematical learning through play

There is great scope for mathematical learning through play and with the interaction of adults and/or older children in early years settings. It is important to create opportunities for children to:

■ hear mathematical language used, such as bigger, smaller, fewer, more;
■ make mathematical marks, such as scoring for a game or counting objects;
■ use a score board;
■ celebrate birthdays and display birthday cards;
■ record what they do on post-its for example;
■ name products in shops and giving them a price;
■ use simple coins in reception class;
■ count how many teeth when going to the dentist;
■ work in small groups;
■ use the outdoor environment – numbers on walls for scoring when playing with balls, counting petals on flowers, counting and identifying leaf shapes leaves on trees and number of trees can all be achieved in a playful way.

It is very possible to build mathematics into children's play. As children hunt for minibeasts, they record as a tally and then as numerals the numbers of spiders, worms, caterpillars and woodlice they found in the undergrowth of the outdoor setting. Another group of children making kebabs on an outdoor fire talk about the different lengths of their kebabs and notice the repeating patterns on them. Cutting toast or sandwiches into shapes provides the opportunity for children to identify shapes such as triangle, rectangle, square or circle. Role-play areas set up as a lost property area leads to children sorting the clothes by size, shape and colour. Play-based learning provides a very relevant context for developing early mathematical concepts. Notwithstanding how easily mathematical learning can be encouraged in play, a recent Ofsted survey (2015b) commented on the less frequent time devoted to mathematical development in all pre-school age groups. This was partly attributed to the lack of confidence by the staff and their own negative experiences at school.

Teaching mathematics in the early years

To avoid only having an emphasis on mathematical development generated by the games children play, it is important to define what early years practitioners need to do to develop children's mathematical understanding. A recent Ofsted survey (Ofsted, 2015b) found that staff in early years settings were resolute that this area of learning was just as important as literacy. The view held was that there was less of a priority given to mathematics and a lack of national initiatives. A first step to address this is to ensure that literacy and mathematics are allocated the same amount of time for focused teaching however this takes place in an early years setting. Mathematics can easily be incorporated into many playful activities. The example cited by Ofsted praises how a setting built mathematics into children's play. My own guilt is evident as I check the case studies for this chapter and note the absence of any related to mathematics! However, to rectify this the case study of children hunting for minibeasts demonstrates just how easily children's mathematical interest and motivation is garnered.

CASE STUDY 10.4 Mathematical learning

The children recorded as tally marks, then as numerals the numbers of spiders, caterpillars and woodlice they could find in the undergrowth of the outdoor setting. At another setting, children were asked to name the shape of their toast at snack time. A role-play lost property shop required children to count the numbers of items for sale in each category. There are too all the routines of the day that require counting – number of children, the returning numbers of toys etc. as children tidy up and return items to storage. The key is the expectation of the practitioners to encourage counting to consolidate children's understanding and the purpose behind counting.

Mathematical research for the early years

The findings of a longitudinal research study (Sylva et al., 2004) emphasised the long-term benefits of pre-school mathematical learning. They found that children who received a rich variety of home learning before they started school achieved measurably better results in mathematical tests at age 10. There are similar findings too for children with special educational needs. Sure Start evaluation reports (Melhuish et al., 2008) highlight the difficulties centres have in getting to those hard to reach families and help parents and their young children to access support. There are key pointers from the William's review (2008) which have influenced the guidance provided to practitioners. The review places a priority on providing practitioners with guidance on mathematical mark-making, as well as recommendation to include time and capacity in the early learning goals. Crucially, the review comments on mathematical pedagogy in the early years and especially mathematical learning through play activities. The review cites the findings of the *Effective Provision of Pre-School Education project* (Sylva et al., 2004) and fully endorses the findings that effective pedagogy includes interaction traditionally associated with the term 'teaching', the provision of instructive learning environments and 'sustained shared thinking' to extend children's learning (DCSF, 2008: 33). Chapter 6 goes into more detail about 'sustained shared thinking', 'joint involvement episodes' and 'schema'. The interrelationship between the home environment and the early years setting is of great importance, with the parent (or carer) seen as the most important educational influence in a young child's early development. The key features of effective mathematical pedagogy are:

- skilled practitioners interacting with children in a rich, stimulating and interesting environment;
- practitioners' use of mathematical language in open-ended discussions;
- building on play;
- making the most of everyday routines and spontaneous learning to develop mathematical skills and concepts;
- practitioners supporting, challenging and extending children's thinking and learning through sustained shared thinking and the use of accurate mathematical language;
- giving children opportunities to record their understanding and thoughts in early mathematical mark-making.

The final point is the key and an area in which, historically, practitioners have not encouraged children to mark-make in a mathematical context. The groundbreaking practitioner research by Elizabeth Carruthers has led to new approaches in early years settings and the inclusion of mathematical learning in the DCSF publication on mark-making.

Mathematical mark-making

Carruthers and Worthington (2003) coined the term 'mathematical mark-making' or 'graphics' to describe children's own marks and representations that they use to explore and communicate their mathematical thinking. This is evident in the scribbles, drawings, writing and tally-type marks which lay the foundations for understanding mathematical symbols and later use of standard forms of written mathematics (Carruthers and Worthington, 2006). It is through mark-making that a child is truly creative. A single drawing, for example, may help a child to develop concepts relating to problem-solving, reasoning and numeracy or knowledge and understanding of the world, as well as improving their physical coordination (DCFS, 2008: 3). Mark-making is thinking on paper (Carruthers and Worthington, 2006). It is useful for practitioners to recognise this in planning and assessing early mathematical skills.

Counting and recognising number ('numerocity') and calculation

Historically, much research into mathematical learning is in the area of numeracy, with a marked change in the findings of researchers in recent years. There are aspects of counting that need consideration in early years settings. The traditional 1:1 matching activities of objects as a first step towards counting is less effective in helping children learn object to word. The 1:1 principle is more likely to be learned through 1:1 number word to object matching when modelling counting. So instead of matching sets of objects by 1:1 correspondence, more should be made of recognising equivalence, greater than and less than when comparing sets (Thompson, 2008). It is further postulated by other researchers that there can be confusion for children in the cardinal principle, in that the count word assigned to the final object indicates the cardinality (how many) of the whole set. This can confuse children and it is suggested that there could be more attention in early years to the idea that number words and written symbols represent quantity rather than being a function of counting and the relationship between consecutive counting numbers as representing one more or one fewer (Sarnecka and Carey, 2008). When items added to, or removed from a set of hidden objects babies recognised this, thus indicating an innate understanding of calculation. (McCrink and Wynn: 2004). Other researchers have noted that 3-year-olds understand such tasks with larger numbers, recognising which sets would have more when there are additions or removals of objects. Children demonstrate an innate understanding of addition and subtraction at the age of 3, which is not evident in children's emergent counting abilities. What this research is showing is the value of informal mathematical learning in the early years which can embed understanding in a practical context that lays the foundation for later understanding in more formal school mathematics. Are there enough opportunities created for this informal understanding of calculation? Later problems can arise when children are lacking in confidence in counting forwards or backwards. This has implication for practices such as counting words forwards, backwards and from a given number rather than one, in order to aid subsequent calculation strategies. Once children start to count fluently, they recognise small quantities without counting. This is known as subitising. Children continue to subitise when looking at dice and patterns. Table 10.7 lists some key vocabulary for this area of learning and Table 10.8 is a planning example based on Goldilocks and the Three Bears.

There is an evidence base that states that achievement in mathematical activity on entry to school is a clear indicator of subsequent achievement in later years (Aubrey et al., 2006 in England and other researchers in the United States and Finland). Young children are much more likely to develop an understanding in socially contextual activities than non-contextual mathematical contexts. The early years could have a greater emphasis on number words as representing a quantity rather than a function of counting (Sarnecka and Carey, 2008). There needs to be lots of informal learning in the early years. For example, being able to count on and back is a first step to being able to solve addition or subtraction problems later. However, there is research reported by Aubrey (2003) of a European study which shows that beginning formal instruction at an early age does not improve subsequent mathematical achievement.

TABLE 10.7 Key mathematical language in the early years

- More/less
- Bigger/smaller
- Longer/taller/shorter
- Higher/lower
- Full/empty
- Heavier/lighter
- Wider/narrower
- Faster/slower
- Too much/too little
- Same/different
- Before/after
- Balance
- Both
- Altogether
- Add/take away
- Share
- In/out/on/under/besides
- Above/between/behind/in front
- Names of numbers, shapes, days, months, year, coins
- Round/flat/straight/curvy/corner/line

TABLE 10.8 Example of a mathematical activity linked to Goldilocks and the Three Bears

Day	Objective	Activity	Evaluation
Tuesday	Gain an awareness of one-to-one correspondence, distinguish between quantities recognising that a group of objects is more than one (16–26 mths). Use some number language such as 'more, and 'lot' (22–36 mths). Compare two groups of objects, saying when they have the same number (30–50 mths). Sometimes match number and quantity correctly (30–50 mths).	Introduce toy bear (mummy bear) with one sock glove, claim she has muddled all of the socks/gloves and cannot find the corresponding one. Ask children for their help. Encourage children to give their ideas for sorting and use maths. Vocabulary such as 'more' and 'lot'.	Student to record success and understanding against the objectives and those who talk about the sorting and matching.

Understanding the world

This area of learning is especially important for providing the context for the prime areas of learning and absolutely fundamental for young children's development and understanding about places, people and what they do. There are the beginnings of historical and geographical understandings relating to their immediate environments.

The technology aspect of this area of learning is separated to highlight the growing use of technology in early learning. The scope for topics on understanding the world are considerable. The list below is of the topics accessible via the Internet (Teaching resources TES):

- Animals
- Festivals and celebrations
- Friends
- Homes and buildings
- Minibeasts
- Ourselves
- People and communities
- People who help us
- Plants
- Seasons and weather
- Space and planets
- Special days
- Toys
- Transport
- Where we live.

get the dragon out of his
in the session we saw him
the easel.
breathe fire," he wrote.
fingers a superb sketch of
head raised, claws
with flames shooting from
was keen to upscale this
a beutifully proportioned

FIGURE 10.8 A dragon painting

TABLE 10.9 Early learning goals for understanding the world

Understanding the world
People and communities ■ Children talk about past and present events in their own lives and in the lives of family members. ■ Children know that other children do not always enjoy the same things and are sensitive to this. ■ Children know about and similarities and differences in relation to places, objects.
The world ■ Children know about similarities and differences in relation to places, objects, materials and living things. ■ Children talk about features of their own immediate environment and how environments might vary from one another. ■ Children make observations of animals and plants and explain why some things occur, and talk about changes.
Technology ■ Children recognise that a range of technology is used in places such as homes and schools. ■ Children select and use technology for particular purposes.

The learning environment is the best teaching tool we have. Direct access to resources and experiences, both real and imaginary, that children do not receive at home, replicate everyday situations – fire fighters, docks, paramedics, sailors. Understanding of the world provides a secure basis for learning concepts, attitudes and skills in all areas of learning. Explorations, investigations and enjoyment experienced by children in the outdoor environment are central. Ideas and the plans of practitioners provide a valuable context for children's learning. They are not to straitjacket children into doing things they do not wish to do. This is such an easy claim to make with regard to this area of learning, which along with expressive art and design are at the heart of children's learning and enjoyment. Adults are likely to be the spur for triggering an understanding of the world, whether it is an understanding of people's work, places and experiences children undergo or a developing understanding of places and technology. Specific areas of learning are culturally determined, whereas prime areas are universal to all societies. The revised area of learning has an increased emphasis on the 'concentric approach to learning'. This is a recognition that children learn first about themselves and the people and the things that are important to them. It then focuses on the inter-relationship of people and communities and of living and non-living things. There is an increase on the focus on children using a computer. This is a reflection on the growth of children's understanding of the application of many types of technological device. I am sure practitioners will agree with this explanation and welcome the child-centred approach. A child's first encounter with early years provision is often in the form of a record 'All About Me'. In a previous edition I wrote, 'the opportunity to apply communication, numeracy, literacy, observational and investigational skills to practical situations is at the heart of knowledge and understanding of the world…this area of learning is fundamental to young children's learning' (Rodger, 2003: 152). The activities and experiences in which children take part ensure they deepen their understanding about themselves, their friends and families. For example, watching the traffic passing and counting the lorries rumbling past provides a context for the application of basic skills in a meaningful way. The activity is about recording how many vehicles they see. It is also about observing similarities and differences between different types of vehicles. Where are they going, where have they come from? That activities such as counting the bulbs as they are planted is described as geography or mathematics, or personal and social development is largely irrelevant. The subject or area of learning label is for the adults to know about for their assessment and record keeping and to inform their planning. Children benefit from the richness and first-hand nature of a range of experiences. They use all their senses to hear the traffic, to see the different vehicles, to record the number seen or simply to tell someone about it. The experience is everyday, within the child's understanding and importantly will have some meaning for that child, who will begin to identify with the world around him/her.

A key principle of EYFS that 'the environment plays a key role in supporting and extending children's development and learning' is fundamental to this area of learning. The importance of the outdoor environment is reiterated in the description of the learning environment necessary for children.

- Being outdoors has a positive impact on children's sense of well-being and helps all aspects of children's development.
- Being outdoors offers opportunities for doing things in different ways and on different scales than when indoors.

■ It gives children first had contact with weather, seasons and the natural world and the opportunity to be active and exuberant.

(DCSF, 2008)

Therefore, it is well worth thinking of this area of learning holistically. This is demonstrated admirably in the following case study about Ben, a 3-year-old with special educational needs in a northeast nursery school.

CASE STUDY 10.5 Outdoor learning

I am reminded of Ben (3 years old) who had special educational needs at the end of his nursery experience. Fortunately for him his parents want him to go to school in the area. There is no suitable school catering for his special needs and so he stays in the nursery full-time until a suitable school can be found. He has his own teacher for two hours every day. His parents want him to go to the school his brothers attend, across the road from the nursery. The head of the school is not so sure. Ben has profound hearing loss and is partially sighted. His communication skills are minimal. He communicates via signing (a little) and expresses delight by hugging anyone around. He has just spent half an hour of his daily two hours allocation of a special educational needs support teacher in the quiet room, where they work through a programme of literacy and numeracy activities recommended by the support service. He can count to five now. The support teacher is a very experienced former nursery teacher. She is making little headway with Ben as she struggles to sustain his attention on the picture book they are sharing. Ben and she go outside and head for the climbing platform in the middle of the field near the railings which separate the nursery field from the main road. She cajoles him to climb to the centre where they can easily see both main roads coming to a junction. Once again she gets out the picture book and encourages Ben to point to the lorry and say 'l-o-r-r-y'. Squirming and wriggling Ben's attention wanders. Suddenly, rumbling round the corner comes a builder's lorry. Pointing excitedly Ben cries out, 'LORRY!' and hugs his teacher, who smiles and glows at this tremendous achievement.

It is clear from the examples of planning that this indeed is how practitioners are planning for *Understanding of the World*. By providing a context to enable children to find out about themselves, where they live, what people around them do and how they make sense of the environment, you are helping children to make sense of the world. You are recognising that children learn most effectively when they are actively involved and interested. The three key learning characteristics that are assessed by practitioners provide an excellent prompt as to what kinds of activities and experiences should be available to young children. To remind you these are *playing and exploring, active learning* and *creating and thinking critically*. However, what is critical as children attend nursery is the enrichment that needs to be provided to extend learning and maintain children's interest. I recently observed children in a nursery unit learning about living outdoors – in tents, a tree house and gazebo. It was the tents that generated all the interest because once inside they provided privacy and security for the children.

CASE STUDY 10.6 How many areas of learning?

A group of reception class boys are playing with some miniature animals in the rainforest area of the classroom. They are in the second term of their time in this class and have attended part-time in the school nursery.

DAMIEN: Look at mine hanging off (about the monkey).
PAUL: Mine's hanging.
PAUL: Right! Crocodiles can't fly.
JOHN: Crocodiles can't fly. They can't jump.
DAMIEN: Jaguar's can't climb.
JOHN: Snakes can slither. You don't know where my monkey is?
DAMIEN: Sss, Sss, Sss.
PAUL: Two jaguars come out of the forest.
DAMIEN: We haven't got five.

All the boys count the animals together, one, two, three, four, five, six, seven eight.

JOHN: There are seven (There are seven).
PAUL: I've got three (He has).
JOHN: Where does the monkey live?
DAMIEN: On top of the trees.
JOHN: Which live on the bottom?
PAUL: I know, the spiders.

The boys continue with their play describing to other children who come to the table the movements of each of the animals. The activity lasts about 15 minutes.

The case study above exemplifies the range of learning taking place in an activity that was planned to help the children learn what animals can do and how they live and did not include any reference to mathematics. Nonetheless, the boys accurately applied their numeracy knowledge, demonstrating the case for this as a 'specific' area of learning.

A key principle of EYFS that 'the environment plays a key role in supporting and extending children's development and learning' is fundamental to this area of learning. The importance of the outdoor environment is reiterated in the description of the learning environment necessary for children.

- Being outdoors has a positive impact on children's sense of well-being and helps all aspects of children's development.
- Being outdoors offers opportunities for doing things in different ways and on different scales than when indoors.
- It gives children first had contact with weather, seasons and the natural world and the opportunity to be active and exuberant.

(DCSF, 2008)

I have observed many excited and enthusiastic young children exploring their outdoor localities. There is nothing more inspiring than turning over a large stone to see what might be lurking underneath. The time to encourage children to play and learn outside is paramount in maintaining enthusiasm, motivation and concentration. This is well-described in the case study below.

CASE STUDY 10.7 Many areas of learning

Children have been finding out about mini-beasts (see Table 10.10) for the medium-term plan. They have read stories, such as *The Very Hungry Caterpillar* (Carle, 2014) and *The Bad-Tempered Ladybird* (Carle, 2010). They know that insects are found outside and they sometimes fly. A small group of children armed with information books, pooters and magnifying lenses set off to gather small creatures and hopefully to find ladybirds and caterpillars. Very carefully their findings are collected in transparent containers and taken back to the classroom for further observation. Great care and concern is shown by the teacher and the children as they allow the ladybirds to rest on their hands while they count their spots and number of legs, talk about the colour of their bodies and their relative size compared to a butterfly which was found outside earlier in the day. The children are engrossed. They are using and acquiring a range of scientific and language skills initially. The teacher does not want to lose the momentum of their interest and enthusiasm so she quickly provides each child with a selection of coloured play dough to make their version of the ladybird.

TABLE 10.10 Medium-term planning for the mini-beast hunt

Topic: mini-beasts	Area of learning: CLL & UW Learning characteristics: all	Term: Summer 2/2
Learning intentions – link to CLL, UW, MD, PSED, PD	**Areas/resources, inside/out. Self-initiated**	**Adult-directed activities**
Children know the similarities and differences between the creatures (legs, size, colour, wings) link to MD.	Collection of mini-beasts made from around the outdoors.	Children encouraged to sing 'We're all going on an insect hunt' with NN.
Children observe the mini-beasts, talk about what they see.	Children use the magnifiers and pooters correctly and observe the insects.	CT asks children to describe the insects they see (Assess).
Some children talk about the insects' habitat.	Children go the library to get information books.	Teacher encourages talk about insect similarities and differences (Assess).
Some children use reference book to identify insects.	Children engage in role play outside to make an insect hide, home, as they decide.	Children make a ladybird from playdough with help.
Children use the magnifiers with skill.	Children draw, paint their insects from observation and with support.	Children draw and label with help.
Children listen to *The Hungry Caterpillar* and *The Bad-tempered Ladybird* stories.		Stories in the book corner linked to activity.
Children draw an insect and some add a caption.		Movement linked to how the insects move on outside grassy area.
Children take turns and share the tools.		Talk about caring for creatures.

A research perspective

The findings of research suggest that children make sense of the world by seeking out patterns that connect different objects and experiences. These patterns are known as schema. The schema become templates for looking at, acting and explaining the world (Evangelou et al., 2009). The schema provide a focus of interest for a child's intellectual energy. This is evident in the way 2-year-old Estelle gathered together a selection of boxes and lids, as an example of the way she searched for objects and experiences which were able to fit her 'schema' and confirmed her expectations and is seen to be highly motivating. Schemas provide a focus for action. When children acquire a new capability, whether it is as stated above, or constructing a garage, or jumping up and down, they apply it as often as possible and the achievement of mastery, as the achievement of understanding is said to be particularly rewarding (Bruner, 1983) carried out research to try to establish what knowledge young children possess about the physical world and how they attain this knowledge. Following several experimentations, Bruner concludes that early years children behave as if they are formulating rules and how events might operate, with experience they revise and refine these rules and elaborate their concepts about how things work. Five-year-old Ethan very swiftly began to refine the rules related to saving a goal between two posts by reducing the width of the goal net to prevent his opponent scoring a goal. A common feature of this theory is that infants realise that objects continue to exist even when they are hidden.

Technology

> Young children today are growing up in a world which not only contains but is also increasingly shaped by ICT. More and more children encounter a computer before they go to school.
>
> (Siraj-Blatchford and Whitbread, 2003)

The use of ICT in children's cognitive development

Young children in the twenty-first century are becoming aware of the technological aspects of that world. They are the children of the digital age (Marsh, 2005: 3). A survey in the USA of children's experiences with electronic media from six months to six years (Rideot et al., 2003) concluded that there is evidence of young children growing up immersed in media. To corroborate this statement, Aubrey and Dahl (2008) concluded that technology can impact positively on early years development in three main ways:

1   Developing dispositions to learning that thread through personal, social and emotional development across EYFS in general.
2   Extending knowledge and understanding of the world in the broadest sense of communication and language, literacy, problem-solving, reasoning and numeracy, creative development and recreational/play behaviour.
3   Acquiring operational skills.

How are young children's communication and language skills supported at home and in early years settings…?

(Formby, 2014)

If there is an area of learning that has become much more dominant in the lives of children, it has to be technology. From their earliest years, children should be finding out about and using technology in their everyday lives. They are very likely to be familiar with games on iPhones, iPads, laptops and programmable toys in their homes. The increased familiarity and use of information and communication technology (ICT) in the home will for many children be the norm that will need to be developed further in early years settings. It is a number of years since Blatchford (2000) identified the following seven general principles for determining the effectiveness of ICT applications or uses of ICT in the early years to help practitioners provide the best possible experiences:

1   Ensure an educational purpose.
2   Encourage collaboration.
3   Integrate with other aspects of the curriculum.
4   Ensure the child is in control.
5   Choose applications which are transparent.
6   Avoid applications containing violence or stereotyping.
7   Be aware of health and safety issues.

It goes without saying that parental involvement should go hand-in-hand with these experiences.

The statutory requirements for technology are:

- Children recognise that a range of technology is used in places such as homes and schools.
- Children select and use technology for particular purposes.

Research findings

A recently published book, *iPads in the Early Years: Developing Literacy and Creativity* (Dezuanni et al., 2015), praises the success of tablet computers for their potential in the early years due to the speed with which 3- and 4-year-olds are able to master the use of the device and its associated apps. It is versatile, can be used anywhere, is very portable and has many apps suitable for young children. The authors warn of the impact apps could have on early literacy. As a requirement of the statutory EYFS framework, I felt it was necessary to include information about how technology features in the daily range of activities in early years settings. Concern because of the cost implications for settings to provide the necessary hardware and software were at the front of my mind and the impact of ICT on other methods of communication. I am very aware of the presence of technology in the home environment and the capabilities of children as young as 2 years old as they confidently surf the net for familiar websites on an iPhone or iPad. This was recently brought to my attention in a report that Birkbeck's Department for Psychological Sciences wishes to understand how technology influences early child development (*Sunday Times*, 14 June 2015). The Leverhulme Trust-funded TABLET (Toddler Attentional Behaviour and Learning with Touchscreens) project aims to document the huge increases in touch screen devices in family life, and the enthusiasm most children show for using them, and also the concerns that parents express. The presence of technology in the early years environment was also further highlighted in an unexpected way in a recent newspaper headline:

Give babies iPads: they'll learn faster than with books.

(*Sunday Times*, 14 June 2015)

The gist of the article according to research by Annette Karmiloff-Smith of the University of London is that babies learn faster when they are given iPads rather than books to look at. It is claimed that iPads give babies more sensory stimulation. Parents are advised to give them to babies almost as soon as they are born. 'Tablets should be a part of a baby's world from birth,' she claims, citing babies' skill at scrolling up and down text. I can vouch for this by a 2-year-old who was able to use her mother's iPhone to swiftly locate her favourite photographs. Karmiloff's research was with thirty-six babies in two groups: one of 6-month-old and another of 10-month-old babies. The research team found that the babies recognised the number 3 more quickly when presented with the number in lights, sounds and moving images on an iPad. An ongoing research project involving hundreds of babies aged 6 months to 3 years is underway with half the babies given tablets from birth and remainder only limited access to the devices. The expectation is that the babies given iPads will go on to have better motor control, visual attention and even behaviour than those who are not. It is also worth saying that there are notable academic critics. It is claimed that over exposure to screens can damage children's brain development. Karmiloff's advice to parents in response to criticism is to stay with the child while they are using the iPad. They can point to things on the screen and talk their baby through what they are doing or play games on tablets with them.

The statistics show that over one in four children aged 3 to 4 uses a tablet computer at home (Ofcom, 2013). Bearing in mind that it is what parents do rather than who parents are (Sylva et al., 2008). Any judgements made about the use of technology by children has also to consider home and pre-school. Do we know if this is affects children's outcomes at the age of 5? Is the rapid onset of technology raising any worrying concerns regarding children's communication and language skills? Do parents spend less time reading to their children? Currently, it is likely that only a fifth of children have access to a tablet computer. Research carried out by the Literacy Trust (Formby, 2014) suggests that in settings there is an equal amount of attention given to using a tablet with children and looking at books. Practitioners say that children are very to fairly confident using a tablet computer without an adult. Children are slightly less confident looking at books on their own or with an adult. Overall practitioners say that children are able to use tablets and enjoy doing so slightly more than they do looking at books on their own. This may be a result of greater exposure to the tablets in the home. Interestingly, practitioners in PVI settings make greater use of tablet computers. The majority of practitioners would like greater access to touch screens. It is widely acknowledged that new technology provides a central support to children's language and communication development and to be literate today children must learn to effectively use a range of media. Many schools have very limited resources to allow children daily access to tablet computers for example, but those that do have them find that adults and pupils use the computers readily throughout the week.

How practitioners use technology to extend communication, language and reading development

Apps are used regularly for phonics and mathematical learning. Creative and very cross-curricular activities include retelling a story, innovating the story to make it the children's own, voice recording of the story on the iPad and recreating scenes from the story which were photographed. The work done by children was put together as a movie. The use of the iPads for independent games is popular. The skills required by practitioners to scaffold children's activities are extensive:

- Suggest or select appropriate programmes.
- Explain how to use technology.
- Suggest alternative actions.
- Demonstrate how to use tools – for example, how to delete.
- Move children to a more appropriate level.
- Offer help after errors.
- Provide feedback.

Clearly, explaining how to use a programme was the commonest support given. Other ways in which technology is used to stimulate children's interests is through the use of interactive whiteboards for mark-making and writing. The use of 'magic pencils' are one way to do this. Aspects of physical development, moving and handling are widespread in technology as children develop a range of electronic skills, directional skills and language and various control actions. What is particularly well developed is the stimulation of children's imagination.

Expressive arts and design

The expressive arts and design area of learning is a very important aspect of children's learning and development and is central to their enjoyment whatever setting they attend (Table 10.11). Opportunities for children to explore and play with a wide range of media and materials should be encouraged to develop their imagination through imaginative play, through art and design, music, dance, role play and stories. The emotional strand is also prevalent in this area

TABLE 10.11 Early learning goals for expressive arts and design

Expressive arts and design
Exploring and using media and materials
■ Children sing songs, make music and dance, and experiment with ways of changing them.   ■ Children use and explore a variety of materials, tools, techniques, experimenting with colour, design, texture, form and function.
Being imaginative
■ Children use what they have learned about media and materials in original ways, thinking about uses and purposes.   ■ Children represent their own ideas, thoughts and feelings through design and technology, art, music, dance, role play and stories.

FIGURE 10.9 Observational drawing (fish)

when children are encouraged to represent their own ideas, thoughts and feelings (Sharp, 2004). There are creative and psychological processes involved in developing creativity in young children. This is an area of learning that stays with many of us as adults through the way we all develop our self-confidence, curiosity and motivation. These too are personality traits that we are anxious to develop in the children we teach. There are also emotional processes that are developed in young children in the emotional fantasy that is so common in play, the pleasure children get in a challenge and how they become tolerant of anxiety. Through fantasy play cognitive abilities are developed; for example, divergent thinking and sensitivity to problems. The focus is much more clearly on *children's experience* of exploring and learning about creative and artistic expression in parallel with their desire to express and represent their learning in diverse ways. The intention is to emphasise the children's aesthetic experiences, which are defined as, 'belonging to the appreciation of the beautiful' (Fowler and Fowler, 1964). Is this really how one would define 'aesthetic experiences' for young children? One can look to a seminal educational publication by HMI in 1989, which describes aesthetic and creative areas of learning as 'central to learning' (HMI, 1989: 29).

The stages children go through when beginning to draw are listed in Table 10.12.

TABLE 10.12 The development of children's drawing

Children	
Birth–1 year	■ Imitate actions and movement using their whole body. ■ Are aware of patterns which have strong contrasts and resemble the human face. ■ Make intentional marks, for example, with food using finger and hand and are aware that movements result in a mark.
1–2 years	■ Make a variety of marks, sometimes described as scribbling. ■ Are aware that different movements make different marks. ■ Grip pen or crayon using palm of hand. ■ Make marks that record and represent the movement of their bodies and other objects. ■ Draw overlapping and layered marks.
2–3 years	■ Use pincer grip to hold graphic materials. ■ Produce continuous line and closed shape to represent inside and outside. ■ Combine lines and shapes. ■ Produce separate but linked shapes.
3–4 years	■ Name marks, and symbolic representation is emerging. ■ Experiment with the variety of marks that can be made by different graphic materials, tools and surfaces. ■ Unaided, use a circle plus lines to represent a person, often referred to as a 'tadpole person'. ■ Start to produce visual narratives.
4–5 years	■ Are able to produce a range of shapes and sometimes combine them, for example to produce a sun. ■ Draw shapes and figures that appear to float in space on the page. ■ Draw figures which include more details, such as arms, legs, hands, fingers, eyebrows. ■ Subdivide space on page to show higher and lower.
At 6 years	■ Draw figures that are grounded and use lines for ground and the sky. ■ Display depth by making figures in the distance smaller to indicate further away. ■ Include more details in their drawings, for example, windows, doors and chimneys on buildings. ■ Drawings have more narrative features, for example, may feature a number of episodes of the same story.

Source: Matthews, 1994

The creative classroom

Creativity needs to be part of every day in an early years environment. The list below provides a good starting point for the ways in which this can be achieved.

■ Story time
■ Building in the construction area

- Playing outside
- Modelling, making, cutting and sticking materials
- Sand and water play
- Role play in the home corner/hospital/shop
- Painting by comparing artists' work and painting self-portraits
- Model making linked to a special occasion (Christmas, Easter, holidays, light and dark theme)
- Digital media.

The last experience cited on the list above will become more commonplace in the near future as more and more children begin to have access to digital media in their homes through video games and interactive fiction. As stated earlier it is already acknowledged that today's children are likely to have the skills to search websites for pictures and skilfully play games. This too is an important part of creativity. It is acknowledged by some academics that children have the skills to learn to read using technology.

Topics for discussion

- Share the ways you organise learning in your setting, identifying how you manage indoor/outdoor learning in reception class settings.
- Research suggests that less priority is given to mathematical learning in the early years. Discuss what is happening in your setting.
- As trainee early years practitioners what are the key areas causing you most concern?
- Discuss your priorities for the early years curriculum.
- Share the ways in which you balance your priorities and time allocations to indoor/outdoor learning.
- Discuss the usefulness or otherwise of the categories prime and specific areas of learning.

Further reading

Early Education (2013) *Development Matters in the Early Years Foundation Stage.* www.foundationyears. org.uk/files/2012/03/Development-Matters-FINAL-PRINT-AMENDED.pdf

Conclusion

I would like this conclusion to be optimistic and hopeful for the future of our youngest children in whatever setting they attend. 'Research has never been clearer – a child's early education lasts a lifetime, securing a successful start for our youngest children, and particularly those from disadvantaged backgrounds is crucial' (Ofsted, 2015b). However, this is not always how it looks like developing based on research evidence and reports by experienced and committed early years researchers and academics. The aim for everyone must be that the bar for early years qualifications needs to be raised to enable setting-based training for staff. There is a demand to have graduate leaders in all settings, especially those serving disadvantaged areas. This is the key to high-quality provision as currently the most disadvantaged children are likely to be those attending early years settings with less well-qualified staff. As stated in the introduction, there are many graduate and postgraduate routes to early years qualifications. This needs to be applied to all early years settings. A considerable boost in their funding to be able to employ graduate members of staff needs to be a priority. A recent newspaper heading, 'The early years matter most, but good quality childcare still eludes us' (Toynbee, June 2, 2015) is too true. The accuracy of the gloom that surrounds early years in the UK is starkly brought to bear when one compares the quality of provision and access to childcare in comparisons with other countries.

HMCI's annual report (2015a) for the early years is positive about early years in many respects, but primarily that irrespective of the type of provision, 80 per cent of provision is good or outstanding. It is further claimed that early years practitioners understand that they are there to teach children, not just to provide childcare. This finding is accompanied by a big jump in the proportion of children reaching a good level by the end of their reception year. At a national level, early years is enjoying a political profile that is unprecedented. Cost, capacity, accessibility and quality are centre stage. A level of discord arises, however, when one reads reports from headteacher conferences (September, 2015).

The recent government pledge in 2015 to provide 30 hours free childcare for working parents is not a solution for disadvantaged families and will not be in place until 2016. The most recent government report *Foundation Years: Sure Start Children's Centres* (House of Commons Education Committee, 2013–14, vol.1) raises several concerns about the closure of Sure Start Centres. In April 2010, for example, there were 3,631 Children's Centres in England and three years later this had decreased to 3,116 centres. The variation between authorities was marked with twenty local authorities decreasing their Children's Centres by 50 per cent. The use made of the existing closed Sure Start Centres in my own authority suggests that the accommodation is now used by charitable groups and as outreach centres for early years staff working with families experiencing various levels of disadvantage as a result of a cross-party government report (2014–15). The impact of benefit cuts in recent months is reported to likely effect 330,000 children from low income families with single mothers being the hardest hit. Further reports (Centre on Migration, Policy and Society (COMPAS)) at the University of Oxford warns that thousands of children are living well below the poverty line in the UK – often in dangerous and squalid conditions as a result of changes to government immigration and benefit policies. Charities are seeing an increase in the number forced into destitution – with some families living on as little as £1 per day. This is because there are too many NRPF (no recourse to public funds) families. The increase in families from Syria seeking asylum into the country is likely to create further hardships in what is one of the richest countries in Europe! The research base for these findings is robust, based as it was on 137 children's services departments in England and Wales and 105 voluntary sector organisations. Councils have a legal duty to protect children from destitution, but the report says there is evidence that councils have had their central funding cut by 40 per cent since 2010 according to the Local Government Association.

Can there be hope in the reports from Ofsted? Can the parents of children in London be hopeful that their new mayor will be able to create a £60 million fund for Sure Start in London? I turn to Head Start – the centrepiece of US President Lyndon Johnson's Great Society fifty years ago. Young children, he said, 'are inheritors of poverty's curse, not its creators'. The resounding success of Head Start remains with thirty-two million Head Start children emerging to be thankful for their success. To quote Darren Ford, president of the Ford Foundation, who recalls sitting on the porch of 'our little shotgun shack in Ames, Texas' with his mother, when she was approached to offer a Head Start place for her son:

> It changed my life. It allowed me to imagine, to think creatively about the world beyond my environment and what my life might be.

As a result of this study, a Labour group followed a group of children on a highly structured Head Start type scheme in Ohio, comparing them with a control group. While the children did not 'soar up aspirational ladders', two intensive years of pre-school cognitive and emotional support protected many from disaster. By the age of 40, some 46 per cent fewer Head Start children went to jail, fewer girls had unplanned babies, fewer drew welfare or needed mental treatment, while more stayed at school and had jobs. Early years provision in England is inadequate in many respects for those disadvantaged children under 3 and their parents who need the most support. A common theme throughout this edition is that by the time children start school, it is too late for many who have not had the kind of upbringing, stimuli and comfort so many of us take for granted.

Research also shows that, by the time children arrive for their first day at school, the life chances of a significant number of them have been closed down. What happens to children before they ever see their primary school teacher is more important in determining what kinds of jobs they will gain than all the public expenditure spent on them over their entire school career. Cathy Nutbrown made nineteen recommendations related to the level of qualifications required by staff working in the early years sector with a 70 per cent proportion possessing a 'full and relevant' Level 3 to count in the staff:child ratios. This level should be increased to all cover all staff by 2022. However, the welcome to these proposals was mixed due to suggestions that the Early Years Professional Status (EYPS) qualification is not good enough and that there needs to be one way forward and that would be QTS. In response to the Nutbrown review, the government stated that training for early years teachers would commence in September 2013 and there would be improvements to the standards for EYPS so they more closely match teaching standards for classroom teachers, but will not confer QTS. In September 2014 prospective early years teachers were required to pass the same skills as classroom teacher trainees before they start their courses. Academies, independent schools and all other private and voluntary providers are not required to have a teacher with QTS. As stated in the introduction, the crisis looming in the early years sector is gathering momentum as nurseries struggle to afford the majority of free places they have to offer working parents from 2016 and allow 2-year-olds from disadvantaged homes to attend. Added to that, recently there has been the prospect of parents with very young 4-year-olds delaying their entry to reception class for a year. Will there be room for these children in the pre-schools? Good-quality childcare and education is a basic need and requires appropriately trained staff. Many good-quality childcare providers will fail to make ends meet and fold, leaving families having to find somewhere else for their children to get their early years care and education. There has to be a solution found to the dark days that are yet to come.

Bibliography

Aasen, W. and Waters, J. (2006) The new curriculum in Wales: A new view of the child? *Education 3-13* 34(2), 123–129.

Abbott, L. and Rodger, R. (1994) *Quality Education in the Early Years*. Buckingham: Open University Press.

Abbott, L. and Langstone, A. (Eds) (2005) *Birth to Three Matters-Supporting the Framework of Effective Practices*. Maidenhead: Open University Press.

Alexander, R. (2009) *The Cambridge Primary Review*. University of Cambridge and Esmee Fairbairn Trust. www.esmeefairbairn.org.uk/upload

Allen, G. and Duncan Smith, I. (2008) *Early Intervention, Good Parents, Great Kids, Better Citizens*. London: The Centre for Social Justice and The Smith Institute.

Athey, C. (1990) *Extending Thought in Young Children*. London: Paul Chapman.

Aubrey, C. (2003) Count me in: Taking in early early mathematical experiences. *Primary Mathematics* 7(3), 17–20.

Aubrey, C., Dahl, S. and Godfrey, R. (2006) Early mathematical development and later achievement: further evidence. *Mathematics Education Research Journal* 18(1), 27–46.

Aubrey, C. and Dahl, A. (2008) *A Review of the Evidence on the Use of ICT in the EYFS*. Coventry: Becta. http://dera.ioe.ac.uk/1631/2/becta_2008_eyfsreview_report.pdf

Avon Longitudinal Study of Parents and Children (ALSPAC) (2007–2012) Children of the 90s. University of Bristol.

Bandura, A. (1997) *Self- Efficacy*. New York: W.H. Freeman.

Barber, S., Akhter, S., Jackson, C., Bingham, D., Hewitt, L., Routen, A., Richardson, G., Ainsworth, H., Moore, H., Summerbell, C., Pickett, K., O'Malley, C., Brierley, S., and Wright, J. (2015) Preschoolers in the playground: A pilot cluster randomised controlled trial of a physical activity intervention for children aged 18 months to 4 years. *Public Health Research* 3(5).

Bennet, J. (2004) The OECD Thematic Review of Early Childhood Education and Care Policy. *Educational and Child Psychology*. Vol. 21. No.4.

Bertram, T. and Owen, C. (2014) Raise your game. *Nursery World* 107(4074), 10–11.

Bilton, H. (2010) *Outdoor Learning in the Early Years*. London: Taylor and Francis.

Bowers, A.P. and Strelitz, J. (2012) *Equal Start: Improving Outcomes in Children's Centres: An Evidence Review*. London: UCL Institute of Health Equity.

Bradshaw, J. and Richardson, D. (2009) An index of child-wellbeing in Europe. *Child Indicators Research* 2(3), 319

Brewer, M., Brown, J. and Joyce, R. (2011) *Child and Working age Poverty from 2010 to 2020*. London: Institute of Fiscal Studies.

Brooker, L., Rogers, S., Ellis, D., Hallet, E. and Roberts-Holmes, G. (2010) *Practitioners' Experiences of the Early Years Foundation Stage*. Research Report DFE-RR029. London: DfE. www.gov.uk/government/uploads/system/uploads/attachment_data/file/181479/DFE-RR029.pdf

Brooks, (2011) *Preschoolers Nutrition and Fitness*. Raisingchildren.net.au

Bruce, T. (1997) *Early Childhood Education*. London: Hodder and Stoughton.

Bruner, J. (1977) *The Process of Education*. New York: Vintage Books.

Bruner, J. (1983) *Children's Talk: Learning to Use Language*. New York: Norton.

Burnett, C. (2010) Technology and literacy in early childhood settings: A review of research. *Journal of Early Childhood Literacy* 10(3), 247–270.

Carle, E. (2014) *The Very Hungry Caterpillar*. London: Puffin.

Carle, E. (2010) *The Bad-tempered Ladybird*. London: Puffin.

Carruthers, E. and Worthington, M. (2003) Making sense of mathematical graphics: The development of understanding abstract symbolism. Presentation at the *European Education Research Association* (EECERA) conference, September, University of Strathclyde.

Carruthers, E. and Worthington, M. (2006) *Children's Mathematical Making Marks, Making Meaning*. London: Sage.

Davies, S. (2013) *Annual Report of the Chief Medical Officer. Our Children Deserve Better: Prevention Pays*. gov.uk/government/uploads/system/pdf

DCSF (2009) *Breaking the Link Between Disadvantage and Low Achievement in the Early Years*. www.teachernet.gov.uk/publications

DCSF (2008) *The National Strategies Early Years: Social and Emotional Aspects of Development*. Nottingham: DCSF. www.foundationyears.org.uk/wp-content/uploads/2011/10/SEAD_Guidance_For_Practioners.pdf

DCSF (2008a) *Every Child Matters. Outcomes for Children and Young People* (Archived content for Every Child Matters).

DCSF (2009) *Learning, Playing and Interacting*. London: DCSF.

DCSF (2010) *Challenging Practice to Further Improve Learning, Playing and Interacting in the EYFS*. www.foundationyears.org.uk/wp-content/uploads/2011/10/Challening_Practice_to_Further_Improve_Learning_Playing_and_Interacting_in_the_EYFS.pdf

DfE (2008) *Practice Guidance for the Early Years Foundation Stage*. London: DfE.

DfE (Department for Education) (2008) *The Impact of Sure Start Programmes on Five-year-olds and their Families*. London: DfE.

DfE (2010) *The Impact of Sure Start Local Programmes on Five Year Olds and Their Families*. Research Report RR067. www.gov.uk/government/uploads/system/uploads/attachment_data/file/182026/DFE-RR067.pdf

DfE (2011a) *The Impact of Sure Start Local Programmes on Seven Year Olds and Their Families*. The National Evaluation of Sure Start (NESS) Institute for the Study of Children, Families and Social Issues, Birkbeck, University of London. www.ness.bbk.ac.uk.

DfE (2011b) *Practitioners' Views of the Early Years Foundation Stage*. London: DfE.

DfE (2012a) *Supporting Families in the Foundation Years*. London: DfE.

DfE (2012b) *Progress Check at Age 2: A Know How Guide*. London: DfE.

DfE (2012c) *Foundations for Quality: The Independent Review of Early Education and Childcare Qualifications. Final Report (Nutbrown Review)*. www.gov.uk/government/uploads/system/uploads/attachment_data/file/175463/Nutbrown-Review.pdf

DfE (2012d) *Statutory Framework for the Early Years Foundation Stage 2012*. London: DfE.

DfE. (2013) *Early Years Foundation Stage Profile Results: 2012 to 2013*. London: DfE.

DfE (2014a) *Statutory Framework for the Early Years Foundation Stage. Setting Standards for Learning, Development and Care for Children from Birth to Five* All publications. DFE-00023-2012. www.dfe.gov.uk/publications/standards/

DfE (2014b) *Reforming Assessment and Accountability for Primary Schools*. www.gov.uk/reformingassessmentandaccountability for primary schools.

DfE (2014c) *Students Educational Development Outcomes at Age 16. Effective Prer-school, Primary and Secondary Education (EPPSE 3-16) Project*. www.gov.uk/government/uploads/system/uploads/attachment_data/file/351496/RR354_-_Students__educational_and_developmental_outcomes_at_age_16.pdf

DfE (2014d) *Advice on the Admission of Summer Born Children*. London: DfE.

DfE (2015a) *Reception Baseline Assessment: A Guide to Signing up Your School*. London: DfE. www.gov.uk/government/publications/early-years-years-outcomes

DfE (2015b) *Special Educational Needs and Disability Code of Practice:0 to 25 Years*. www.aguidetothesen codeofpractice.co.uk

DfES (2007) *National Standards for Leaders of SureStart Children's Centres*. Nottingham: DfES.

Dezuanni, M, Dooley, K., Gattenhot, S. and Knight, L. (2015) *iPad in the Early Years: Developing Literacy and Creativity*. London: Routledge.

Dixon-Woods, M., Cavers, D., Agarwal, S., Annandale, E., Arthur, A., Harvery, J., Hsu, R., Katbamna, S., Olsen, R., Smith, L., Riley, R., and Sutton, A. (2006) Conducting a critical interpretive synthesis of the literature on access to healthcare by vulnerable groups. *BMC Medical Research Methodology* 6(1), 35.

Dombey, H. (2013) Language debates. https://languagedebates.wordpress.com/tag/henrietta-dombey.

Donaldson, M. (1978) *Children's Minds*. Glasgow: Fontana.

Donby, H. (2013) *Synthetic Phonics is Not Enough: Teaching Young Children to Read and Write English*. 18th European Conference on Reading 'New Challenges – New Literacies', Jonkoping, Sweden 6–9 August.

Dunlop, A. (2008) *A Literature Review of Leadership in the Early Years* (update of 2005 review). http://www.educationscotland.gov.uk/resources/a/leadershipreview.asp

Early Education (2012) *Development Matters in the Early Years Foundation Stage. (EYFS)*. London: British Association for Early Childhood Education. www.early-education.org.uk/default/files/ Development%Matters%20FINAL%20PRINT%AMENDED.pdf. www.education.gov.uk/publications

Education Children and Families Committee (2014) *The Early Years Strategy Progress Report*. www.edinburgh. gov.uk/download/meetings/id/43172/item_72_-_early_years_strategy_progress_report

Edwards, C., Gandini, L. and Forman, G. (1998) *The Hundred Languages of Children. The Reggio Emilia Approach*. London: Ablex Publishing.

Elfer, P., Goldschmied, E. and Selleck, D.Y. (2012) *Key Persons in the Early Years: Building Relationships for Quality Provision in Early Years Settings and Primary Schools*. London: Routledge.

Ellis, S. (2010) University of Strathclyde, *The Guardian,* July 2007.

Evangelou, M., Sylva, K., Edwards, A. and Smith, T. (2008) *Supporting Parents in Promoting Early Learning*. Report No. DCSF RR039. London: DCSF.

Evangelou, M., Sylva, K., Kyriacou, M., Wild, M. and Glenny, G. (2009) *Early Years Learning and Development Literature Review*. Report No. DCSF RR176. London: DCSF.

Evangelou, M. and Soukakou, E. (2012) *Measuring the Quality of Inclusive Early Years Practices in Early Years Settings*. Oxford: University of Oxford.

Evangelou, M., Goff, J., Hall, J., Sylva, K., Eisenstadt, N., Paget, C., Davis, S., Sammons, P., Smith, T., Tracz, R., and Parking, T. (2013) *Evaluations of Children's Centres in England. Strand 3: Main Report*. London: DfE.

Feinstein, L. (2003) *Very Early Evidence*. cep.lse.ac.uk/pubs/download/CP146.pdf

Formby, S. (2014) *Parents' Perspectives: Children's Use of Technology in the Early Years*. National Literacy Trust.

Gambaro, L., Stewart, K. and Waldfogel, J. (2014) *An Equal Start? Providing Quality Early Education and Care for Disadvantaged Children Access to High Quality Early Education and Care*. Bristol: Policy Press.

Gambaro, L., Stewart, K. and Waldfogel, J. (2013) *A Question of Quality: Do Children from Disadvantaged Backgrounds Receive Lower Quality Education and Care in England?* CASE Working Paper. London: CASE, London School of Economics. http://sticerd.lse.ac.uk/dps/case/cp/CASEpaper171.pdf

Gamboro, L., Stewart, K. and Waldfogel, J. (2014) (eds) *An Equal Start? Providing Quality Education and Care for Disadvantaged Children*. Bristol: Policy Press.

Garrick, R., Batu, C., Dunn, K., Maconochie, H., Willis, B. and Wolstenholme, C. (2011) *Children's Experience of the Foundation Stage*. Research Report DFE-RR071. www.gov.uk/government/uploads/ system/uploads/attachment_data/file/182163/DFE-RR071.pdf

Gaunt, C. (2014) Inspections Should be Tailored to the Early Years. *Nursery World* 10 October.

Glover, A. (1999) The role of play in the development and learning. In E. Dau (ed.), *Child's Play. Revisiting Play in Early Childhood Settings*. Sydney, Australia: Maclennan Pretty.

Goddard, S. (2014) *Why Young Children can be Described as a Terranaut*. Blog. Sally Goddard.

Goodhead, S. (2013) *National Portage Association Survey – Autumn*. www.portage.org.uk/wp-content/ uploads/2011/01/NPA-survey-Autumn-2013-November-2013.pdf

Gordon, M. (2005) *Roots of Empathy*. www.rootsofempathy.org

Goswami, U. and Bryant, P. (1990) *Phonological Skills and Learning to Read*. Hove: Psychology Press.

Harris, A.W., Thompson, S.D. and Norris, D.J. (2007) Defining quality childcare: Multiple stakeholder perspectives. *Early Education and Development* 18(2), 305–336.

Hechman, J.J. (2006) *Investing in Disadvantaged Young Children is an Economically Efficient Policy*. Unpublished manuscript, University of Chicago, Economics Department.

Her Majesty's Inspector of Schools (2005) *Transition from Reception to Year 1*. London: HMSO.

Hillman, J. and Williams, T. (2015) *Early Years Education and Childcare*. www.nuffieldfoundation.org/sites/default/files/files/Early_years_education_and_childcare_Nuffield_FINAL.pdf

Hopkins, R., Stokes, I. and Wilkinson, D. (2010) *Quality Outcomes and Costs in Early Education*. Report to the Office for National Statistics. London: National Institute of Economic and Social Research.

House of Commons Education Committee (2013) *Foundation Years: Sure Start Children's Centres*. Fifth Report of Session 2013–14. London: The Stationary Office.

Jackson, N. and Coheart, M. (2001) *Routes to Reading Success and Failure*. Hove: Psychology Press.

Jarvis, P. (2015) It's against human nature to send two-year olds to school. *The Conversation* 1 May.

Kahn, T. (2006) *Involving Fathers in Early Years Settings: Evaluating Four Models for Effective Practice Development*. London: DES.

Kalas, I. (2013) *Recognising the Potential in ICT in Early Childhood Education*. UNSECO Institute for Information Technologies in Education.

Kendrick, D., Elkan, R., Hewitt, M., Dewey, M., Blair Robinson, J., Williams, D., and Brummell, K. (2000) Does home visiting improve parenting and the quality of the home environment? *Archives of Disease in Childhood* 82(6), 443–451.

Kochanska, G., Coy, K. and Murray, J.T. (2005) The development of self-regulation in the first four years of life. *Child Development* 72(4), 1091–1111.

Kwom, Y. (2002) Changing Curriculum for Early Childhood Education in England. *Early Childhood Research and Practice* 4(2), 1–15.

Learning and Teaching Scotland (2006) *Early Education Support: The Reggio Emilia Approach to Early Education*. Glasgow: Learning and Teaching Scotland.

Law, J. and Harris, F. (2001) *Sure Start Promoting Speech and Language Development*. London: City University.

Learner, S. (2014) *Activity Collection Provides Physical Development for Under 3*. www.daynurseries.co.uk/news

Lindon, J. (2005) *Understanding Child Development: Linking Theory and Practice*. London: Hodder Education.

Luberman, J.N. (1977) *Playfulness: Its Relationship to Imagination and Creativity*. New York: Academic Press.

Marmot Review Team (2010) *Fair Society Healthy Lives. Strategic Review of Health Inequalities in England post 2010* (The Marmot Review). www.instituteofhealthequity.org/projects/fair-society-healthy-lives-the-marmot-review

Marsh, J. (Ed) (2005) *Introduction in Popular Culture, New Media and Digital Literacy in Early Childhood*. London: Routledge Falmer.

Mathers, S., Eisenstadt, N., Sylva, K., Soukakou, E. and Ereky-Stevens (2014) *Sound Foundations: A Review of the Research Evidence on Quality of Early Childhood and Care for Children under Three*. The Sutton Trust and University of Oxford.

Mathers, S., Singler, R. and Karemaker, A. (2012) *Improving Quality in the Early Years: A Comparison of Perspectives and Measures*. www.education.ox.ac.uk/wordpress/wp-content/uploads/2012/03/Early-Years-Quality-Mathers-et-al-Final-Report-2012.pdf

Mathers, S. and Smee, R. (2014) *Quality and Inequality: Do Three and Four Year olds in Deprived Areas Experience Lower Quality Provision?* Nuffield Foundation.

Matthews, J. (1994) *Helping Children to Draw and Paint in Early Childhood (0-8 Years)*. London: Hodder and Stoughton.

Maude, P. (2006) 'How can I do this better?' From movement education into early years physical education (1996), in Whitebread, D. (ed.), *Teaching and Learning in the Early Years*. London: Routledge.

Maynard, T. (2007) Forest Schools in Great Britain: Initial Exploration. *Contemporary Issues in Early Childhood Education* 8(4), 320–31.

McCrink, T. and Wynn, K. (2004) Large number edition and subtraction by 9 month old infants. *Psycho. Sci.* 15(11), 776–781.

McLean, C. (2015) Promising More from Nursery Care is One Thing, Delivering it is Another. *The Conversation,* 1 May.

McNeill (2012) *Why Should Vulnerable Families be a Concern for Deep End General Practices.* 12 October. pdf www.gla.ac.uk

Meadows, S. (1993) *The Child as Thinker.* London: Routledge.

Meadows, S. and Cashdan, A. (1988) *Helping Children Learn.* London: David Fulton.

Meadows, S. (1993) *The Child as Thinker: The Development and Acquisition of Cognition in Childhood.* London: Routledge.

Melhuish, E., Belsky, J., Leyland, A., Anning, A., and Hall, D. (2008) *The Impact of Sure Start Local Programmes on Five Year Olds and their Families:* London: DfE.

Melhuish, E., Belsky, J., Leyland, A., Anning, A., and Hall, D. (2010) *The Impact of Sure Start Local Programmes on Five Year Olds and their Families:* London: DfE. Available at ness.bbk.ac.uk/impact/documents/RB067.pdf.

Melhuish, E. (2011) *Early Years Experiences and Long-term Child Development: Research and Implications for Policymaking.* Paris: OECD.

Montie, J., Xiang, Z., and Schwienhart, J. (2006) Preschool experiences in 10 countries: Cognitive and language performance at age 7. *Early Childhood Research Quarterly* 21, 313–331.

Morris, E. (2014) Early learning – the fights we do not need. *The Guardian,* 22 April.

Moylett, H. (2014) Valedictory Report from Outgoing President. *Early Education.* www.early-education.org.uk/news/valedictory-report-outgoing-president-helen-moylett

Mucavelle, P., Wall, C. and Sharp, L. (2013) *Eat Better, Start Better.* Programme in Gloucestershire. Evaluation Report.

Mullin, A. (2012) Defining Vulnerable Families Relevance to General Practice? www.gla.ac.uk/media/media_244195_en.pdf

National Children's Bureau (2012) *The EYFS Progress Check at Age2. A Know How Guide.* www.gov.uk/government/publications/a-know-how-guide-the-eyfs-progress-check-at-age-two

Nutbrown, C. (1997) *Recognising Early Literacy Development.* London: Paul Chapman.

Nutbrown, C. (2006) *Threads of Thinking.* London: Paul Chapman.

Nutbrown, C. (2015) Re-examine the Baseline. *Nursery World,* 26 January. www.sheffield.ac.uk

Oberhuemer, P. (2005) International perspectives on early childhood curricula. *International Journal of Early Childhood* 37(1), 27–37.

O'Brian, L. and Murray, R. (2007) Forest schools and its impact on young children: Case studies in Britain. *Urban Forestry and Urban Greenery* 6(4), 249–265.

OFCOM (2013) *Children and Parents: Media Use and Attitudes Report.* Stakeholders.ofcom.org.uk. cmr13

Ofsted (2006) *Inclusion: Does it Matter where Children are Taught?* www.ofsted.gov.uk

Ofsted (2011) *The Impact of the Early Years Foundation Stage.* London, DfE.

Ofsted (2012) *From Training to Teaching Early Language and Literacy.* Ofsted Early Years and Childcare. Ref 120031. London: DfE.

Ofsted (2013a) *Getting it Right First Time. Achieving and Maintaining High Quality EYFS Provision.* London: DfE.

Ofsted (2013b) *Unseen Children Educational Access and Achievement 20 Years On.* London: DfE.

Ofsted (2014) *Conducting Early Years Inspections.* London: DfE.

Ofsted (2015a) *The Report of Her Majesty's Chief Inspector of Education, Children's Services and Skills 2015. Early Years.* www.gov.uk/government/uploads/system/uploads/attachment_data/file/445730/Early_years_report_2015.pdf

Ofsted (2015b) *Teaching and Play in the Early Years: A Balancing Act.* www.gov.uk/government/uploads/system/uploads/attachment_data/file/444147/Teaching-and-play-in-the-early-years-a-balancing-act.pdf

Ofsted (2015c) *Parents as Partners in Teaching: Trimdon Grange Infant and Nursery School.* www.gov.uk/government/uploads/system/uploads/attachment_data/file/443912/Trimdon_Grange_Infant_and_Nursery_School_-_good_practice_example.pdf

PACEY (2013) Professional Association for Childcare and the Early Years. www.pacey.org.uk

Palmer, S. (2007) *Toxic Childhood: How the Modern World is Damaging Our Children and What We Can Do About it.* London: Orion.

Pepper, D. and May, T. (2009) *Early International Themes*. Final Report. Slough: NFER.

Piaget, J. (1929) *The Child's Conception of the World,* London: Routledge & Keegan Paul.

Piketty, T. (2014) *Capital in the Twenty-First Century*. Cambridge, MA: Harvard University Press.

Pordes Bowess, A., Strelitz, J., Allen, J. and Donlin, A. (2012) *An Equal Start Improving Outcomes in Children's Centres*. www.instituteofhealthequality.org

Pugh, G. and Duffy, B. (2014) *Contemporary Issues in the Early Years*. London: Sage.

Reece, E. and Newcombe, R. (2007) *Child Development*. Wiley Online Library.

Reed, H. (2012) *In the Eye of the Storm: Britain's Forgotten Children*. Blog post report.

Rideot, V. (2003) *Zero to Six. Electronic Media in the Lives of Infants, Toddlers and Preschoolers*. The Henry Kaiser Foundation.

Robb, S. (2014) Primary School Assessments for Pupils Must Not Just be a Test. *4Children*. www.4children. org.uk/News/Detail/Primary-school-assessments-for-pupils-must-not-just-be-a-test

Roberts, J., Donkin, A. and Pillas, D. (n.d.) *Measuring What Matters: A Guide for Children's Centres*. UCL Institute of Health Equity.

Rodger, R. (1998) Using structured play to promote language development in the early years. In Halsall, R. (ed.), *Teacher Research and School Improvement*. Buckingham: Open University Press.

Rose, J. (2008). *Independent Review of the Primary Curriculum: Final Report*. www.teachernet.gov.uk/publications

Roulstone, S., Law, J., Rush, R., Clegg, J. and Peters, T. (2011) *Investigating the Role of Language in Children's Early Educational Outcomes*. Research Report DfE RR134. www.gov.uk/government/publications/investigating-the-role-of-language-in-childrens-early-educational-outcomes

Samuelsson, I. and Carlsson, M.A. (2008) The play learning child: Towards a pedagogy of early childhood. *Scandinavian Journal of Educational Research* 52(6), 623–654.

Sarnecka, B.W. and Carey, S. (2008) How counting represents number: What children must learn and when they learn it. *Cognition* 108, 662–647.

Save the Children (2014) *Read on. Get on*. London: Save the Children. www.savethechildren.org.uk/sites/default/files/images/Read_On_Get_On.pdf

Scott, K. (2010) Phonics: Lost in translation. *The Guardian*, 19 January. www.theguardian.com/education/2010/jan/19/phonics-child-literacy

Scottish Government (2013) *Play Strategy for Scotland: Our Vision* and *Play Strategy for Scotland: Our Action Plan*. Edinburgh: Scottish Government. www.gov.scot/resource/0043/00437132.pdf

Scottish Government (2014) *Building the Ambition: National Practice Guidance on Early Learning and Childcare*. Edinburgh: Scottish Government. www.gov.scot/Resource/0045/00458455.pdf

Sharp, C. (2004) Developing young children's creativity: What we can learn from research? *Topic Issue 32.*

Sharp, C. (2006) 'Making the transition from foundation stage to key stage' *Presentation to Early Years 2006 conference*. NFER. https://www.nfer.ac.uk/publications/early-years. cfm

Siraj-Blatchford, I. (2003) *The Effective Provision of Pre-School Education (EPPE) Project*. London: DfEE.

Siraj-Blatchford, I. (2000) *Developmentally Appropriate Technology in Early Childhood Education (DATEC) Final Report*. B.A.E.C.E. (British Association for Early Childhood Education).

Siraj-Blatchford, I., Sylva, K. Simmons, P. and Melhuish, E, (2007) *The EPPE Case Studies. Technical Papers 10*. London: Institute of Education.

Soukakou, E., Eriky-Stevens, K., Sylva, K., Eisenstadt, N. and Mathers, S. (2014) *A Review of Research Evidence on Quality of Early Childhood Education and Care for Children under Three*. London: University of Roehampton.

Sylva, K., Melhuisg, E., Sammons, P., Siraj-Blatchford, I., and Taggart, B. (2004) *The Effective Provision of pre-School Education (EPPE) Project. Findings from Pre-school to end of Key Stage 1*. London: DFEE.

Sylva, K., Melhuish, E., Sammons, P., Siraj-Blatchford, I. and Taggert, B. (2008) *Final Report from the Primary Phase: Pre-school. School and Family Influences on Children's Development during Key Stage 2 (Age 7-11)*. RR061. London: DCSF.

Taguma, M., Litjens, I., and Makowiecki, K. (2013) *Quality Matters in Early Childhood Education and Care: Sweden 2013*. OECD Better Policies for Better Lives.

Tickell, C. (2011) *The Early Years: Foundations for life, Health and Learning. An Independent Report on the Early Years Foundation Stage to Her Majesty's Government*. London: DfE. www.educationengland.org.uk/documents/pdfs/2011-tickell-report-eyfs.pdf

Thompson. I. (2008) *Teaching and Learning Early Numbers*. Buckingham: Open University Press.

Toynebee, P.(2015) The early years matter most. *The Guardian* 2 June.

Vygotsky, L. S. (1978) *Mind in Society*. Cambridge, MA: Harvard University Press.

Walker, M., Bartlett, H., Sainsbury, M. and Mehta, P. (2013) *Evaluation of the Phonics Screening Check: First Interim Report*. Slough: NFER.

Wetton, P. (1997) *Physical Education in the Early Years*. London: Routledge.

Williams, P. (2008) *Independent Review of Mathematics Teaching in Early Years Settings and Primary Schools*. London: DCSF.

Wood, E. (2014) *Play, Learning and the Early Childhood Curriculum*. London: Sage.

Wood, E. and Attfield, J. (1996) *Play Learning and the Early Childhood Curriculum*. London: Paul Chapman.

Woodman, I., Allister, J., Raffi, I., De Lusignan, S., Peterson, I., and Gilbert, R. (2012) A simple approach to improve recording of concerns about child maltreatment in primary care records: Developing a quality improvement intervention. *British Journal of General Practice* 62(600), 478–486.

Yeh, S.S. and Connell, D.B. (2008) Effects of rhyming, vocabulary and phonemic awareness instruction on phoneme awareness. *Journal of Research in Reading* 31(2), 243–256.

Index

Note: Page numbers followed by 'f' refer to figures and followed by 't' refer to tables.